D1349970

NAZI WOMEN
HITLER'S SEDUCTION OF A NATION

CATE HASTE

First published in March 2001 by Channel 4 Books, an imprint of Macmillan Publishers Ltd, 25 Eccleston Place, London SW1W 9NF, Basingstoke and Oxford.

Associated companies throughout the world.

www.macmillan.com

ISBN 0 7522 1936 7

9 8 7 6 5 4 3 2 1

A CIP catalogue record for this book is available from the British Library.

Designed and typeset by Jonathan
Printed by Mackays of Chatham plc

This book accompanies the television programmes:

Hitler's Women, made by Blakeway Associates for Channel 4
Executive Producer: Denys Blakeway
Director: Fiona Procter
Researcher: Grace Chapman

Hitler's Brides, made by Flashback Television for Channel 4
Executive Producer: Taylor Downing
Director: Cate Haste
Producer: Dunja Noack

Picture credits: page 1 – (above left, above right, below left) Ullstein Bilderdienst, (below right) Bavarian State Library, Munich; page 2 – (above left) David Gainsborough Roberts, (above right) Ullstein Bilderdienst, (below) National Archives; page 3 – National Archives; page 4 – (above) Ullstein Bilderdienst, (below) National Archives; page 5 – (above) Süddeutscher Verlag, (below) Mary Evans Picture Library; page 6 – (above) Ullstein Bilderdienst, (middle, below) Bavarian State Library, Munich; page 7 – Flashback Television; page 8 – (above) David Gainsborough Roberts, (below) AKG London Ltd

The publishers have made every effort to trace the owners of these photographs, and apologise for any omissions.

CONTENTS

Introduction   7

1   Utopian Designs   13

2   Munich Matrons   27

3   Obsession: Geli Raubal   37

4   Secrecy: Eva Braun   51

5   Married to Germany   61

6   The Ideal Nazi Woman   73

7   The Racial State   101

8   The 'Grand Seduction of Youth'   129

9   The Road to War   141

10   Conquest   161

11   Plunder   177

12   Bombed Out   195

13   Collapse   217

Bibliography   240

Index   251

INTRODUCTION

'If only our generals had been as brave as you.'

When Hitler spoke these words on 22 April 1945, he was deep underground in his Berlin bunker. In the distance, he could hear the thud of artillery as the Russians advanced into the heart of the city. He had just conceded that the war was hopelessly lost and raged in fury against the leaders and generals who had betrayed him, and the German people who had let him down. However, he expressed nothing but gratitude and praise for the four women in his tiny inner circle who remained loyal to him to the last – his mistress Eva Braun, his dietician Constance Manziarly and his two younger secretaries, Traudl Junge and Gerda Christian. He had spent all his private moments and taken all his meals with them during the past months, as the Third Reich crumbled around him.

Hitler had ordered the women close to him to escape from Berlin while the few remaining routes were still open. But, dumbfounded by his final admission of defeat, and knowing that he now intended to take his own life, each in turn refused to leave his side. Their loyalty at that moment was immutable. Shortly afterwards, Eva Braun took her fealty to the extreme when she committed suicide alongside Hitler. The others escaped, and with that, broke free from the trance in which they had lived under Hitler's rule.

Throughout most of his life, Hitler relied on the devotion and support of women, even though he banished them to the periphery of political life and often treated them with indifference in private. His narrow, cramped views on women's role determined the destiny of millions of ardent female supporters during and after the twelve destructive years of the Third Reich.

This book is about a man who was incapable of forming a normal affectionate attachment to any one woman, a man dominated by the will to power and a rage to possess and destroy. And yet, he was able to seduce women into giving him their support and active participation in a system which ended in the annihilation of the very core of what he claimed to revere as women's world – the family and the home.

Nazi Women starts with his early life, a story which has been told in numerous biographies. The focus here is on his formative relationships with the opposite sex, for here may be found the clues to his emotional emptiness, his sexual 'awkwardness', and his romanticised view of women. Here also is the evidence of his self-absorption, his messianic belief in his own 'genius', and his indifference and lack of compassion. His views on the ultimate role women would fill in the New Germany were already evolving. He saw them as people whom he could use - as playthings to entertain him, or subjects who would idolise him. Women were set apart from men, cordoned off in a different world and by their very 'nature' incapable of participating in the masculine spheres of thought and politics. Women were to be revered for their capacity for self-sacrifice, and for the tenderness they showed in serving others.

Women's loyalty in private was as essential to him as their unquestioning allegiance in public. His mother's devotion was absolute, and provided him with the only real emotional tie he ever had. Hitler's relations with the opposite sex from then on were troubled. An adolescence marked by prudishness and shyness towards women led to a life which, as far as we know, was spent almost exclusively in the company of men until his late twenties.

Once Hitler embarked on his political career, he transferred his belief in his genius as an artist to his conviction of his destiny as 'saviour' of Germany. Women were among his earliest and most steadfast supporters, and he honed his oratorical skills to appeal to the crowd's irrational instincts, which he defined as 'feminine'. A strong leader with a dominating will, he believed, could always force the masses into submission.

Hitler shunned marriage. The image he shaped as leader was of a man who sacrificed his personal life for Germany, a 'saviour' unhindered by domestic ties, and an ascetic unsullied by sex. Being 'married to Germany' meant that all women could idolise him. He could flatter them freely, and mould for them a role of service to him. He sought their adulation because he needed their support in building the New Germany. But having no woman at his side also suited his private inclinations. A man driven by rage, ambition, self-absorption and hatred – which many called 'genius' – had little capacity or space for the 'ordinary' affections of a human being.

Once in power, out of this uneven experience of women, spliced with prevailing reactionary ideas of women's 'place', and an idealised image of motherhood, he was in a position to impose on Germany's women their role in building the Thousand Year Reich. They had always been barred from participation in the essentially misogynist Nazi Party. The compensation for their exclusion from formal politics was the esteem they could expect in their prescribed role as wives and mothers – the bearers of children to build the future Reich, the carriers of Nazi German culture into the next generation, and the source of eternally patient suffering and enduring love.

The reward for their adulation of Hitler was participation in what they believed, as everyone did, to be the revival of German honour and dignity, and the creation of a stable society in which their future as the generative 'soul' of the nation was assured. It also entailed the willing sacrifice of their individual freedom for the higher national good, and unprecedented State intervention in their private lives, including their right to marry and reproduce. And it led to their collusion with the ideology of a racial State headed by fanatics, who wrought destruction on a vast scale, not only on the targets and victims of their racial policies, but also on their own families and homes and, indeed, on the entire moral landscape of Europe.

*   *   *

This book grew out of two films for television, commissioned by Channel 4 – *Hitler's Women*, produced by Blakeway Associates, and *Hitler's Brides*, produced by Flashback Television. In writing it, I have been able to draw on the sources, research and interviews used in the series – the experts and witnesses who added their fresh and valuable insights into Hitler's early relations with women, and the influences which moulded the man who would later control, and destroy, the lives of so many: Professor Ian Kershaw, John Lukacs, Brigitte Hamann, Ron Rosenbaum, Brett Kahr, Reinhardt Spitzy, and Herbert Döhring. I have also drawn on the interviews with the ordinary women whose first-hand experience and oral testimony is the backbone to the chapters dealing with how women experienced life in the Third Reich: Luise Bierbaumer, Susanne von der Borch, Dorothea Buck, Gertrud Draber, Hedwig Ertl, Lilli Gentzen, Helga Lohniger, Traudl Junge, Liselotte Katscher, Lotte Lasch, Elly Napp, Jutta Rüdiger and Ilse Schmidt. In all cases their role or position is indicated in the text.

In such a book, the personal testimony of witnesses from the time is particularly valuable, especially in an area so well trodden by historians, since it can introduce the more subtle shades of feeling and experience into the spectrum, which can startle as well as illuminate wider understanding of the events. I am particularly indebted to Alison Owings book, *Frauen*, a collection of interviews with women, which filled in some gaps left by our interviewees. Most of those we interviewed were in their early teens when Hitler came to power, and in their twenties when the war ended. Older women, who experienced the Third Reich as adults, are mostly no longer with us, but their testimony survives. Published autobiographies and biographies of those living at the time have also been used, with care.

Several historians have been invaluable as sources for the book, and for their excellent comprehensive perspective on the subject of women, notably Claudia Koonz, *Mothers in the Fatherland*; Lisa Pine (whom we consulted for the film), *Nazi Family Policy*; Jill Stephenson (also consulted), *Women in Nazi Society*; Dalia Ofer and Leonore J. Weitzman, *Women in the Holocaust*; Elisabeth Heineman, *What Difference Does a Husband Make*; and Gisela Bock, 'Racism and Sexism in Nazi Germany', among others. I have also consulted the three major biographies of Hitler: Ian Kershaw's *Hitler, Hubris 1889-1936* and *Nemesis 1936-1945*; Joachim Fest's *Hitler*; and Alan Bullock's *Hitler, a Study in Tyranny*; and works on the social history of the Third Reich by

INTRODUCTION

Michael Burleigh, David Schoenbaum, Richard Grunberger and Hans Peter Bleuel, among others.

I am indebted to the wholehearted co-operation given to me by the *Hitler's Women* team – Fiona Procter (director), Grace Chapman, (researcher) and Denys Blakeway (executive producer), all of Blakeway Associates. Without the team at Flashback Television, none of this would have been possible for me. I am particularly delighted that Taylor Downing (managing director and executive producer), along with Dunja Noack (producer and originator of the idea), invited me in to direct the film *Hitler's Brides* in the first place, and then encouraged me to write the book, thereby condemning me to a life filled entirely with a cast of the Third Reich, with not much time to do anything else. I had the pleasure of working on the film with a first-rate team: Dunja Noack, who also found our interviewees and was always ready with her extensive knowledge, Aileen McAllister (film researcher) who burrowed deep into the archives for original material, Claire Otway (production manager), Gareth Johnson (film editor), Leo Kelly and Una Schinners. We are all delighted that Channel Four's commissioning editors, Tim Kirby and Janice Hadlow, took on the ideas in the first place and were supportive to the end.

I am also indebted to my agent, Faith Evans, for her comments and support, and to my editor Gillian Christie at Channel 4 Books, and Christine King, who have worked overtime to catch a crushing deadline, and been both encouraging and efficient at every stage. My particular thanks go to Sue McConachy, whose wide experience of working on films of the period, and unrivalled knowledge of the Third Reich and the people living through it, she generously shared with me while writing this book.

And to my family, willing and welcome cheerleaders in this enterprise.

1
UTOPIAN DESIGNS

Hitler's mother, Klara, died on 21 December 1907. Adolf was eighteen. He would not allow the neighbours to come in and remove the body, and he sat for hours and hours by his mother's bedside, sketching her. In the final weeks before her death, from breast cancer, he had been constantly at her side. He moved his bed into her room to be with her every moment. When she died, Dr Bloch, the Jewish doctor who had attended her during the months of her illness, reported that he 'had never seen a boy so completely bereft'. For the rest of his life, Hitler carried a photo of his mother in his breast pocket wherever he went. To many who have written about Hitler, this was the closest love attachment he had to any woman throughout his life. He romanticized his mother, and it was from her image that he shaped an ideal of motherhood, which became the centrepiece of women's place in Nazi ideology.

Hitler's home life, like all his personal relationships, was troubled. His mother, Klara Pölzl, had married Alois Hitler in 1885 in the Waldviertal, a mainly poor, mainly peasant area of Austria. She was, according to their family doctor Dr Bloch, 'a simple, modest, kindly woman. She was tall, had brownish hair which she kept neatly plaited, and a long, oval face with beautifully expressive grey-blue eyes.'[1] In historian Ian Kershaw's view, she was 'submissive, retiring, quiet, a pious churchgoer, taken up in the running of the household' and the care of the children and stepchildren. Paula Hitler, Adolf's younger sister, spoke of her mother as 'a very soft and tender person'.[2]

Klara was twenty-four when she married, after being intermittently employed in Alois's household as a serving girl for almost six years. Alois was a forty-seven-year-old customs official with considerable ambition, who had risen steadily through the civil service from a minor post to the highest rank possible for a man of his education. Though Hitler claimed he came from a dirt-poor background, the family was comfortable, although not well-off. It was Alois Hitler's third marriage, and he had been twice widowed. Klara, the daughter of a smallholder, was actually related by blood to Alois: she was the daughter of his cousin, or – quite possibly, because Alois was illegitimate and his parentage was uncertain – his niece. Klara called him 'uncle'. She was already pregnant with their first child when his second wife, Franciska, died of tuberculosis.

Before Adolf was born, Klara had given birth to three other children, but in the winter of 1887–88, tragedy struck the family. In the space of three weeks, the infant Otto died at just three days old, then Gustav, aged two and a half, and Ida, aged just over a year, died of diphtheria. Klara became pregnant with Adolf within six months of their deaths, and gave birth to him on 20 April 1889 at Braunau am Inn. The effect on Klara of losing virtually her entire family can only be surmised. She had little time, psychiatrist Brett Kahr notes, 'to get over the very natural depression which a young mother would experience when all three of her children die so suddenly, so tragically, leaving her feeling, I think, quite guilt-stricken, quite helpless'. Klara, he suggests, would have been very depressed at the time of Adolf's birth, and for some time afterwards: 'It's not unreasonable to suggest that at the time that Klara became pregnant, there were a number of perhaps messianic fantasies floating around in the Hitler family, in the hope that a new child who would be born would become such a special, spectacular child, that he or she could replace all these previously dead babies.'

During Adolf's early years, when he was 'a sickly child', it is likely that Klara was anxious and over-protective towards her son. Their home life was unsettled, and they moved several times as Alois changed jobs. There were severe tensions in the family. Alois was a typical provincial civil servant, pompous, strict, humourless and domineering. His passion was bee-keeping, which kept him out of the house; he smoked heavily, and often went to the local inn after work. He had an unpredictable temper, and was a stern disciplinarian and an often tyrannical father and husband, prone to beating both his wife and children, including his two eldest, Alois and Angela, from his previous marriages. Young Alois left home at the age of fourteen, never to return. Angela recalled that Adolf was subject to 'regular beatings' at his father's hands. After Alois retired in 1895, he was at home almost all the time, and Adolf got the full force of his sometimes drunken fury. Adolf's sister Paula recalled: 'It was especially my brother Adolf who challenged my father to extreme harshness and who got his sound thrashing every day.'[3] Hitler later told others that his father had sudden outbursts of temper and would hit out; that he did not love his father, but he feared him.[4] He wrote in *Mein Kampf*, 'I had honoured my father, but loved my mother.' Whatever good qualities this stern and distant father, Alois, possessed, they were not much remembered by his children.

Klara was submissive to her husband, but highly protective towards her son. Paula thought she was 'the compensatory element between the almost too harsh father and the very lively children who were perhaps somewhat difficult to train. If there were ever quarrel[s] or differences of opinion between my parents, it was always on account of the children.' Her mother would intercede after rows between Adolf and Alois: 'How often... did my mother caress [Adolf] and try to obtain with her kindness what the father could not succeed [in obtaining] through harshness.'[5] She attempted to shield him from his father's outbursts. A later friend, Henriette von Schirach (daughter of Hitler's photographer, Heinrich Hoffmann), reports that at the age of eleven, Adolf would have to fetch his father, who was often irascible, from the inn. When Alois tried to hit the boy, the mother and his sisters stood in front of him to protect him, 'so Hitler must have seen women and girls as guardian angels from an early age'.[6]

Hitler later spoke of how his poor beloved mother lived in constant concern about the beatings he had to take, sometimes waiting outside the door as he was thrashed.[7] To Goebbels, he described his father as 'a tyrant in the home' and 'a fanatical father', while his mother was 'a source of goodness and love' (Goebbels Diary, 9 August 1932, 15 November 1936). Ian Kershaw concludes: 'Hitler's mother lived in the shadow of her husband, this somewhat brutal, authoritarian, dominating, tyrannical father... and as a compensatory factor for that, [she] evidently smothered the young boy with affection, spoilt him terribly, pandered to his every whim.'

Klara supported Adolf in his growing ambition to be an artist. Adolf had stubbornly fought against his father's wish that he should follow him into a respectable career in the civil service. 'She was the one who defended him when he let it be known to his stern father that... he wanted to pursue an artistic career,' Ron Rosenbaum, author of *Explaining Hitler*, says. 'The father was apparently quite annoyed or more at this, and the mother defended this softer side of Hitler.' She shared his growing appetite for books, as he read to overcome loneliness. When his father was away, according to Henriette von Schirach, Adolf gave his mother his schoolbooks and then other books, so that she could read them too, and exchange ideas.[8] She read them all, except the Karl May boys' adventure stories, which Hitler would continue to read into adulthood. Dr Bloch, the family doctor, later wrote of Adolf: 'Outwardly, his love for his mother was his most striking feature. While he was not a "mother's boy" in the usual sense, I have never witnessed a closer attachment.'[9]

When his father died suddenly in 1903 – at the local inn, as he was about to take a drink – Adolf became the man of the house. This liberated him from his father but, as the eldest of Klara's children, he became even more the focus of his mother's attention. Her devotion 'might have had a number of impacts on his growing development', Brett Kahr suggests. 'One is that it might have exacerbated his tendency to what clinicians would refer to as a narcissistic personality structure... [that is] one which has very little compassion or concern for other people, but a real sense of self-absorption, self-preoccupation.' Dr Bloch described him at this time as a frail-looking young man, who 'lived within himself'.

At school, Hitler found little pleasure or sense of achievement. He had done reasonably well at junior level, but his results deteriorated when he moved up to secondary school. He was only any good at physical education and drawing, and in every other subject he was judged unsatisfactory or 'mediocre'. As well as being indolent, his class teacher later described the boy Hitler as stubborn, dogmatic and hot-tempered –

characteristics he shared with his father. Adolf later recalled his adolescence as 'painful'; he was left 'with an elemental hatred' towards his school and most of his teachers.[10] Nor did he make any school friends. His only friend from his adolescence was August 'Gustl' Kubizek. Franz Jetzinger, who researched Hitler's youth, concluded that there was 'no contact between him and his school-fellows, for Adolf was not interested in having a companion on an equal footing, but someone who would follow and admire, and admiration was Gustl's strong point'.[11]

Having persuaded his mother in 1905, when he was sixteen, that he should leave school, he spent the next two years lazing around Linz, dressing up in dandyish clothes – black coat, dark hat and a black cane with an ivory handle. He made no attempt to get a job, and nursed fantasies of becoming a great artist or architect. When he expressed a passion for music, his mother bought him a grand piano. She looked after him, as did his sister and half-sister and an aunt, while he painted, read, wrote poetry, went regularly to the theatre and the opera (Wagner was his favourite), and worked out grandiose schemes to redesign Linz. Once, he bought a lottery ticket and, with August Kubizek, now an aspiring musician, he planned an elaborate vision of a future residence, where the pair would live an artistic existence, visiting places of culture while being looked after by a middle-aged lady. Hitler was furious when he failed to win.

His massive self-absorption, his preoccupation with his image, his cultivation of fantastic schemes and his firm opinions on everything appealed to 'Gustl' Kubizek. The pair were, for a while, inseparable. 'He had to speak, and needed someone to listen to him,' Kubizek explained. Kubizek shared in Hitler's life for over two years, and witnessed his contact with young women. At school, Hitler had shown no interest whatsoever in girls, according to classmates.[12] One spring day in 1906, Hitler, out strolling with his friend in Linz, noticed an elegant, blonde young lady walking arm-in-arm with her mother. He was smitten. 'You must know, I'm in love with her,' he confided to Kubizek. Her name was Stefanie Jansten, and she was the seventeen-year-old daughter of a government official. He composed love poems to her, which he read out to Kubizek, but never sent. Hitler decided he was going to marry her, and set about making architectural plans for their future family home. For two years he was infatuated with her, but not one word ever passed between them. 'He plainly took a fancy to this girl in a sort of idolizing, distant fashion,' says historian Brigitte Hamann. 'He was already, in certain respects, living in a fantasy world... and Stefanie fitted into this fantasy world... One always had the impression that he didn't really want to see this girl directly. He didn't want a relationship. All he wanted was the illusion of a girl who would suit him, if he had ever the courage to speak to a woman. He seemed to have learned from a book how a German woman should be: blonde, tall, unapproachable, and chaste.'

When Kubizek suggested he introduce himself to this girl and her mother, Hitler told him: 'Between such exceptional beings as himself and Stefanie there was absolutely no need for the usual form of spoken communication. He told me that exceptional people arrive at mutual understanding through intuition.'[13] His self-absorbed, distant and idolizing infatuation caused him anguish; after he found out that she danced with young men at balls he threatened to drown himself in the River Danube.

When he left for Vienna, he wrote to her, promising to come back and marry her, but left the letter unsigned. Six years later, in 1913, Hitler sent an anonymous greeting in a Linz paper to the 'girlfriend' he had not seen since he was eighteen. Even during the Second World War, he would reminisce fondly in his 'Wolf's Lair' headquarters in East Prussia about his 'first love'. The woman in question was, by 1908, engaged to an army officer whom she later married. Years later, an Austrian historian sought out Stefanie, who recalled only that: 'I once received a letter in which the writer said he was now going to attend the Academy of Fine Arts, but I was to wait for him, he would return and marry me... I couldn't imagine who had sent it.'[14] This 'relationship' had been nothing but a fantasy on Hitler's part.

In 1907, Hitler made up his mind to study at the Vienna Academy of Fine Arts. He had been profoundly impressed by the grandeur of Vienna's buildings, and the culture, art and opera he had seen on his first visit there the previous year. Though his mother was by now ill with cancer, he took himself off to Vienna in time to take the preliminary examinations for the Academy in September 1907, convinced that he would soon be moving to Vienna to study there. He was rejected in October. 'It struck me as a bolt from the blue,' he recorded in *Mein*

Kampf. He had been 'convinced that it would be child's play to pass the examination'. He sought out the Rector of the Academy, who explained that his drawings 'incontrovertibly showed my unfitness for painting', and suggested to him that his talents lay more in the direction of architecture. Hitler felt 'for the first time in my young life at odds with myself' – not surprisingly, since his self-image was by now rooted in his belief in his genius as a painter. This would transfer later to his conviction of his genius as the saviour of Germany.

Meanwhile, his mother's condition was deteriorating rapidly. Kubizek visited her, after neither had heard from Hitler for a fortnight:

> Frau Klara seemed more careworn than ever. Her face was deeply lined. Her eyes were lifeless, her voice sounded tired and resigned. I had the impression that, now that Adolf was no longer there, she had let herself go, and looked older and more ailing than ever. She certainly had concealed her condition from her son to make the parting easier for him. Or perhaps it was Adolf's impulsive nature that had kept up her vitality. Now, on her own, she seemed to me an old, sick woman.[15]

She was forty-seven. Hitler returned to Linz and the news that there was no hope for his mother. Deeply upset, he nursed her and devoted his dutiful and 'indefatigable care' to her until her death in December. Brett Kahr surmises the long-term effect on Hitler: '[Her death] really damaged Hitler tremendously, and I think the reason that he couldn't forge relationships with young girls his own age when he was a teenage boy, or then later, with grown-up women when he was a grown-up man, is because he still remained deeply, deeply psychologically faithful to Klara. I think he could never let Klara go.'

Within the space of three months, Hitler had suffered a severe blow to his self-esteem with his rejection by the Academy, and 'he lost the one person for whom he had ever felt close affection and warmth'.[16]

Early in 1908, Hitler returned to Vienna. His ambition to study art was not accompanied by any effort to work for the entrance examination, which he took later in the autumn, and failed again. He persuaded

Kubizek to join him in the small room he had rented in February, and concealed from him his first rejection by the Academy. Cushioned by an orphan's pension, he shunned work, and pursued his life of idleness, spiced with visits to museums and art galleries and the opera (he saw *Tristan and Isolde* 'thirty to forty times'). He continued to draw up ever more grandiose and utopian architectural designs, pursued drawing and painting, at one time making a small living copying postcards of Viennese scenes, and attempted to write several dramas based on Germanic mythology, including an opera on the Wagnerian scale, based on a myth he looked up in his book *Gods and Heroes*. He oscillated between bitterness and hectic activity. Kubizek noted with some concern his fits of despair and fury, and his violent denunciation of those he believed were persecuting him: 'Choking with a catalogue of hates, he would pour his fury over everything, against mankind in general who did not understand him and by whom he was persecuted and cheated' – in particular, those at the Academy who laid traps for him 'for the sole purpose of ruining his career'. Kubizek concluded: 'Altogether, in those early days in Vienna, I had the impression that Adolf had become unbalanced.'[17] His paranoia was shaping itself, as was his passion for secrecy. He continued the fiction of his studies, not least because that was the condition of his financial support. Very soon, Hitler's contact with the remaining family, and his past in Linz, faded.

Hitler had only passing contact with women in Vienna. What might have been shyness was combined with a kind of prudishness. Kubizek remembers him living in 'strict, monk-like asceticism, having too high an opinion of himself for superficial flirtation or a merely physical relationship with a girl'. When Hitler interrupted a lesson with a female pupil in their room, he was furious with jealousy, thinking it was a girlfriend, and then, when he found she was a pupil, he ranted about the pointlessness of women studying. Kubizek was deterred by Hitler from involvements with women: 'Any step in that direction would have necessarily meant the end of our friendship.' He thought Hitler's attitude amounted to a deep disgust and repugnance at sexual activity.[18] Another associate from the Vienna days, Reinhold Hanisch, believed Hitler 'had very little respect for the female sex, but very austere ideas about relations between men and women. He often said that, if men only wanted to, they could adopt a strictly moral way of living.'[19]

This prudishness may have been shored up by his contact with political ideas circulating in Vienna at the time, including the aggressive Pan-Germanism expounded by Georg Ritter von Schönerer, who, as Joachim Fest summed up, was 'obsessed by fears of drowning in a sea of foreignness', and 'saw deadly threats to his Germanism all around him', chief among them Jews and the Catholic Church.[20] Schönerer titled himself Führer, used the 'Heil' greeting, and was virulently anti-Semitic. Matching his nationalism and anti-Semitism was Karl Lueger, then Mayor of Vienna and leader of the Christian Social Party, whose ability to command the masses through propaganda and an appeal to base instinct and emotion impressed Hitler.

Though the evidence points to the fact that Hitler's early political ideas had not yet crystallized, it is possible that they influenced his later thinking. Spliced into the political philosophy was their moral teaching, which glorified the ideal of the blond German male, who was fit and ready to fight in defence of a beleaguered Germania. One method of attaining readiness for this, expounded in Pan-German texts such as *Unadulterated German Words*, was sexual continence until the age of twenty-five: 'Nothing is as advantageous to young people as exceedingly long absti-nence. Every muscle becomes light, the eye begins to glow, the mind is quick, the memory fresh... And out of a sense of strength, one sees the world as if through a multi-coloured prism.' Dietary selection was recom-mended – 'food which stimulates the genitals should be avoided: this includes first of all meat'.[21] Hitler, who gave up smoking, and later became a vegetarian as well as a non-drinker, would regale Kubizek on the virtues of sexual purity to protect 'the flame of life'. Another strand, whose influ-ence on Hitler is uncertain, was propagated by the misogynist and anti-Semite, Jörg Lanz van Liebenfels, who asserted the superiority of the Aryan–German race, and warned young men against corruption by contact with young women, especially prostitutes, to avoid infection, including 'racial' infection. They were duty-bound to safeguard German dominance over other races by ensuring the 'purity of blood and race' in the next generation, and to ensure German male dominance over women by the wife's complete subordination to her husband.

In a city seething with sexual opportunities, with prostitutes openly offering their services day and night, and men encouraged to 'sow their wild oats', Hitler stood aloof. He recoiled from any sexual encounters. On visits to the opera, Kubizek noted how Hitler, dressed up in his finery and with his piercing blue eyes, attracted the glances of young girls. Hitler always looked away, as Brigitte Hamann relates:

> He had the shy ways of a man who didn't know anything, and of course that's very attractive for women, including older women. Older women thought this dear young man so nice and kind, and, in fact, there must have been a number of advances from them, in any case, more than were made to his friend Kubizek, who was very short and not very handsome. But Hitler always ran away. As soon as he saw that a woman was getting serious, he panicked, and ran away.

He was afraid of women. But one evening, after seeing Frank Wedekind's play, *Spring Awakening*, which was scandalizing Vienna with its scenes of pubescent angst, rape and homosexuality, Hitler grabbed his friend by the arm and steered him off to the red-light district, to observe at first hand what he called the 'cesspool of iniquity'. The play seems to have awakened in Hitler a lurid sexual fascination, as Kubizek relates:

> We walked along past the low one-storey houses. The windows, which were at street level, were lighted so that we could see directly into [them]. The girls sat there, some behind the window pane, some at the open window... In their scanty and slovenly attire they sat there, making up their faces or combing their hair or looking at themselves in the mirror... I was of the opinion that the one experience would have sufficed, but Adolf was already dragging me along the lighted windows... He grew angry at the prostitutes' 'tricks of seduction'.

Hitler used it as an occasion for a rant against the evils of prostitution. Ian Kershaw comments: 'Hitler took [Kubizek] back and gave him a lecture about prostitution and dirt and syphilis and everything else, but it was all done in this distant fashion, almost of voyeurism, on the one hand, but with the strongest antipathy to any actual contact with sex, on the other.' By the time he was well into his twenties, it is reasonably certain that Hitler had no sexual experience at all.

Some observers have suggested that the seeds of Hitler's anti-Semitism may have been nurtured by his early horror of prostitution, as author Ron Rosenbaum observes: 'There is some evidence that he used to be a reader of a scurrilous pornographic publication known as *Ostara*, which was filled with tales of beautiful, innocent, Aryan maidens being pursued and corrupted by lascivious Jews. So perhaps you could say that his emotional life, or his view of sexual life, was distorted during the Vienna period by this peculiar kind of pornographic, anti-Semitic litera-ture.' In the cultural and political flux of turn-of-the-century Vienna, this would be only a small strand in an evolving anti-Semitism, though the image was reproduced extensively in the anti-Semitic propaganda of the Third Reich, including in children's school text books.

Hitler's prudishness continued into the war. From 1909, when he descended from a relatively comfortable bohemian existence into poverty, he was almost exclusively in the company of men. In October 1908, possibly because of a second rejection by the Academy, he abruptly ended his relationship with Kubizek without a word of explana-tion. He moved out of the room he had shared with him, leaving only a note, and never saw or contacted his friend until his arrival as the saviour of the Germanic people when he annexed Austria in 1938. But, as the money he had got from his aunt Johanna (Klara's sister) for his 'studies' and his orphan's pension began to run out, his circumstances deteriorated rapidly. Over a period of three and a half years, he first slept rough, then lived among the poor in doss-houses and eventually men's homes. He became thin, bedraggled, unkempt and down-at-heel. Later, he shuddered at the memory of those days – of 'sordid scenes, of garbage, repulsive filth, and worse'. Characteristically, as Joachim Fest points out, 'he felt no compassion'.[22] He made few friends, though he set up a 'business partnership' with a fellow occupant of the men's home, Reinhold Hanisch, and then Josef Nauman, a Jew, to garner a paltry living hawking his paintings of Viennese street scenes.

In 1913, when he was being pursued for not registering for the

Austrian national service, he packed his bags and moved to Munich. Here, describing himself as 'an architectural painter', he continued his lonely drop-out existence, loitering in cafes where he might discuss politics with other customers, browsing in libraries, sketching and selling his paintings. When the military authorities caught up with him, he was found to be unfit for the army anyway. But when war was declared in August 1914, Hitler immediately and enthusiastically volunteered to fight in the Bavarian Army.

At the western front, Hitler, a corporal and dispatch rider, was a committed and dutiful soldier, eventually winning the Iron Cross First Class. He was called the 'monk' by his fellow soldiers. They thought him a little odd. He never had any letters from home. Though he would sometimes join in, he was more often to be found sitting apart from the group, reading. He never joined the others on visits to brothels. 'What about looking for a French mamsell?' a telephonist suggested. 'I'd die of shame looking for sex with a French girl,' Hitler is reported to have said, as the others burst into laughter. 'Look at the monk,' another said, to which Hitler retorted, 'Have you no German sense of honour left at all?' Another time, a soldier companion, Balthasar Brandmayer, asked, 'Haven't you ever loved a girl?' Hitler solemnly replied, 'I've never had time for anything like that and I'll never get round to it.'[23]

Ian Kershaw sums up in an interview the effect that period had on Hitler's character:

> The personal failures that he had in his life, with the inability to enter the Art Academy, his lack of self-esteem, the inability to match up to the image which he had of himself, sinking down in the Viennese period quite literally into the gutter and finding himself in the doss house for a while – this, against his whole self-image, left an enormous gulf, much larger than in the average human being. This carried on through to the end of the First World War. In the war he seemed to be finding some type of satisfaction in what he thought was Germany's coming victory. When the defeat happened in 1918, that was an additional trauma, where his world seemed to be falling apart.

NOTES

1   Bloch, Eduard, 'My Patient, Hitler' in *Collier's* (15 March 1941)
2   Interview with Paula Wolf (Hitler) – Adolf's sister – at Berchtesgaden, 5 June 1946, cited Kershaw, Ian, *Hitler: Hubris, 1889–1936*, Penguin, London, 1998, p. 12
3   ibid., p. 13
4   Schroeder, Christa (ed.), *Er war mein Chef: Aus dem Nachlass der Sekretärin von Adolf Hitler*, (ed.) Anton Joachimstaler, Munich, 1985, p. 63
5   Interview with Paula Wolf, cited Kershaw, *Hitler: Hubris*, p. 13
6   von Schirach, Henriette, *Frauen um Hitler: Nach Materialien von Henriette von Schirach*, F. A. Herbig, Munich and Berlin, 1983, p. 15
7   Schroeder, *Er war mein Chef*, p. 63
8   von Schirach, *Frauen um Hitler*, p. 15
9   Bloch, 'My Patient, Hitler'
10 Kubizek, August, *Young Hitler: The Story of Our Friendship*, Tower, New York, 1954, p. 61
11 Jetzinger, Franz, *Hitler's Youth*, Hutchinson, London, 1958, p. 88
12 ibid, p. 71
13 Kubizek, *Young Hitler*, pp. 63–4
14 Jetzinger, *Hitler's Youth*
15 Kubizek, *Young Hitler*, p. 77
16 Kershaw, *Hitler: Hubris*, p. 25
17 Kubizek, *Young Hitler*, pp. 182, 163
18 ibid., p. 237
19 Hanisch, Reinhold, 'I Was Hitler's Buddy', *New Republic*, 19 April 1939
20 Fest, Joachim, *Hitler*, Penguin, London, 1977, p. 64
21 Cited Hamann, Brigitte, *Hitlers Wien: Lehrjahre eines Diktators*, Piper, Munich, 1996
22 Fest, *Hitler*, p. 82
23 Cited Kershaw, *Hitler: Hubris*, p. 92

2
MUNICH MATRONS

Following Germany's defeat and surrender, Hitler stayed on in the Army. In the chaos of post-war Bavaria, he was selected to be sent on an anti-communist political education course, which involved tuition in public speaking. He found that he excelled in oratory. One of the teachers there, historian Karl Alexander von Müller, was leaving a lecture when he saw a group had gathered round one speaker: 'I saw a pale, thin face under a drooping, unsoldierly strand of hair, with close-cropped moustache and strikingly big pale blue eyes gleaming coldly with fanaticism.'[1] Shortly afterwards, Hitler joined the small, nationalist, anti-Semitic German Workers Party, led by Anton Drexler. He addressed a group of 111 people in 1919, and there, he claimed in *Mein Kampf*, he found his vocation: 'I spoke for thirty minutes, and what before I had simply felt within me without in any way knowing it was now proved a reality. I could speak. The people in the small room were electrified.' What he spoke of was German humiliation and hatred of the Jews, and he hit a nerve with audiences of demobilized soldiers in Bavaria. When Hitler found he could 'speak', Ian Kershaw suggests, it meant:

> Now he's finding someone who's listening to him. He's no longer just an eccentric somewhere, but his outward projection is now meeting a ready response on the part of his audiences... so that the secretive inner self which he's never disclosed, even in his closest circle, is compensated for in an

outward self. And in sexual terms, it's perhaps not going too far to say that the lack of inner sexual satisfaction is compensated for by this almost orgiastic response to the cheering and adulating masses.

By 1921, Hitler had taken over the leadership of the newly branded National Socialist German Workers Party and gathered around him a band of loyal followers, and what amounted to a small army of stormtroopers – his SA thugs – many of them rootless war veterans who regularly engaged in fighting and street brawls with their communist and socialist left opposition. As for speaking, Hitler was refining his 'voice' and his message for what he believed was maximum impact: 'Cruelty impresses. People need a good scare. They want to be afraid of something. They want someone to make them afraid. Haven't you noticed, after a brawl at a meeting, that the ones who get beaten up are the first to apply for membership of the party? What is this rot you talk about violence? The masses want that. They need something to dread.'[2]

Observers at the time noted how Hitler engineered his speeches to command a 'feminine' form of adulation, for, in his mind, the 'crowd' behaved like a woman, 'whose psychic feeling is controlled less by abstract logic than by indefinable sentimental yearning for complementary strength... the masses love a man who commands, not a man who begs'. The stage-management of crowds was carefully and cynically honed. He went on: '[The masses] understand neither the audacity used to terrorize them spiritually, nor the outrageous infringement of their human freedom, for they are totally unaware that the doctrine is delusional. They see only the unreasoning force, the brutality and the purpose of its manifestations, and, in the end, they always give in' (Mein Kampf).

Though his audiences were largely male, women were also present: 'Women's gushing adulation, carried to the pitch of pseudo-religious ecstasy, provided the indispensable stimulus that could rouse him from his lethargy,' Hermann Rauschning surmised. Hitler would begin 'in a low, slow tenor voice, and after about fifteen minutes, something occurs that can be described only by the ancient primitive metaphor – the spirit enters into him.' In the front rows at rallies were 'elderly women of a certain type, married and single. Anyone looking down from the platform on these front seat women and watching their expression of rapturous self-surrender, their moist and glistening eyes, could not doubt the character of their enthusiasm.'[3]

Though Hitler needed to court women's support, no woman had any place in the Nazi Party from its foundation:

> I detest women who dabble in politics. And if their dabbling extends to military matters it becomes utterly unendurable. In no section of the Party has a woman ever had the right to hold even the smallest post... In 1924 we had a sudden upsurge of women who were interested in politics... They wanted to join the Reichstag, in order to raise the moral level of that body, so they said. I told them that 90 per cent of the matters dealt with by parliament were masculine affairs, on which they could not have opinions of any value... Gallantry forbids one to give women an opportunity of putting themselves in situations that do not suit them.[4]

Gallantry, on the other hand, was indispensable in binding women to his cause.

As Hitler's notoriety in Munich increased, his support base broadened. It was not enough to hold the beer halls spellbound. Through one of the earliest members of the Party, Dietrich Eckart, a poet and playwright, Hitler gained access to the salons of Munich and a coterie of mainly older women who became willing benefactors to the cause, and gave him a new respectability. 'The young Hitler, whose newspaper was much discussed, whose meetings attracted so many, and about whom one actually knew so little, soon became a welcome guest, much sought after,' wrote Henriette von Schirach, daughter of Hitler's personal photographer.[5] Ernst 'Putzi' Hanfstaengl, a rich, cultured socialite who converted to Hitler's way of thinking after hearing him speak ('an astonishing spectacle of suggestive influence of the mass psyche,' he wrote), opened the doors of his glittering mansion and his extensive contact list to Hitler.

This young outsider with a reckless air and an awkward, rough edge to him fascinated them. His eccentricity was now a bonus. There is little evidence that politics was the main motive, though his nationalist, anti-Bolshevik, anti-Semitic rhetoric may have struck a chord. Curiosity about this 'revolutionary' appears to have been the initial pull. Putzi's sister Erna – a 'true *grande dame*, eccentric and generous', and a former child beauty who cycled through town in white breeches and was one of the first women to drive a car – invited a group to meet Hitler:

[We] were already sitting at the polished mahogany table by the window when the doorbell rang. Through the open door I could see him in the narrow hallway politely and almost servilely greeting our hostess, laying aside riding whip, velour hat and trench coat, finally unbuckling his cartridge belt with revolver attached and likewise hanging it on the clothes hook. It all looked very odd, reminiscent of Karl May's American Indian novels. As yet we did not know how precisely each of these trivialities in clothing and behaviour was even then calculated for effect... but something curiously awkward still clung to him, and one had the uneasy feeling that he sensed it and resented anyone's noticing it. His face, too, was still thin and pale, with something like an expression of suffering... This time, too, he spoke very little; most of the time he listened with marked attentiveness.[6]

To Hitler, who was building up the party's influence and finance, the Munich 'Muttis' (mothers) were useful, with their money, their contacts and their valuable support. With older 'safe' women, Hitler could call out, and manipulate, as he had with his mother, feelings of protective loyalty. He began to feel at ease with women who welcomed, and then adored, him. 'He was an odd-looking man, and he gave the impression that he was very lonely... His eyes always appealed to women, he had large piercing blue eyes, and some of the women of the very conservative-cum-nationalist circles in Munich took him up almost as if he were an adopted son... some of them were fond of him as a young man who deserves to be protected,' explains John Lukacs, author of *The Hitler of History*.

Elsa Bruckmann, small and graceful, a former Rumanian princess and wife of the owner of an extreme nationalist publishing house, held a famous salon in Leopoldstrasse, a business residence with rooms lined with their famous collection of works of art, and genuine Renaissance furniture. Here, she introduced Hitler to writers and thinkers, as well as industrialists and members of the aristocracy. As a child she had suffered from smallpox, leaving scars on her face, so her salons, at which she sat beside a dim lamp, never started before dusk. Hitler thought that her understanding and kindness made you forget the scars. Elsa extended her kindness to Hitler, and bought him the pale, English officer's coat that became his trade-mark for a time, and pandered to his taste in accessories by buying him a whip made of hippopotamus hide; it had a silver knob with 'EB' engraved on it, which, with a rifle hook attached, served as a dog lead. Later, she read the proofs of *Mein Kampf.*[7]

It was from the Bruckmanns' balcony that Hitler first noticed a small palace on Briennerstrasse, owned by an Englishman whom Hitler had met through Elsa Bruckmann. Hitler decided to buy it for his party headquarters. His associate Rudolf Hess raised the necessary 1.5 million Reichsmarks from industry – steel magnate Frank Thyssen arranged a Dutch credit of 300,000 RM – and from donations from party members. Hitler called in architect Paul Ludwig Troost to redesign the Brown House, based on Hitler's initial architectural jottings. Troost's wife, Gerdy, did the interior decoration, and became Hitler's adviser on decoration from then on.

Hitler's glitterati contacts gave him a useful veneer of respectability, which in turn gained him wider social access. Bavarian industrialist Emil Gansser was instrumental in getting Hitler to speak twice at the influential National Club in Berlin in 1922, which resulted in financial contributions from two leading Berlin industrialists, Ernst von Borsig and Werner von Siemens, and others, including executives of the Daimler Company and the Bavarian Industrialists Association.[8]

Helene Bechstein, wife of the piano manufacturer, regularly invited him to stay at their various residences in Berlin and Bavaria, and to supper at their suite at the exclusive Bayerische Hof. The Bechsteins had a villa at Obersalzberg, and it was through them that Hitler was able to buy Haus Wachenfeld, the property that he would later turn into his mountain retreat, the Berghof. When Hitler needed surety against a loan of 60,000 Swiss francs for the party funds, she lent the party her jewellery, and persuaded others of her circle, including Gertrud von Seidlitz, to do the same. 'I wish he were my son,' she said. She even claimed to be his adoptive mother in order to visit him in Landsberg prison, after his failed putsch against the Bavarian government in November 1923.[9]

They also introduced Hitler to the Wagner circle at Bayreuth, where he satisfied his appetite for opera and influence by regularly attending the festival. Winifred Wagner overcame her initial impression of him as 'rather common' (he had turned up in lederhosen, thick woollen socks and an ill-fitting short blue jacket – the Bavarian national dress) and concluded shortly that he was 'destined to be the saviour of Germany'. Her husband, the composer Wagner's son, Siegfried, decided Hitler was 'a fraud and an upstart' but failed to quell his wife's enthusiasm. While many of Hitler's friends rejected him after the 1923 putsch, Winifred wrote an open letter: 'All Bayreuth knows that we have a friendly relationship with Hitler.' She sent him packages in Landsberg, visited him in Munich after his release, encouraged him to continue with the struggle, and kept up regular contact with him from then on.

These stately ladies took him under their wing, and helped knock away a few of his rough edges. Putzi Hanfstaengl had noted on Hitler's first visit that 'his awkward use of knife and fork betrayed his background'. When he found Hitler sugaring a vintage wine, he was appalled, but added, patronizingly, 'he could have peppered it, for each naïve act increased my belief in his homespun sincerity'.[10] Hitler's taste in clothes also alerted Putzi to the need for change; he had turned up in a blue suit, purple shirt, brown waistcoat and a red tie, and the bulge at his hip betrayed his revolver. When Pfeffer von Salomon, later his chief stormtrooper, first saw him wearing an old tailcoat, tan shoes and carrying a knapsack, he refused to be introduced. 'He seemed concerned less with making his appearance attractive than with making it memorable,' historian Joachim Fest concludes.[11] Hitler, aware of how useful his new patrons could be to him, was a willing student. Munich's society ladies tidied him up: 'Helene Bechstein bought him a tailcoat, a dinner jacket, the right hats and decent clothes. She taught him how to behave at the dinner table, that one had to make small-talk before finally getting to what one really wanted to talk about. And he appreciated her and was as obedient as a child. He knew: "I have to learn",' says author Brigitte Hamann. Though his quaint Austrian style of hand-kissing charmed them, clicking his heels on being introduced was thought to be going a bit far.

But they failed to puncture his egotism in conversation. It was only in his yelling speeches that he lost his awkwardness, as Hermann Rauschning observed at the time:

> A quiet conversation with him was impossible. Either he was silent or he took complete charge of the conversation. Hitler's eloquence is plainly no natural gift, but the result of the conquest of certain natural inhibitions which, in intimate conversation, still make him awkward. The convulsive artificiality of his character is specially noticeable in such intimate circles; particularly noticeable is his lack of any sense of humour. Hitler's laugh is hardly more than an expression of scorn and contempt. There is no relaxation about it. His pleasures have no repose.[12]

His conquest of 'society' women gave him a new confidence and ease in female company, and he no longer retreated into solitude, shunning women. Their adoration helped justify his inclination to remain single. Aware of the political need to gain women's support, he also had a personal investment in it – the need to be idolized: 'Lots of women are attracted to me because I am unmarried,' he told Albert Speer later. 'That was especially useful during our days of struggle. It's the same as with a movie actor; when he marries, he loses a certain something for the women who adore him. Then he is no longer their idol as he was before.'[13] Hitler was fond of relating stories about women who became jealous of his attentions. 'I knew of one woman whose voice became raucous with emotion when I spoke in her presence to another woman,' he claimed. Frau Bruckmann once refused to re-invite a 'very pretty' woman, after she had shown an 'untimely' interest in him.[14]

The signs of vanity are unmistakable. His preoccupation with his photographic image began at this time, when he acquired his loyal personal photographer, Heinrich Hoffmann. Until he found a man he could trust, he forbade any photographs to be taken of him, and his associates dealt summarily with intruders, smashing up both the offender and his photographic plates. In the privacy of Hoffmann's studio, he would practise for hours with poses and gestures to perfect his platform style. He tended to favour the matinee idol image in close-up portraits; photos were only ever released after his approval.

In Munich, he began to take delight in being associated with beautiful women. 'What lovely women there are in the world!' he reflected later, recalling, like some ageing movie actor, a reception at the Bayrischer Hof. 'There were splendid women there, elegant and covered with jewels. A woman entered who was so beautiful that all the others were eclipsed. She wore no jewels. It was Frau Hanfstaengl. I saw her again with Mary Stuck at Erna Hanfstaengel's. Three women together, one more beautiful than the others. What a picture!'[15] 'The beautiful Helene' Hanfstaengl was the target of one of his more clumsy advances, but she was safe because, though young and blonde, she was Putzi's wife. He paid court to her. On one occasion, he fell on one knee in front of her and told her that if things had been different, and she wasn't married, and he didn't have a high historical mission, she would be his ideal. According to her son, Egon, she had felt sorry for him. When she related the episode to her husband, she told him not to worry: 'Putzi, I tell you he's a neuter.'[16] However, her loyalty extended to sheltering Hitler in her house for several days before his arrest following the failed putsch in 1923.

By that time, the Nazi Party had 55,000 members, more than half from the lower middle classes. Afterwards, with Hitler incarcerated in Landsberg prison, support among the social elite, apart from the inner circle of women, temporarily waned. But it had revived again on the national level by 1932, when society hostesses provided the Nazis with valued entrée to the drawing rooms of Berlin. These included Helen von Carnap, wife of the Kaiser's last Chamberlain; Manna von Winterfeld, wife of an army general; and the monarchist Victoria von Dirksen, who entertained the highest aristocracy and members of the royal family, and had, according to Bella Fromm, society correspondent for the *Vossische Zeitung*, 'for years been an eager hostess of the National Socialists in her magnificent palace', acting as 'a mediator between the National Socialists and the old courtiers' (19 October 1932). Bella Fromm noted in her diary on 29 January 1932: 'Society slowly gets accustomed to the originally plebeian National Socialist movement. People from the upper crust are coming to Hitler.' She informed her readers: 'They get in everywhere, these National Socialists. They are patient, they bore from within and from without.' Victoria von Dirksen's brother attended the parties 'in the full splendour of his SS uniform... and both the hostess and her youngest daughter wear the swastika pinned conspicuously on their bosoms.'[17]

By then, the Nazi Party, after gaining over a hundred deputies in the Reichstag election of 1930, had become a major political player, and was recruiting the aristocracy steadily into the ranks of the SA and the SS. Many of the leading positions in the SA were already held by ex-officers of the nobility, and they joined in ever increasing numbers between 1930 and 1933. Heinrich Himmler, head of the elite SS, and dedicated to promoting racial purity, deliberately targeted the aristocracy: 'If you take a look at the individuals involved, you have to admit there is some damned good blood among them... We must try to fill the sons and daughters of those who are now opposed to us with our ideology, which after all is not so very far removed from the ideological principles of the nobility.' By 1938, the nobility made up almost 20 per cent of the SS top leadership, the Obergruppenführer.[18]

NOTES

1 von Müller, Karl Alexander, *Im Wandel einer Welt: Erinnerungen 1919–1932*, Munich, 1966
2 Rauschning, Hermann, *Hitler Speaks*, Thornton Butterworth, London, 1939, p. 89
3 ibid., pp. 258–9
4 *Hitler's Table Talk 1941–1944*, introduction by Hugh Trevor Roper, Weidenfeld and Nicolson, London, 1953 (26 January 1942), pp. 251–2
5 von Schirach, *Frauen um Hitler*, p. 29
6 von Müller, *Im Wandel einer Welt*, p. 129
7 von Schirach, *Frauen um Hitler*, p. 30
8 Noakes, Jeremy, 'Nazism and High Society' in Michael Burleigh (ed.), *Confronting the Nazi Past: New Debates on Modern German History*, vol. 4, Collins and Brown, London, 1998, p. 54; Fest, *Hitler*, p. 249
9 Fest, *Hitler*, p. 202
10 Hanfstaengl, Ernst, 'I Was Hitler's Closest Friend', in *Cosmopolitan*, March 1943
11 Fest, *Hitler*, p. 201
12 Rauschning, *Hitler Speaks*, p. 68
13 Speer, Albert, *Inside the Third Reich*, Weidenfeld and Nicolson, London, 1970, p. 92
14 *Hitler's Table Talk*, p. 359
15 ibid., p. 247
16 Hanfstaengl, Ernst, *15 Jahre mit Hitler, Zwischen Wiessem und Braunem Haus*, Piper, Munich, 1980, p. 61
17 Noakes, 'Nazism and High Society', p. 56
18 Cited ibid., p. 58

3
OBSESSION: GELI RAUBAL

While Hitler was being fêted by the matrons of Munich, he discovered that he held both a political and personal attraction for women. He flirted with beautiful women, needed to feel that they were attracted to him, and enjoyed being photographed in public with them; but there was no hint of sexual involvement with his patronesses, or with unmarried women of his own age. They were simply useful to him on his 'high mission'. He seems to have focused any sexual attentions on young and submissive women. Later, he declaimed: 'A girl of eighteen to twenty is as malleable as wax. It should be possible for a man, whoever the chosen woman may be, to stamp his own imprint on her. That's all the woman asks for, by the way.'[1]

After his release from prison – where he spent only thirteen months of his five-year sentence, and wrote *Mein Kampf* – he plunged back into political activities. The Nazi Party was in disarray, and had splintered into rival factions during his absence, though it had only ever been a marginal party in a wider grouping of extreme right-wing nation- alists. Hitler's experience in prison crystallized his messianic belief in himself as the saviour of Germany. Banned from public speaking throughout most of Germany, he set about reviving the Party, but spent an increasing amount of time at Obersalzberg. It was here in 1926 that he met Maria ('Mimi') Reiter, a blonde sixteen-year-old. Her mother had recently died, and she was helping run the family clothes shop beside Deutsches Haus, the hotel where Hitler was staying.

Hitler, by now thirty-seven, introduced himself to her when their paths crossed while walking their dogs. He pursued her, flirted with her, took her out on trips in his Mercedes and invited her to a meeting he was to address. She was impressed by his celebrity, and by his dress – by this time, breeches, light velour hat, riding whip and a coat held closed by a leather belt. In her later account, she recalls him taking her to dinner, feeding her cakes like a child, and touching her leg with his knee under the table. Hitler told her that she reminded him of his own mother, especially her eyes, and suggested they visit her mother's grave. There, she recalled, Hitler was overcome – 'moved by something he did not want to tell me'. He allegedly muttered, 'I am not ready yet.' After this, Hitler asked her to call him by his favourite nickname 'Wolf'.[2]

On one occasion, Hitler shocked her when, in a show of harsh dominance, he beat his dog with his whip after it had attacked her dog: 'It was necessary,' he said, when she protested. On several of their excursions, he put his arms round her, and once took her to a remote forest glade, stood her up against a tree, kissed her passionately, calling her his 'wood-nymph', and declared his wish to marry her – but not at the moment. He had no time to think of such things – he had his duty, his mission.[3] Mimi, at sixteen, was clearly infatuated by him. Soon afterwards he was off to Munich. She wrote him fond letters and sent him embroidered cushions; he sent her a leather-bound copy of *Mein Kampf* for Christmas. When he wrote to her in February 1927, thanking her for a present, he was paternalistically caring, but distant:

> My dear, good child, I was truly happy to receive this sign of your tender friendship to me... I am given a constant reminder of your cheeky head and your eyes... As regards what is causing you personal pain, you can believe me that I sympathize with you. But you should not let your little head droop in sadness and must only see and believe: even if fathers sometimes don't understand their children any longer because they have got older not only in years but in feelings, they mean only well for them. As happy as your love makes me, I ask you most ardently to listen to your father. And now, my dear treasure, receive warmest greetings from your Wolf, who is always thinking of you.[4]

This could be construed as a clear attempt to disengage from the relationship.

Mimi met Hitler briefly in Munich at the Cafe Heck, where, in her somewhat romantic account, he pressed her with endearments. But when he returned to Berchtesgaden, he did not visit her. Mimi was distraught at his inattention and his failure to respond to her, and she attempted suicide, the first of a number of women who were driven to despair by Hitler. She tried to hang herself, but her brother-in-law rescued her at the last minute. Mimi's account continues with a visit to Hitler's flat in 1931, after she had married and been estranged from her husband. The date is thought to be unlikely, and the story of 'how I let everything happen' with Hitler, embellished. Though she claims Hitler made further protestations of love for her, and Hitler's lawyer, Hans Frank, helped her initiate divorce proceedings, the affair petered out. Ian Kershaw concludes:

> I think it was the infatuation of a young girl for someone who is already well known, famous and, in a sense, on the way to stardom. I think Hitler played her along. He found her an attractive young thing, she was somebody that he could simply string along. She worshipped at the shrine, so to say. She could be used by him and then later on she was just dropped when it didn't suit any longer... But the stories she later on painted I think have to be treated with more than a dose of scepticism, for example that she spent the night with Hitler in 1931.

By 1927, Hitler was fully occupied with politics. Although still banned from public speaking, he spent a great deal of his time in Munich's cafes and beer halls, holding forth about 'revolution'. Women were peripheral to his politics. 'Very occasionally, a woman would be admitted to our intimate circle, but she never was allowed to become the centre of it, and had to remain seen and not heard,' Hitler's personal photographer, Heinrich Hoffmann, recalled. 'She could occasionally take a small part in the conversation, but never was she allowed to hold forth or contradict Hitler.'[5] But shortly, Hitler would launch into an 'affair' with a woman half his age, which most historians believe was, after his mother, the most important personal relationship in his life.

In Obersalzberg, which he regularly visited, Hitler found a house to rent in 1927. In March, he brought in his half-sister, Angela, with whom he had made only intermittent contact since his departure from Linz, to act as housekeeper. Angela was joined shortly afterwards by her daughter, Geli, who had just left school. Hitler was enchanted by Geli. He was twice her age: she was nineteen when she arrived at Haus Wachenfeld, and he was thirty-eight. Any relationship between Hitler and Geli was possibly incestuous, since she was his half-sister's daughter or, loosely, his niece. She called him 'Uncle Alf', and he called her his 'princess'.

Geli, according to her friend, Henriette Hoffmann (later von Schirach), was 'big, cheerful, and self-confident... She had what Hitler valued in women: courage and understanding – and... cheerful determination.'[6] Julius Schaub, Hitler's adjutant, described her as a 'brown-eyed brunette, five feet, six inches tall, well-built, with a blooming appearance, exceptionally full of animal spirits and a pleasing voice... By nature she was an open character, always ready for a joke... She was extraordinarily self-possessed. Sometimes inclining towards obstinacy.'[7] Ian Kershaw reports: 'From the start, Hitler was evidently attracted by her. She wasn't, physically, a stunning beauty, but she exuded a strong sexuality and she had a number of short-lived affairs and flirtations. Very flighty type of flirtatious girl, full of life and full of fun, and Hitler was not exactly that type, but this contrast somehow had its appeal, and a very strong bond, certainly from Hitler to her, developed.'

Psychologist Brett Kahr finds the similarity with Adolf's parents' relationship 'extraordinary':

There's almost a mirror image between Alois and Klara's relationship on the one hand, and the relationship between Adolf and Geli Raubal. For starters, the age difference... is almost identical. Hitler's father, Alois Hitler, was exactly twenty-three years older than Hitler's mother, Klara, and the age difference between Adolf and Geli is almost the same, nineteen years. And the blood relationship between the two pairs is also very, very similar indeed. Alois Hitler was the second cousin of Klara, and Adolf's half-sister bore a daughter, Geli, so you had these two very similar cousinly, aunty-uncly sort of relationships...

And I think by going for Geli, who was the younger woman, younger by two full decades, he was trying to find in a very overt way a mother substitute.

In some obscure way, he may have identified Geli with his mother. Geli's mother, Angela, was three months pregnant with Geli when she went to Klara's funeral, and perhaps Geli represented some sense of renewal of life after his mother's death.

Hitler enjoyed Geli's company: 'Her cheerful laughter always gave me hearty pleasure, her harmless chatter filled me with joy. Even when she sat quietly by my side working a crossword puzzle, I was enveloped in a feeling of well-being,' he reminisced to Otto Wagener, a member of his entourage. 'I can sit next to young women who leave me completely cold. I feel nothing, or they actually irritate me. But a girl like the little Hoffmann [Henriette Hoffmann] or Geli – with them I become cheerful and bright, and if I have listened for an hour to their perhaps silly chatter – or I have only to sit next to them – then I am free of all weariness and listlessness. I can go back to work refreshed.'[8]

Hitler became increasingly obsessed with Geli. The relationship would last four years. She registered as a medical student at Munich University in autumn 1927. Hitler found her a room, first in the Königstrasse, not far from his extremely drab room, and then, after a year, a room in the house of a singing teacher, Adolf Vogl, just beside his in Thierschstrasse. When Hitler moved into a nine-room apartment on Prinzregenzplatz, in November 1929, he arranged for Geli to come and live there in her own room.

Soon Hitler was taking her everywhere with him – to the Cafe Heck and the Osteria restaurant, where he had a regular table and kept open house. They drove around in his large Mercedes and often went on picnics together. 'She would put her arms around Hitler's neck with a winning smile and say: "Onkel Alf, let's go on a picnic on the Chiemsee," and he usually gave in to her wishes.' Emil Maurice, Hitler's chauffeur, drove them, Henriette Hoffmann recalled. Hitler kept caps in the glove compartment to protect their hair, white linen in summer, brown leather in winter, along with peppermints, sweets and Bahlsen biscuits. 'Hitler never swam. He lay in the woods and read... He took his shoes and socks off and paddled with his white feet in shallow water. He looked for flat, round stones, and, stooping down, he would skim them at an angle over the water, like a little discus, so they would bounce again and again... sometimes ten or twelve times.' Putzi Hanfstaengl was often there, and Henriette's father, Heinrich Hoffmann. The men sat around and read. The girls changed in the bushes and swam naked, and then dried in the sun to get brown. 'On the way home, Hitler would turn round to us and say, "Talk or sing, so the driver doesn't fall asleep"... But he never joined in.' Hitler often went shopping with Geli, waiting patiently while she tried on hats or selected perfumes. For the first time, Hitler was enjoying a social life divorced from politics. He took her to all the new opera productions, then afterwards went on with her to the Osteria and met up with others. 'She exercised the sweet tyranny of youth and he liked it. He was more cheerful, happier.'[9] The chauffeur Emil Maurice concurred: 'He liked to show her off everywhere; he was proud of being seen in the company of such an attractive girl. He was convinced that in this way he impressed his comrades in the party.'[10]

Hitler went further – he allowed her to become the main attraction. He would normally hold forth in company, but, 'When Geli came to Munich it all changed. He took her with him and she won everyone's heart. He was no longer the centre of attention – Geli was.'[11] Most of the men around Geli enjoyed her company, as Baldur von Schirach recalled.

> We liked her. When she was there, Hitler almost never started on the dreadful and often really painful scenes with endless monologues and uninhibited recriminations he bestowed not only on his political enemies but also on friends and fellow-fighters. Geli's presence relaxed and released him... Geli was allowed to laugh at her Uncle Alf and adjust his tie when it had slipped. She was never put under pressure to be specially clever or specially witty. She could be simply what she was – lively and uncomplicated.[12]

Nor did Geli show any interest whatever in Hitler's politics. The one time she heard him speak, it seemed to Henriette that she found her uncle strange.

Hitler was intensely possessive of Geli, but whether a sexual relationship existed between them remains a matter of speculation. Historian Ian Kershaw comments:

> I think I'd agree that Hitler was in some ways sexually attracted to Geli, and that this transcends anything that had apparently taken place earlier on. Certainly it was a very different relationship, all those around him recognized that and saw it as different. And Hitler was different in her presence. So I think that there was this sexual attractiveness that she somehow emitted, and that Hitler was taken by, and that presumably was one of the reasons why the possessiveness became so chronic on his part, but whether the sexual attraction that Hitler felt for her was reciprocated is a very moot point indeed. It almost certainly wasn't, and Geli didn't find the sexual attraction in her uncle who was nineteen years older than her. She found it interesting to be with all these cronies and to be ferried around and taken here, there and everywhere and treated like a little princess, which Hitler frequently called her, but that there was a mutual sexual attractiveness is, I think, highly unlikely.

Hitler ordered Geli's life more and more. He arranged for her to take singing lessons, though unfortunately her teacher did not believe she had any talent, and moreover he pronounced her lazy. He circumscribed her social activities. Once on the way home from a picnic, they saw a fire and went to investigate. It was to celebrate the shortest night, when boys and girls sat round the fire singing and then they jumped the flames. One of the boys took Geli's hand and they jumped. Almost immediately there were two short hoots on the car horn – Hitler's signal for them to go, and Geli had to leave.[13] She loved going to balls, but Hitler insisted she was chaperoned by older men. Once, her escort Heinrich Hoffmann told Hitler he thought Geli was unhappy, she was too protected. According to Hoffmann, Hitler replied: 'You know, Hoffmann, I'm so concerned about Geli's future that I feel I have to watch over her. I love Geli, and could marry her. Good! But you know what my viewpoint is. I want to remain single. So I retain the right to exert an influence on her circle of friends until such time as she finds the right man. What Geli sees as compulsion is simply prudence. I want to stop her falling into the hands of someone unsuitable.' Hoffmann concluded that, though it flattered Geli that her uncle was so fond of her, and she was charmed by his gallantry and generosity, it seemed, 'simply intolerable to this child of nature that he should want to mother her every step and that she shouldn't be allowed to speak to anyone without his knowledge'.[14]

When Hitler detected signs of affection between Geli and his chauffeur Emil Maurice, whom he employed to chaperone her, he was furious. They seem to have planned to get engaged. Henriette remembered that Emil had come one day and told her that he and Geli had been laughing at something in the flat. Suddenly Hitler appeared in the room and grabbed Emil – 'I thought he wanted to shoot me.' Geli watched in silence: 'She realized how powerless she was.' Hitler effectively insisted they break it off. Geli wrote to Maurice on 14 December 1927: 'Uncle Adolf is insisting that we should wait two years. Think of it, Emil, two whole years of only being able to kiss each other now and then and always having U.A. in charge... I can only give you my love and be unconditionally faithful to you... I love you so infinitely much... Uncle A is being fearfully nice. I'd like to give him great happiness but I don't know how... But Uncle says our love must be kept completely secret.'[15] Under these constraints, presumably as Hitler had intended, the relationship petered out.

But Geli was feeling the strain: 'Hitler was driven by an intense possessiveness towards her. It was like a clammy hand all round her and she was like the proverbial bird in the gilded cage, who could not get away from her uncle who was stifling her very existence. She was a fun-loving girl who wanted normal relationships and so on, and ultimately this must have driven her to a position where she felt there was no way out of it,' says Ian Kershaw.

Her friend Henriette Hoffmann noticed the change: 'In the years when she lived so close to Hitler, she became introverted and serious. She did not want to be protected, she was ready to try new things, she was hungry for experiences.' In the last summer before she died, when Henriette enjoyed all sorts of things, such as mountain hikes with other students, Geli wasn't allowed by Hitler to go. 'She was the Queen in Hitler's game of chess, his valued object.' Geli confided to Heinrich Hoffmann that she loved a man in Vienna who had no money. For her, being in love was the centre of her existence. Henriette once asked her: 'Which would you rather – to love, or be loved?' Without hesitation she answered 'But of course, I want to love. To be loved isn't interesting, but to love someone, you know, *love,* that's the whole point of life. And if you are loved back then that is paradise.'[16]

After her death, a letter was found in Geli's room. The sender's name is not known, but it is dated June 1929, and suggests that she had wanted to get engaged to a young man, but her mother, under pressure from Hitler, had put them off for a year:

> Now your uncle, who knows how much influence he has over your mother, is trying to exploit her weakness with boundless cynicism. Unfortunately we won't be in a position to fight back against this blackmail until you're twenty-one. He's putting obstacles in the way of our mutual happiness although he knows that we're made for each other. The year of separation your mother is imposing on us will only bind us together more closely... but your uncle's behaviour towards you can only be described as egoistic. He quite simply wants you to belong to him one day and never to anyone else... Your uncle still sees you as the 'inexperienced child' and refuses to acknowledge that in the meantime you've grown up and want to take responsibility for your own happiness. Your uncle is a force of nature. In his party they all bow down to him like slaves... He's hoping to succeed this year in changing your mind, but how little he knows your soul.[17]

The trail on this relationship peters out here, but it illustrates Hitler's obsessive control over Geli's life, and other people's supposition of his intentions – that she should never belong to anyone else but him.

On 19 September 1931 Geli was found dead in Hitler's flat, having shot herself with his gun. The previous evening, Hitler left for Hamburg as part of his electioneering in North Germany. It was alleged that they had quarrelled before his departure; she wanted to go to Vienna, and he had told her she couldn't go, though Hitler vehemently denied this. It was rumoured that she had a lover there. Angela Raubal, Geli's mother, later said she had wanted to marry a violinist from Linz, but she and her half-brother had forbidden her to see the man. Others claimed, implausibly, that she was pregnant by a Jewish lover in Vienna.

Heinrich Hoffmann had picked Hitler up from the flat the previous day. His daughter, Geli's friend, recorded what the housekeeper, Frau Winter, had seen and heard that evening: 'Hitler had run back up the steps to say goodbye again. He stroked her cheek gently and whispered something in her ear, but Geli reacted angrily. She went back into the flat with Frau Winter and shut the door, then she said, and these were her last words: "Really, nothing ties me to my uncle any more." She told Frau Winter that she was going out with friends and did not want any supper. So Frau Winter did not worry when she did not see Geli again that evening.'[18] When Hitler was told, he rushed back to Munich. By then, a flurry of rumours was circulating about her death. A top-level conference of Munich Nazis was immediately convened in his flat, to decide how to contain the imminent scandal. As the mystery of her death remains unsolved, speculation is rife.

It is most likely that Hitler's possessiveness drove Geli to her death. But another theory was put forward by American intelligence during the war. 'A Psychological Profile of Adolf Hitler' was compiled by the US Office of Strategic Services in 1943. It was based on the testimony of two of Hitler's former associates, Putzi Hanfstaengl and Otto Strasser, both of whom had very serious grievances against him by that time, and both had fled in fear of their lives. Under the heading 'Masochistic Gratifications', the report talked about Hitler's copraphagic tendencies, how he felt compelled to degrade himself in the eyes of the loved one and eat their dirt. In Geli's case, it was of the utmost importance to him that she squat over him in such a way that he could see everything.

This detail is based on the testimony of Otto Strasser, not by any means a close friend of Geli's, who alleges that Geli told him that there were things that Hitler made her do which were disgusting. From this claim is spun the theory that Geli could stand this no longer, and it drove her to suicide. Ian Kershaw comments: 'The evidence that we have about sexual perversions comes from very dubious or unsatisfactory sources. A lot of them went back to rumours put around Munich and elsewhere at the time by Hitler's political enemies, so I tend to be sceptical or cautious in dealing with these.' Psychologist Brett Kahr is also sceptical about the sources, but adds: 'It is not outside the realms of psychological possibility, of clinical possibility, that the allegations about Hitler's sexual perversions could be true. We know that Hitler as a child had to endure a number of extremely humiliating situations in the family home, and it is not unreasonable to suggest that Hitler might have tried to turn those early experiences of humiliation into something more pleasurable by enacting them with his female mistresses in later life.' Ron Rosenbaum, author of *Explaining Hitler*, suggests another reason for the persistence of the stories:

> People would like to find a connection and be able to say, 'Well, Hitler was monstrous personally in his private sexual life, therefore that explains the monstrousness of his political fantasies.' But, in fact, I think that what underlies all this attempt to find a sexual explanation is fear. Fear in some way that in the absence of some wild perversion, you might have to realize that Hitler in some way is normal, and then a Hitler who is normal is in some way more frightening than a Hitler who is hugely perverse. Because Hitler's normality in some way implicates our own normality.

Historian John Lukacs, author of *The Hitler of History*, draws a different conclusion about Hitler: 'I am nearly convinced that his sexuality was normal... Hitler was an under-sexed person, normal, but under-sexed. But, by and large, not only after he becomes successful, relationships with women were never a principal thing in his life.'

Hitler was devastated by Geli's death. He sank into depression, refused to see anyone for a while and retreated to the house of his publisher. He made Geli's room a shrine, in which nothing was to be moved; he kept the keys and allowed no one in. As with his mother's death, Hitler refused to let her go. Rudolph Hess claimed he was near to suicide himself and thought of giving up the whole thing; rumours had circulated that he had shot Geli and, Hess reported, he had been 'so fearfully vilified by this new campaign of lies that he wanted to make an end of everything. He could no longer look at a newspaper because this frightful filth was killing him.' Hoffmann reported when he met him on Tuesday 22 September that he looked 'like a broken man'.[19] He paced his room for two whole nights, refusing to eat. One of his major concerns was the possible political repercussions on the Party when it was just manoeuvring its way into prominence and respectability. Another may have been fear of his arrest if allegations of murder got out of hand. Strenuous attempts, largely successful, were made by the Party to shut down the investigation into Geli's death and keep it from becoming a political issue. When, on the day after the funeral, Hitler addressed a meeting in Hamburg, he was reported to be 'looking very shaken, but speaks very well'.[20]

It was a crucial time for the Nazi Party, and Hitler, though undoubtedly upset, was not depressed for long. There was electioneering to get on with, and within a week of Geli's death the Party made important gains in city elections all over Germany, building on their success in the 1930 Reichstag election, when their representation went up from twelve to 107 seats. Hitler was preparing to campaign for the presidency of the republic, which would place him firmly at the centre of national politics. There were votes to be gained, people and constituencies to be won over, and crowds to be wooed. Hitler salved his wound, which was undoubtedly deep, moved on, and let the outer self take over from the private inner emptiness as he returned to 'the struggle'.

Geli's friend, Henriette Hoffmann, sadly noted the aftermath: 'After Geli's death, much changed in our lives. Picnics didn't happen. Nobody talked about Geli, it was as if she had never existed. Her room was closed, the clothes remained in the wardrobe, the pullovers, the pleated skirts, the hats she'd brought back from Vienna, the long evening dresses she'd worn at the Bayreuth Festival... Only the blood was washed away, in so far as it was possible to get rid of bloodstains.' Six months later, on her wedding day, Henriette went into Geli's room. All her things were there untouched, the air 'was perfumed with withered roses, with perfectly fresh early freesias', which the housekeeper, Frau

Winter, had put there: 'Though everything appeared unaltered, as if it had only just been abandoned, the room seemed to me like an Egyptian burial place.'

Henriette drew her own conclusions: 'Geli lived for four years with her uncle and then killed herself with his pistol in his flat. He had so limited her life, driven her into a corner, that she saw no other way out. In the end she hated her uncle, actually she wanted to kill him. She couldn't do that so she killed herself to hurt him deeply, to destroy him. She knew nothing else could wound him. He knew that and was in despair because he knew it was his fault.'[21] Her father, one of Hitler's most loyal acolytes, 'noticed a big change in Hitler. He became inhuman – he had destroyed what he had loved. The revolutionary had become a tyrant, merciless to himself and others.' Ron Rosenbaum is critical of the 'no more Mr Nice Guy' theory: 'Hitler's ruthlessness, his murderousness is evident in the 1920s long before Geli Raubal's death.'

The episode revealed more clearly his profound inability to sustain personal relationships. As with his mother, he could not let Geli go, keeping her room in his flat locked and unchanged from the day of her death. Something of the destructiveness and rage at the heart of the man infected his relationships with women, and his narcissism and self-preoccupation precluded concern and compassion for others. Locked in a rigid vision of an idealized woman, the intricacies of personal tenderness were beyond him.

Geli had, by all accounts, touched his deeper feelings. Her death confirmed him in his conviction that, for his public image, no one woman could ever be seen to be too close to him. Women in his personal life were periphery to his purpose. But he needed their support politically. As he shaped the leader cult, his image as the lonely figure, burdened by his task as saviour of Germany, sacrificing his personal life for the nation, became central to his appeal. In his cynical and grandiose way, he declared himself 'married to Germany'. From this lofty platform, he could pontificate endlessly on the role and purpose of women in the life of the nation, and, once in power, he had the means to persuade, or seduce, women to his vision.

NOTES

1 *Hitler's Table Talk 1941–1944*, p. 246
2 Rosenbaum, Ron, *Explaining Hitler: The Search for the Origins of His Evil*, Papermac, London, 1999, p. 113
3 ibid., pp. 112–14
4 Cited Knopp, Guido, *Hitler. Ein Bilanz*, Siedler, Berlin, 1995
5 Hoffmann, Heinrich, *Hitler Was My Friend*, Burke, London, 1955, pp. 147–8
6 von Schirach, Henriette, *Frauen um Hitler*, p. 46
7 Cited Hayman, Ronald, *Geli & Hitler*, Bloomsbury, London, 1997, p. 104
8 Wagener, Otto, *Hitler – Memoirs of a Confidant*, ed. Henry Ashby Turner, Yale University Press, 1985, pp. 222, 36
9 von Schirach, Henriette, *Frauen um Hitler*, pp. 55–9, 51
10 Gun, Nerin E., *Eva Braun: Hitler's Mistress*, Leslie Frewin, London 1969, p. 108
11 von Schirach, Henriette, *Frauen um Hitler*, p. 50
12 von Schirach, Baldur, *Ich glaubte an Hitler*, Mosaik Verlag, Hamburg, 1967, p. 106
13 von Schirach, Henriette, *Frauen um Hitler*, pp. 59–60
14 Hoffmann, *Hitler Was My Friend*, pp. 125–6
15 Unpublished letter, Geli Raubal to Emil Maurice, cited Hayman, *Geli & Hitler*, p. 113
16 von Schirach, Henriette, *Frauen um Hitler*, p. 64
17 Schroeder, Christa, *Er war mein Chef*, p. 213
18 von Schirach, Henriette, *Frauen um Hitler*, p. 67
19 Cited Hayman, *Geli & Hitler*, pp. 197–8
20 Cited ibid., p. 197
21 von Schirach, Henriette, *Frauen um Hitler*, pp. 73–5, 79–80

4
SECRECY: EVA BRAUN

Though Hitler was strengthened in his resolve never to marry, women continued to play a part in his life. And young women, in particular. In October 1929, even before Geli Raubal's suicide, he met Eva Braun, who would be his mistress for thirteen years. She was seventeen years old, blonde, fresh-faced, cheerful and apparently pliable. The daughter of a Munich schoolteacher, she was working at the time as an assistant to Heinrich Hoffmann, in the photographic shop next to his studio. Eva described the meeting to her sister:

> I'd stayed on after closing time to file some papers and I'd climbed up a ladder to fetch the files kept on the top shelves of the cupboard. At that moment the boss came in accompanied by a man of uncertain age with a funny moustache, a light-coloured, English-style overcoat and a big felt hat in his hand. They both sat down on the other side of the room, opposite me. I tried to squint in their direction without appearing to turn round and sensed that this character was looking at my legs... That very day I'd shortened my skirt, and I felt slightly embarrassed because I wasn't sure I'd got the hem even. As you know, I don't like to ask Mother to help me. Hoffmann introduced us when I'd climbed down, 'Herr Wolf, our good little Fräulein Eva.'[1]

Hoffmann sent her out to buy beer and sausages, and then invited Eva to join them:

> The elderly gentleman was paying me compliments. We talked about music and a play at the Staatstheater, as I remember, with him devouring me with his eyes all the time. Then, as it was getting late, I rushed off. I refused an offer of a lift in his Mercedes. Just think what Papa's reaction would have been!... But before I left, Hoffmann pulled me aside and asked me, 'Haven't you guessed who that gentleman is; don't you ever look at our photos?' I answered, 'No,' mystified. 'It's Hitler! Adolf Hitler!' he said. 'Oh?' I replied.[2]

After that, when Hitler infrequently dropped by the studio, he would ask for Eva, calling her 'My lovely siren from Hoffmann's'. For Christmas 1929, he sent her, as he sent all the Hoffmann staff, a signed portrait of himself in uniform.

Eva Braun had just completed her Catholic convent education, and was living at home with one of her two sisters and her parents, who were protective towards her. When she mentioned Hitler to her father after their meeting, he was hostile and dismissive of him. Hitler had recently moved to his larger flat in the Prinzregentenplatz, and Geli had moved in. There is little sign that Eva Braun was infatuated with Hitler, or that he paid more than occasional attention to her during 1930.

Henriette Hoffmann knew Eva Braun, who worked in her father's studio. She recalled that '[Eva] had pale blonde hair, cut short, blue eyes, and, although she had been educated in a Catholic convent, she had learnt feminine wiles – a certain look, and swaying hips when she walked, which made men turn their heads.'[3] She had the 'sweet girl' look, popular at the time. They would go bicycling together, and swim in pools, where Eva was noticeably athletic, diving and doing hand-stands. Often, Hitler gave away theatre or opera tickets to Henriette, Eva and others: 'She was given theatre tickets like I was, and she thanked him with a curtsey.' Sometimes Hitler asked her to go to the opera. Henriette did not see Eva as a rival to Geli, but Hitler's housekeeper, Frau Winter, reported that a torn-up letter was found in Geli's room on the night of her suicide in September 1931, which read: 'Dear Herr Hitler, Thank you again for the wonderful invitation to the theatre. It was a memorable evening. I am most grateful to you for your kindness. I am counting the hours until I may have the joy of another meeting. Yours, Eva.'[4]

Whatever went on before, Eva Braun increased her interest in Hitler after Geli's death. According to Henriette, she wrote letters expressing her sympathy for his despair, and smuggled them into his trench-coat as it was hanging up, so that he would find them in his pocket. A few weeks after Geli's death, Hitler invited Eva to the Troubadour. Henriette believes the affair began then, although it may have been later, in the spring of 1932. Frau Winter remembers that Eva was often at Hitler's flat: 'Eva Braun was there often when Hitler was in Munich. She was always running after him, insisting on being alone with him. She was a most demanding woman.'[5] Nerin Gun observed from her subsequently discovered photograph albums that from this time almost all the photos are of Hitler. Whatever the relationship was, he appears to have made frequent protestations of love, and Eva believed them, and became infatuated with him.

From the start, their relationship was conducted in secrecy, not least because Hitler did not want to be associated in public with any one woman. Eva lived at home, and her parents were strict. Hitler, almost totally preoccupied with politics, was rarely in Munich. Eva was kept firmly in the background of his life. The pattern of secrecy that began their relationship suited Hitler, and continued to its end. And so did the pattern of despair. In November 1932, Eva Braun attempted suicide by shooting herself with her father's pistol, but she then rang Hitler's doctor, who came in time to save her, and the whole thing was hushed up. Hitler came to visit her with flowers at the clinic where she was recovering. Eva, the shadowy, loyal figure at the periphery of Hitler's life, continued to be frustrated by his neglect. Hitler would turn up at unpredictable times, and his moods shifted between gushing charm and indifference.

In 1935, when Hitler was in power, she again attempted suicide. A fragment of her diary reveals a woman desperately in love, who believed his protestations of love, but was constantly upset by his tormenting behaviour, and often cruelty, towards her. On her twenty-third birthday, 6

February 1935, she recorded that flowers and a telegram were delivered to her by a member of Hitler's staff. 'My office looks like a flower shop and smells like a mortuary,' she commented, dourly. He had failed to deliver the basset puppy she wanted, and she feared she was approaching spinsterhood, but thought she must not despair: 'It's time I learned to be patient.' On the eighteenth, he turned up unexpectedly, and announced he would take her away from the shop where she still worked and buy her a house. 'Dear God, please let this come true and let it happen in the near future... I am infinitely happy that he loves me so much and I pray that it may always remain so. I never want it to be my fault if one day he should cease to love me.' On 4 March, she was 'mortally unhappy again'. He had taken her to the theatre and then she had, 'with his permission', gone on to a ball afterwards. Next day he failed to contact her, despite having promised he would. She 'waited at Hoffmann's like a cat on hot bricks' but he never arrived. 'He won't be back for a fortnight and until then I shall be miserable. I have lost my peace of mind. I don't know why he's angry with me. Perhaps because of the ball. But he himself gave me permission to go. I'm racking my brains to discover the reason why he left without saying goodbye to me.'[6]

A week went by and she heard nothing. She was not allowed to write to him: 'Why do I have to bear all this? Oh, if only I had never met him... When he says he loves me, he thinks it's only for the time being. The same with promises, which he never keeps. Why doesn't he have done with me, instead of tormenting me?' She consoled herself that politics was keeping him very busy, but when they went to dinner two weeks later, she sat beside him 'for three hours without being able to say a single word to him. As a farewell gesture, he gave me an envelope with some money inside, as he has already done once before... There were days last week when I cried every night as I accepted my "duty".' By 10 May she is resolved to 'wait until 3 June, in other words, a quarter of a year since our last meeting, and then demand an explanation. Let nobody say I am not patient. The weather is magnificent and I, the mistress of the greatest man in Germany and in the whole world, I sit here waiting while the sun mocks me through the windowpanes. That he should have so little understanding and allow me to be humiliated in front of strangers...'

In despair, she sent him a 'decisive letter' and resolved that if he did not reply by 28 May, she would take thirty-five sleeping tablets: 'Is this the mad love he promised me, when he doesn't send me a single comforting line in three months?'[7] When no word came, she took the sleeping pills. It was a *cri de coeur*, and she was found in a coma by her sister and rescued. They decided to disguise it as an accident resulting from excessive fatigue. It did have the desired effect of calling Hitler's attention back to Eva, however. Several months later, he kept his promise to her, renting her an apartment, and the following spring he bought her a villa in a smart district of Munich. She no longer had to be a shopgirl at Hoffmann's. From then on, he phoned her almost daily, even during the war.

Hitler could not afford another scandal over a woman's suicide. Moreover, in a perverse way, Eva Braun had shown her steady loyalty to him, the thing Hitler craved most from women. She was rewarded by being allowed to play a small part in his private, but never his public, life. She adapted to the cramped role he allowed her, despite always secretly hoping to marry him. Later, Hitler would pontificate interminably on marriage, and in particular why he would have none of it: 'My wife would justly have been bored to death. I'd have had nothing of marriage but the sullen face of a neglected wife, or else I'd have skimped my duties. That's why it's better not to get married. The bad side of marriage is that it creates rights. In that case it's far better to have a mistress. The burden is lightened, and everything is placed on the level of a gift... What I've said applies only to men of a higher type, of course.' This followed from his fixed views on women and men's roles: 'A woman who loves her husband lives only for his sake. That's why, in her turn, she expects her spouse to live likewise for *her* sake. The man, on the other hand, is a slave to his thoughts. The idea of his duties rules him.'[8] Eva Braun had learned *her* 'duty'. Albert Speer described her as 'very feminine... a man's woman, incredibly undemanding of herself, helpful to many people behind the scenes – nobody ever knew that – and infinitely thoughtful of Hitler. She was a restful sort of girl. And her love for Hitler was beyond question.'[9]

Presumably cherishing his mistress's love as 'a gift', when Hitler refurbished Haus Wachenfeld (now called the Berghof) in the

Obersalzberg in 1936, she was given a flat, and allowed to make it her home for much of the time. Angela Raubal, Hitler's half-sister and house-keeper, disliked Eva, and saw the drift of the relationship. She left, having allegedly referred to her as 'a stupid cow'. On her identification papers, Eva was marked as 'secretary'. But she gradually became mistress of the Berghof, though only Hitler's 'inner circle' knew of her place in his life. Reinhard Spitzy, aide to Ribbentrop, Hitler's foreign minister, later visited the Berghof, and recalls his astonishment when she appeared:

> Hitler and Ribbentrop were walking up, down, up, down, one hour, two hours, and three hours. And then the door was opened and the small blonde face came in and she said to our Führer, 'Oh, Adolf, please, we must go and have our luncheon!' I was shocked, how this person of no social quality was allowed to speak with him in that way. And I went to the chief ADC and I said to him: 'Uberführer, who is that –' I didn't say lady – 'who is that woman?' And he said, 'Spitzy, listen, you are here, and you will see a lot of things, and you will shut up. And what you have seen here you will forget. And you won't tell it to your mistress, to your parents, or to your friends. Never. Because that would be very dangerous for you. Because our Führer has a right for a private life and she is his mistress – do you understand me?'

Later, Eva was given a small apartment in the Reichschancellery in Berlin, which she entered through the servants' quarters. She was never seen in public with him. Any photograph that showed her face was stamped 'Publication Forbidden'. At the Berghof, she carved out a life for herself, entertaining her women friends in his absence, and appearing only at unofficial functions in his presence. She was never mentioned by name by the staff, though they called her *Chefin* (female chief), and her room was designated the 'guest room'. 'She liked all sorts of things that young women like, and she liked having a good time, and she liked partying, very keen on dancing – Hitler would never dance of course, so she always had to find other partners to dance with – she liked nice clothes, and liked make-up, which Hitler wasn't too fond of. So she had an air of normality about her except for this connection with Hitler,' Ian Kershaw believes.

Henriette Hoffmann (von Schirach by then, having married the Youth Leader Baldur von Schirach) visited Eva at the Berghof: 'Outwardly, she was perfect. She changed several times a day, the hairdresser came and did her hair. But when it got interesting, when guests arrived, Eva was invisible – that was one of the agreements between her and Hitler.' Henriette's earlier friendship with Eva had distinctly cooled. Invited to Eva's flat, she was 'disappointed': 'It was furnished like a guest house, deep armchairs covered in rustic material, pots of flowers, cupboards painted with gentians, whole years' editions of film magazines. She had film stars' clothes copied, knew which star sign they were born under, and was interested in their lives.' Eva had her two dogs by her side and 'was smoking fast and nervously, as she always did when she knew that Hitler was not nearby.'[10]

At dinner with the inner circle only, she went in on the arm of Martin Bormann, and usually sat on Hitler's left for the meal. Reinhard Spitzy thinks that: 'Hitler wanted to be absolutely free, and she should give him a small bourgeois home with cake and tea. Hitler didn't want to have a socially high person. He could have had them, but he didn't want to have a woman who would discuss with him political questions or who would try to have her influence, and that Eva Braun never did. Eva Braun didn't interfere in politics.'

With Hitler controlling her movements, her relations with the other Nazis' wives were sometimes strained. Emmy Göring, who had a country house near the Berghof but had not met Eva Braun by the middle of the war, wanted to get to know her so that, 'People would have no grounds for the silly rumour that I had purposely ignored her.' When Hitler next visited her, she asked him if she could invite 'all the ladies who are your guests' to tea. 'He immediately understood what I meant and went as red as a schoolboy, and said haltingly. "Yes, of course, please do."' Göring was summoned to Hitler, and on return told his wife that Hitler 'did not want Eva Braun to come to see you, he felt she would be too embarrassed, she was actually afraid of you!' Despite Göring's protestation that 'even the very shyest, most timid people would relax after just five minutes' with her [Emmy], there was nothing to be done. Emmy Göring went ahead with the tea for the other guests, and only found out later that 'Fräulein Braun would have very much liked to come, but Hitler wouldn't let her.'[11] Eva Braun was only occasionally allowed 'out' – on skiing trips with Albert Speer and his wife Margret, or to parties.

On the other hand, Eva did have some privileges, which may have caused some resentment, as she was allowed to do what was forbidden to others. 'She was allowed to sing, to dance, to paint her nails with red paint, and she was even allowed to smoke a cigarette outside. Meanwhile, *we* had to go to the loo to smoke,' Reinhard Spitzy recalls. 'And there I met Generals and Ministers and with a towel we pushed out by the window the smoke, because Hitler had a very good nose, and it was forbidden to smoke. But Eva Braun was allowed everything.' And she exercised her role as *Chefin*, mistress of the house. Margret Speer countered her husband's belief that she was 'shy' and 'modest': 'With us women, you know, she was quite aware of her position. If Anni Brandt said, "Let's go sightseeing," but Eva Braun wanted to go swimming, it's swimming we went and that was that.'[12]

After supper, Hitler watched movies; and on some occasions he was seen holding Eva Braun's hand. Or the company would be subjected to one of Hitler's monologues. Margret Speer, who stayed at the Berghof for long periods, was asked by Gitta Sereny about the conversations she had with Hitler. 'He was always very gallant to women, very Austrian,' she said, but they were 'not *conversations* – it wasn't like that... He talked. We listened.'[13] Albert Speer was one of the few who appreciated Eva Braun. In her 'exile', during official functions, he sometimes kept her company: 'She has been much maligned... she was a very nice girl.' He noted how Hitler sometimes cruelly insulted her in public, and remembered his discomfort when, in front of Eva, Hitler pronounced: 'A highly intelligent man should take a primitive and stupid woman. Imagine if, on top of everything else, I had a woman who interfered with my work! In my leisure time I want to have peace...' There were other humiliations. At supper at a Munich hotel, which she had been permitted to attend, Speer saw Eva Braun blush deeply as Hitler walked by without speaking and handed her an envelope, containing money. It was not the first time he had done this in public. 'I felt horribly embarrassed for her,' said Speer.[14]

With a movie camera, Eva Braun recorded the social events of the Nazi inner circle at the Berghof. The men talk, while Hitler usually stands stiff, awkward and preoccupied, or cuddles one child or other, or plays affectionately with his dog, and the women laze on the vast terrace, drinking or chatting or stretching out in the sun. Eva is usually laughing, or posing for the camera. Hitler virtually never smiles. At the heart of life in the Berghof was something empty. When he and Eva spoke, they were distant and formal to each other. Traudl Junge, Hitler's secretary from 1943, visited the Berghof. Her first impression was that the living room was 'too big, too rich, as impressive as everything the Führer had built but far too cold... Later on, when we used to sit there by candlelight around the fire, the same feeling never left me – that room was much too big and the people in it were much too small to fill it.' Though treated as a guest, Traudl Junge 'never felt relaxed at the Berghof... [everyone] lived in an atmosphere of perpetual tension which characterized Hitler's day-to-day existence – an atmosphere which was exhausting, irregular, yet at the same time monotonous'.[15]

As with Geli, the exact nature of Hitler's relationship with Eva Braun is uncertain. Although they had interconnecting rooms, and would often leave gatherings and go to bed within minutes of each other, there were almost no signs of affection. When Eva met him in the mornings in the company of others, he greeted her formally, kissing her hand.[16] Herbert Döhring, Hitler's manservant at the Berghof, got on well with Eva: 'She was friendly, elegant, but she was sometimes moody and morose. Those who knew how the relationship was between them couldn't hold this against her. It was not a love affair – never. This was apparent to my wife before and after we married. She was convinced it was a friendship – a forced, necessary one.'

If Eva Braun ever talked to any of her women friends or relatives about their sex life, no one has breathed a word. Only Albert Speer recalls that once, in 1943, Eva Braun came to him in tears, sobbing that 'the Führer has just told me to find someone else. He said that he can no longer fulfil me.' Speer told Gitta Sereny: 'There are no two ways of interpreting this... She made it quite clear: Hitler had told her that he was too busy, too immersed, too tired — he could no longer satisfy her as a man.' Asked whether Eva Braun thought of taking him at his word, Speer replied: 'It was out of the question for her. Her love for him, her loyalty, were absolute — as, indeed, she proved unmistakably at the end.'[17]

Historian Brigitte Hamann remarks: 'Hitler styled himself as the great saviour and prophet, the rescuer from all misfortune. And this idea of the saviour is part of his self-image. The saviour is a pure man, one unsullied by sexuality And Hitler internalized this view. It was not theory for him, it was life.'

NOTES

1 Gun, *Eva Braun*, pp. 57–9
2 ibid., pp. 58–59
3 von Schirach, *Frauen um Hitler*, p. 224
4 Gun, *Eva Braun*, p. 27
5 ibid., p. 67
6 ibid., pp. 89–90
7 ibid., p. 93
8 *Hitler's Table Talk 1941-1944*, pp. 245–6
9 Sereny, Gitta, *Albert Speer: His Battle with Truth*, Picador, London, 1996, p. 193
10 von Schirach, *Frauen um Hitler*, p. 234
11 Frank, Johannes, *Eva Braun: Ein ungewöhnliches Frauenschicksal in geschichtlich bewegter Zeit*, K.W. Schütz, Preussisch Oldendorf, 1988, p. 163
12 Sereny, *Albert Speer*, p. 193
13 ibid., pp. 193–4
14 Speer, *Inside the Third Reich*, p. 92; Sereny, *Albert Speer*, pp. 192–3
15 Galante, Pierre, and Eugene Silianoff (ed.), *Last Witnesses in the Bunker*, Sidgwick & Jackson, London, 1989, pp. 53–5
16 Gun, *Eva Braun*, p. 196
17 Sereny, *Albert Speer*, p. 193

5
MARRIED TO GERMANY

Eva Braun was not the only woman in Hitler's life after 1931. Many others were swept off their feet by his charisma, or were more than willing to be charmed by him. His fondness for attractive women now had a wider scope. 'What I like best is to dine with a pretty woman,' he later declared.[1] He could now summon women at will, though he preferred them to be unchallenging. 'I always have the most worthy ladies as my dinner partners!' he later protested. 'I'd far rather go on board the *Robert Ley* and pick out some pretty little typist or salesgirl as my partner!'[2] Women of all strata of society were entering his orbit. Few resisted his charismatic spell, or his often awkward advances.

For some women, it ended in disaster. The glamorous actress Renate Müller met him in 1932, when he spent a day watching the shooting of her latest film. When he visited her in the evening, she found his behaviour distinctly odd, according to the account she later gave to director Adolf Zeissler, which he published in a magazine, and was later used as a source in the American OSS report about Hitler's sexual perversions. 'He sat there, not moving at all, looking at me all the time, and then he'd take my hand in his and look some more. He talked all the time – just nonsense.'[3] She was invited to a party at the Chancellery, at the end of which Hitler offered to show her round the building, including his wardrobe of clothes. He arranged frequent meetings and sent her expensive jewels, until one night he took her to his rooms, where, allegedly after a discussion about methods of torture, she claimed she was required to kick and beat him, while he declared himself her slave. After he had excited himself to orgasm, he suggested that they put their clothes on, and they drank a glass of wine and chatted, until he stood up, kissed her hand, and thanked her for a pleasant evening. The reliability of the source, as with the whole OSS report, is however open to question.

Müller's subsequent history was tragic. Allegedly with Hitler's permission, she took a holiday in London, where she spent some time with a former lover who was Jewish, despite being trailed, she believed, by the Gestapo. On her return, she was blacklisted, and rumours circulated that she was to be put on trial for 'race defamation' – having a relationship with a Jew. With her career in ruins, she became addicted to morphine and was sent to a sanatorium. Having asked for, and been refused, permission to see Hitler in 1936, she returned to the sanatorium, but when she saw a car pull up outside, and four SS men get out, she killed herself by throwing herself out of a window. Goebbels sent a wreath to her funeral. Renate Müller was another addition to the tally of women around Hitler who committed suicide.

Unity Mitford was yet another. Daughter of the English aristocrat Lord Redesdale, and sister of several other celebrated Mitford girls, she fell under his spell. She was determined to meet him, and, after hanging around the Osteria restaurant in Munich for some time in 1935, was rewarded with an introduction. Blonde and attractive, her knowledge of the internal workings of the English upper classes was useful to Hitler; her adoration, and her willingness to speak publicly on his behalf at rallies, fetchingly dressed up in Nazi uniform, was another bonus. But when war was declared in September 1939, she took a pistol and shot herself twice in the head in the Englischer Garten in Munich – 'She could not bear a war between England and Germany, she had to put an end to herself.'[4] The attempt failed, and she was despatched for treatment to a private clinic, where Hitler visited her once and sent her flowers. When sufficiently recovered, Hitler agreed that she should be removed from German soil accompanied by one of his doctors. She died in 1948, having been irreparably brain-damaged by the attempt on her own life.

There were a few women whom Hitler respected, and who managed to carve a public position outside the narrow confines of his view of women's 'natural' role as wives and mothers. The ace pilot Hannah Reitsch was one remarkable exception. The other was film director Leni Riefenstahl, who fell under his spell when she heard him speak, at the Sportspalast in February 1932 – the first political rally she had ever attended:

> The Sportspalast was so mobbed that it was hard to find a seat... At last, after a brass band played march after march, Hitler appeared, very late. The spectators jumped from their seats, shouting wildly for several minutes: 'Heil! Heil!' I was too far away to see Hitler's face, but, after the shouts died down, I heard his voice: 'Fellow Germans!' That very same instant I had an almost apocalyptic vision that I was never able to forget. It seemed as if the earth's surface were spreading out in front of me, like a hemisphere that suddenly splits apart in the middle, spewing out an enormous jet of water, so powerful that it touched the sky and shook the earth. I felt quite paralysed. Although there was a great deal in his speech that I didn't understand, I was still fascinated, and I sensed that the audience was in bondage to this man.[5]

Disorientated by his initial impact on her, with its heavy sexual connotations, she then wrote to him declaring her wish to meet him, and was almost instantly sent an invitation. Hitler declared himself greatly impressed by her work, and by her recent major film success, *The Blue Light*, which she acted in and directed. Walking with him on a beach at Wilhelmshaven, he announced, 'Once we come to power, you must make my films.' She protested that she could not make either prescribed or political films, and would never join the Party because of its 'racial prejudices', but he asked her to stay on, saying, 'I seldom get a chance to speak to a real artist.' Later that evening, walking along the beach, Hitler suddenly 'halted, looked at me and slowly put his arms around me and drew me to him... He stared at me in some excitement but when he noticed my lack of response, he instantly let go and turned away. Then I saw him raise his hands beseechingly: "How can I love a woman until I have completed my task?" Bewildered, I made no reply.'

At another rally, she felt herself being drawn in by his persuasive powers: 'He spoke with such force that his words seemed to lash the spectators. He appeared demonic as he swore to them that he would create a new Germany and put an end to unemployment and poverty. When he said: "Collective good takes precedence over individual good," his words struck at my heart... I had lived very egocentrically. I felt ashamed and at this point I felt ready to make the sacrifices he called for.' Afterwards, she had 'only one idea in mind – to get home as fast as possible. It was almost a flight from danger.'[6]

But she did not escape, despite her protestations. Declaring his enormous respect for her as an artist, Hitler persisted in his pressure on her to make films for him, and about him. He succeeded when she agreed (or, she claims, was steadily pulled in further and further) to direct the propaganda epic *Triumph of the Will*, which glorified the 1934 Nuremberg Rally and Hitler, and later, *Olympia*, her mammoth documentary about the 1936 Berlin Olympic Games, which is interpreted by many as an expression of Hitler's aesthetic of beauty and physical perfection.

Propaganda Minister Goebbels also intervened. Leni Riefenstahl was included on the guest list of his wife Magda's parties, while he pursued her relentlessly, declaring his love for her and his mighty respect for her talent. She spurned his sexual advances – a risky course of action for women in the film industry, which he controlled, but she was able to refer directly to Hitler, who invariably gave her his support. 'You alone have the artistic ability to turn real-life events into more than ordinary news footage,' she reports Hitler as saying.[7] Leni Riefenstahl looks back on her relations with Goebbels as being difficult, made worse because she could bypass him and make direct contact with Hitler, though Goebbels, according to his diaries, admired her: 'She is the only one of the stars who really understands us,' he wrote in his diary on 12 June 1933, and then in October 1935: 'Went with Leni Riefenstahl through her Olympic film concept. A woman who knows what she wants.' But by 1936 he was showing exasperation with 'Miss Riefenstahl' who 'tries her hysterics on me. One really can't work with these wild women. Now she wants half a million more and wants to make two films instead of one... She cries, the ultimate weapon of women. But her tears leave me cold' (6 November 1936).

Leni Riefenstahl gives no evidence of any further intimate contact with Hitler, though she was invited to parties, drives and picnics with him and others. She attributes rumours that she was his mistress to the vicious infighting within both the film industry and Nazi Party hierarchy, who were jealous of her access to Hitler and his admiration for her. When film director Joseph von Sternberg asked her point blank if she was his mistress, she replied, 'What nonsense.' Hitler was 'unfathomable and full of contradictions. The unusual thing about him is his hypnotic power, which can make even an opponent change his mind.' But she declared, 'I'm not his type, and he's not my type.'[8]

First Lady

Magda Goebbels, wife of Hitler's rapacious Propaganda Minister, Joseph Goebbels, performed a particularly useful role in Hitler's life. Blonde, elegant and extremely well connected, she would become, for him, the First Lady of the Third Reich. With her family of six children, she came to embody the Nazi ideal of German motherhood. At official receptions, she was called on to welcome the guests. Hitler relied on her to be the hostess at glittering social events. Privately, he spent a considerable amount of his time with the Goebbels household, relaxing at one of their many establishments, and joining them at weekends and on holidays.

Magda Quandt first came across the Nazis in 1930, when she heard Joseph Goebbels speak at a rally at the Sportspalast during the election campaign. She was smitten by his powers of oratory, and walked out of the hall determined to dedicate herself to the cause. She joined the Party and, not long afterwards, having got a job in the Party offices, she walked past Goebbels on the stairs. Goebbels rarely passed an attractive woman without a second glance. Within a short time she was working in his office archives, and it was not long before he declared he was in love with her. His diary for 15 February 1931 suggests they had begun an affair: 'Today I've been going round almost in a dream, so full of sated happiness. It is wonderful to love a beautiful woman and to be loved by her.'

Magda was a particularly good catch. She was beautiful, with shining blue eyes, thick fair hair, a face with well-cut regular features and a slim figure.[9] She was also cultured, and brought her own sophistication to the Nazi movement. The child of divorced parents, she had a strict Catholic upbringing, which was completed at finishing school in Goslar, after which she travelled extensively. Though she had a Jewish step-father, this was overlooked by the Nazis at first. At the age of eighteen, she married Günther Quandt, twenty years older than her and one of the richest business magnates in Germany at the time. She had a stylish apartment, and mixed in German high society. They had one child, Harald. But the marriage was not happy, and she and Quandt completed a relatively amicable divorce in the summer of 1929 when she was twenty-five. Günther gave her a generous settlement of 50,000 marks a year and a smart flat on the Reichskanzlerplatz, and, on completion of the divorce proceedings, he sent her flowers and took her for a meal at Horcher's, Berlin's most exclusive restaurant. Within months she encountered her nemesis.

Goebbels surmised that Magda Quandt, just disengaged from an unhappy marriage, had been looking for something to inspire her. If it had not been the Nazi Party, it could equally well have been the Church that she turned to.[10] The idea of sacrifice for a higher ideal appealed to her. Günther Quandt, whom she still met regularly, became impatient of her constant proselytizing for the Nazi cause, which he opposed, and many of Magda's friends and relations tried to warn her off. Joseph courted her carefully, taking her to meetings and intellectual gatherings, realizing that she, as with other society hostesses such as Frau von Dirksen and Frau Bruckmann, conferred respectability on the Party, which had not entirely lost its red-neck image. He also hoped that her wealthy ex-husband might contribute to party funds, but this Quandt resisted.

Hitler met Magda in 1931 when she joined him for five o'clock tea at the Kaiserhof Hotel. Her son, Harald, was with her, dressed immaculately in a blue uniform she had designed herself. 'From the outset, Magda treated the Führer with the greatest respect, experiencing in his presence a sense of tingling excitement... With true instinct [she] struck exactly the right note with Hitler... The Führer was delighted with her intelligence, her charm, and the interest she showed in his affairs,' wrote her biographer, Hans-Otto Meissner.[11] It was November 1931, shortly after Geli's suicide. Another witness, Otto Wagener, an economics adviser and member of Hitler's entourage, was present at the meeting:

> Even at first glance, Frau Quandt made an excellent impression, which only increased in the course of our conversation... She was dressed well but not excessively, calm in her movements, assured, self-confident, with a winning smile – I am tempted to say enchanting. I noticed the pleasure Hitler took in her innocent high spirits. I also noticed how her large eyes were hanging on Hitler's gaze... No specific next meeting was arranged, but there was no doubt that a closer tie of friendship and veneration between Hitler and Frau Quandt had begun to take shape.[12]

Hitler intimated to Wagener that feelings he thought he had buried with Geli's death had returned. But there was a setback. When the rest of Hitler's group returned later that night, they reported that they had dropped off at Frau Quandt's, and, after midnight, Goebbels had turned up, letting himself in with his own key, an unmistakable sign that he was involved with her. 'That was just a short relapse. Providence was kind to me,' Hitler told Wagener.

Later, Wagener claims, Hitler brought up the subject of Frau Quandt: 'This woman could play an important role in my life, even without my being married to her. In all my work, she could represent the feminine counterpart to my one-sidedly male instincts. She could be a second Geli to me. Too bad she isn't married.'[13] On a journey to a rally at Braunschweig, Goebbels asked Wagener to drive Magda in his car. Wagener took her aside during their picnic and made her a proposal. 'Hitler is a problem in himself, which only a few will succeed in solving, which nobody will be able to master except, perhaps, a woman,' he began. A woman could not arouse, stimulate, control or restrain his 'genius'. What only a woman could do was to 'put Hitler the man in touch with life, with other human beings, to create a hellenic balance within him'. Hitler had refused to marry, he told her, and Frau Quandt could see how difficult this would be: 'I think it is right that Hitler does not marry... He has been a bachelor for too long not to put himself first always. His wife would sometimes, probably often, be only a piece of furniture, a cupboard that occasionally bars his way, or a microphone into which he speaks, or a gramophone on which he wants to hear certain records and which he can turn on and off as it suits him.'

Magda having demonstrated such intuitive understanding, Wagener suggested that she could be this woman, married to another man, but Hitler's close, devoted friend and support, who would rescue him and turn him into a human being. Magda stared at Wagener 'with her large, blue eyes, which held a velvet glow of compassion, love and restrained rapture', as he told her she would have to be married, and preferably to Goebbels, because with him, she could accomplish the difficult task, not merely for Hitler personally, but 'for the welfare of the German *Volk*'. Magda hesitated, before agreeing: 'For Adolf Hitler, I'd be prepared to take everything on myself.' She told him: 'If I get engaged to Goebbels, you will know that I've made the greater commitment at the same time.'[14]

The relationship between Goebbels and Magda Quandt had been going on for some time. They had spent an idyllic summer together. Magda was carried away by his passion, and the new experience of being loved so totally. But shadows were cast by Goebbels's possessive jealousy about her past, and their relationship could sometimes be tempestuous. Promises of eternal devotion were interspersed with rows and irritations. On 15 August 1931, Goebbels wrote in his diary: '...a heated debate about women and their duties and capabilities. I am probably too harsh, but only in principle. In her anger, Magda was very insulting towards me. We part fighting. Long, edgy telephone conversation during the night. Despair.' Magda came running back the next day, but there was still a shadow between them.

Whether Hitler's initiative transmitted via Wagener precipitated the marriage and helped clear away their doubts is uncertain, but it certainly tied Goebbels closer to his Führer. In December 1931, Magda married Goebbels, with Hitler as witness. The civil ceremony was followed by a Catholic service, the altar draped with a swastika banner from the early struggle, and a cross standing on it. Her former husband put the estate at Severin at their disposal. Within a year, the first of their brood of six children was born, and all had names that began with 'H'. There was no hint that any of them were Hitler's, however.

Magda's house was the centre of Hitler's Berlin hospitality, and became his base there. At official functions, she presided with him. He spent weekends at one of their expanding number of country residences, several supplied by grateful donors, including the City of Berlin, where Goebbels was Gauleiter, and the film industry, which he controlled. There, they entertained diplomats and international guests, and Magda frequently hosted parties for artists, actors and members of the intelligentsia, where the focus of attention was Hitler.

The Goebbels family was extolled in propaganda. A newsreel crew filmed the children at their large house by the water at Schwanenwerder as they climbed trees in white dresses with Magda watching, 'like a Fragonard painting'. The commentary was suitably syrupy, emphasizing Goebbels's devotion to family life: 'Men of great creative drive need relaxation to help them recoup their energies. Dr Goebbels derives his capacity for work from the family, that fount of youth and eternal nucleus of the nation.' Magda was not, however, the perfect hausfrau, and neither did she want to be, according to Henriette von Schirach. The food was simple, the champagne never flowed and often the cakes were bought from the baker in the village.[15] Nor was Goebbels the ideal husband. He chased and conquered a very large number of women, and was forever turning up with actresses in tow. His exploits were so notorious that he became known as 'the goat of Babelsberg', or, more cruelly, 'the tadpole', because of his appearance. Those women who refused his advances knew that they put their career in jeopardy, because he had no scruples about blacklisting them immediately.

Magda appears to have taken this in her stride, until he fell for Czech actress Lida Baarova. 'He was the master of the hunt, whom nobody and nothing could escape,' Baarova wrote later. 'His voice seemed to go straight into me. I felt a light tingling in my back, as if his words were trying to stroke my body.'[16] In 1938, matters came to a head when Goebbels turned up with Lida Baarova and announced he intended to have a *ménage à trois*, with the actress as his 'second wife', and hoped – indeed, assumed – that Magda would agree. The arrangement failed to work. When Magda found out that Goebbels had made a promise to Lida Baarova to marry her and leave his family, Magda decided she had had enough, and threatened divorce. He agreed not to see Baarova again, but failed to keep his word. When the 'tadpole' then swore an oath, on the lives of his children, that the affair was over, Magda, who had a letter in her possession indicating the opposite, was appalled. She resolved to get a divorce, and set about finding evidence with the help of Goebbels's assistant, Karl Hanke, who drew up a long – and, he claimed, completely reliable – list of women with whom Goebbels had had affairs. The list was so long and 'so outrageous' that, when he finished reading it out, he, Magda and her sister-in-law looked at each other in silence, and: 'Suddenly, Magda began to laugh, a wild, hysterical, uncontrolled laugh.' The others joined in. 'In view of the length of the list there really was no other possible reaction,' her biographer Meissner concluded.[17]

Magda went to Hitler to pour out her heart, but he would not contemplate the idea that his Propaganda Minister should divorce. This was the man who publicly extolled the virtues of marriage and family life. Hitler could not afford a scandal at the heart of his government. Already, he had had to intervene personally to veto six other divorces requested by his ministers and party leaders. Not letting any sympathy he might still have for Magda override political considerations, he insisted that they drew up a contract agreeing to stay together for a year, after which time Magda could, if Goebbels did not behave himself, divorce him. Hitler was furious at Goebbels's behaviour, particularly because he had lied to him when he denied he was seeing Baarova. 'Where women are concerned, he has no scruples, he even lies to me,' Hitler is reported to have said. 'But where it is a question of politics, I can rely on my Goebbels. Besides, I shall be needing him again soon.'[18]

Goebbels was in disgrace. Hitler only received him officially, refused requests for personal discussions, and made it known that he was banned from his evening parties. But Goebbels kept his post, because Hitler needed him. Slowly and carefully he worked his way back into both Magda's affections and the Führer's confidence. Lida Baarova was banished from Germany. When she sneaked back, Karl Hanke, Magda's supporter (and by this time, allegedly her lover), took several SS heavies and, in broad daylight at the film studios, marched into the office of the executive with whom she was working, and beat him up. Lida Baarova left the country, and heard no more word from Goebbels. Many other actresses, however, continued to be 'hunted' by him.

Magda's loyalty to Hitler remained undimmed to the very end, when she insisted on remaining with him in the Berlin bunker and murdering her six children with poison before committing suicide with Goebbels. She did not kill herself out of love for her husband, Henriette von Schirach believes, but out of love for Hitler. In her last letter to her son, Harald, then fighting on the Russian front, she explained her decision:

> Our glorious ideals of Nazism have been destroyed, and with them everything in my life that has been beautiful, admirable, noble and good. The world which will come after the Führer and National Socialism will not be worth living in. Therefore I have brought the children over with me... We now have only one resolve – to remain true to the death to the Führer. That we can end our lives together with him is a blessing for which we never dared to hope... Harald, my dear child, I bequeath to you the best thing that I have learned from life – be true, true to yourself, true to others, true to your country, in every way, always, in everything... I embrace you with all my deepest, my most heartfelt motherly love.
>
> My beloved son,
> Live for Germany!
> Your mother[19]

*   *   *

In his private life, Hitler's core of destructiveness, rage and egotism cast a shadow over his personal relationships with women. He romanticized women, deifying them as sacred mothers. Or he denigrated them as pretty, irrational beings who gave him some comfort, entertained him and were therefore useful to him. Ultimately he needed to control them. But he also needed their political support. He needed them to sacrifice themselves to his mission, and to the Nazi state. And it was essential to his self-image, and to his messianic task, that they idolized him personally, and surrendered everything to their political faith in him.

NAZI WOMEN

After 1933, the women of Germany were ruled by a man whose private life was empty. He had no capacity for love, only to hate and possess. He had little insight into women beyond a series of fixed images that tied them to marriage, motherhood and sacrifice. But he had power to order and regiment their lives to a racial ideology in which their central, and indeed valued, duty was as mothers who would assist in building the Thousand Year Reich by perpetuating the 'blood purity' of the Aryan race. Armed with a hypnotic allure, as powerful in private as in public, and an ability to rouse women (and men) to almost blind religious fervour and complete trust in his beliefs, he led the nation to disaster. He destroyed what he claimed to revere as the 'woman's world' – their homes, their families, their safety, their love – as surely as he annihilated almost every tie that bound humanity into a moral universe.

NOTES

1 *Hitler's Table Talk*, p. 358
2 ibid., p. 612
3 Cited Hayman, *Geli & Hitler*, p. 146
4 Pryce-Jones, David, *Unity Mitford: A Quest*, Weidenfeld and Nicolson, London, 1976, p. 232
5 Riefenstahl, Leni, *The Sieve of Time: The Memoirs of Leni Riefenstahl*, Quartet, London, 1992, p. 101
6 ibid., pp. 107, 123
7 ibid., p. 144
8 ibid., p. 218
9 Meissner, Hans-Otto, *Magda Goebbels: The First Lady of the Third Reich*, The Dial Press, New York, 1980, p. 28
10 ibid., p. 85
11 ibid., p. 91
12 Wagener, *Hitler – Memoirs of a Confidant*, p. 241
13 ibid., p. 255
14 ibid., pp. 258–9
15 von Schirach, *Frauen um Hitler*, p. 190
16 *Sunday Times*, 21 January 2001
17 Meissner, *Magda Goebbels*, pp. 184–5
18 ibid., pp. 193–4
19 Cited ibid., pp. 271–2

6
THE IDEAL NAZI WOMAN

On 30 January 1933, the Nazis came to power. They celebrated with a huge parade: column after column of uniformed men – swastika banners waving, torches burning and music playing – marched through the Brandenburg Gate and took over the streets of Berlin. In this massive show of political strength, there was not a single woman.

From the foundation of the Nazi Party in 1921, women were denied any position of power in its hierarchy – the only reference to women in its programme was Point 21, which pledged protection for mothers. Since winning the vote in 1918, women had been elected in significant numbers to represent all the other main parties in local and regional government, and in the German Reichstag, where they made up 10 per cent of deputies. In the National Socialist Party there were no women representatives at all.

Hitler's view on their political participation derived from his view of women: 'The woman loves more deeply than the man. But in her, intellect plays no role... In political questions, the woman, even if she is extremely intelligent, cannot separate reason from feeling.'[1] But he knew, cynically, that they had to be wooed: 'I am no friend of female suffrage. If however we must continue with this tomfoolery, then we should draw what advantage we can...Women will always vote for law and order and a uniform, you can be sure of that.'[2]

NAZI WOMEN

The Nazis offered women a special role – as companions to warrior husbands in forging the Thousand Year Reich. Their mission was to be wives supporting their husbands, and mothers breeding the future master race. In this, their 'true' role, they would be valued in the New Germany. 'In my state,' Hitler declared, 'the mother is the most important citizen.' The new state, added Goebbels, Hitler's Minister for Public Enlightenment and Propaganda, would re-establish the 'proper and natural sexual division of labour' which assigned 'clearly distinct domains to men and women, putting an end once and for all to any public disregard of the feminine mission'. Men and women would be equally respected, but in their separate domains. In marriage, family and motherhood, German women would find their true vocation in the service of the whole nation, the *Volksgemeinschaft.*

Others felt less need to be either subtle or seductive. Women served the will of the nation – and that will was male, declared one male follower of Hitler in a Nazi women's magazine: 'The National Socialist movement is an emphatically male phenomenon as far as political power is concerned. Women in parliament are a depressing sign of liberalism. They insult male values by imitating men. We believe that every *genuine* woman will, in her deepest feelings, pay homage to the masculine principle of National Socialism. Only then will she become a total woman!'[3]

Reichsführer Heinrich Himmler enlarged on the Nazi 'total woman': a 'real man' would love her, first, 'as a beloved child to be scolded and perhaps even punished when foolish, but also to be protected and cherished because of her frailty and weakness'. Second, as a companion – 'the loyal and understanding comrade who assists him in life's struggle, always at his side but never shackling or cramping his spirit'. And then as the wife, 'whose feet he must kiss, and whose feminine tenderness and pure, childlike sanctity give him strength to persevere in the thick of the battle and bring him something superlatively divine in the ideal hours of spiritual communion'. Himmler's marriage was a disaster.[4]

When Hitler came to power, almost half of those voting for him were women. His promise to restore order and end unemployment held strong appeal. German women had experienced the anarchy of street fighting between rival political gangs on their doorsteps. Unemployment bred uncertainty and discord at the heart of their family lives. Women who worked to keep their families as their husbands lost their jobs, or who saw their standard of life deteriorate, longed for stability and certainty – feelings successfully tapped by Hitler.

He promised to reassert German pride and greatness, and restore German honour after what he saw as the ignominy and injustices of the Versailles Treaty. He would build a 'national community' – the *Volk* – a New Germany in which individuals sacrificed themselves for the whole nation. Jutta Rüdiger, an early convert and later the Head of the League of German Girls, heard him speak in Düsseldorf in 1932:

> It was a huge hall and everyone was waiting for Hitler to arrive... I must say it was an electrifying atmosphere... Even before 1933 everybody was waiting for him as if he was a saviour. Then he went to the podium. I remember it all went quiet, and he started to speak in his serious voice. Calm, slow, and then he got more and more enthusiastic. I must admit, I can't remember exactly what he actually said. But my impression afterwards was: this is a man who does not want anything for himself, but only thinks about how he can help the German people.

Traudl Junge, later Hitler's personal secretary, remembers him coming to power when she was a schoolgirl:

> In school and generally it was celebrated as a liberation, that Germany could have hope again. I felt great joy then. It was portrayed at school as a turning point in the fate of the Fatherland... There was a chance that German self-confidence could grow again. The words 'Fatherland' and 'German people' [Volk] were big, meaningful words which you used carefully – something big and grand. Before, the national spirit was depressed, and it was renewed, rejuvenated, and people responded very positively.

Hitler was greeted as a saviour who would deliver Germany from economic turmoil, social disarray and national humiliation. The leader cult, his demagogic style and the spectacle of Nazi gatherings were designed to excite religious fervour and unqualified devotion. Women were particular targets. American journalist Louis Lochner observed his charisma at work: 'I have heard the Führer address a group of German women, speaking so tenderly of his mother, expressing such fond concern for the problems of the housewife, tracing so eloquently what the German women had done and could do for the Nazi cause, that the listeners were in tears.'[5]

Katharine Thomas, a British visitor, concluded: 'His words had power. He was emotional. He was sentimental, he was never intellectual... The lonely bachelor, the non-smoker, the crusading teetotaller – the glorious fighter for Germany's honour who had gone to prison for his convictions. It was a richly emotional picture for [the women] to gaze on.'[6] German Nazi convert Guida Diehl fell for the leader as much as the ideology: 'The Führer stands before us: upright, honest, thoroughgoing, God-fearing and heroic – a truly German man of the kind we women yearn for and demand in the Fatherland's hour of direst need.'[7]

Hitler's crowd manipulation was studied. The Catholics had shown him how in darkness or twilight, audiences 'succumb more easily to the dominating forces of a stronger will...' (*Mein Kampf*). He noted and played on what he saw as the crowd's willingness to surrender to force. This was a particularly feminine trait. He told his comrade Ernst Hanfstaengl: 'Someone who does not understand the intrinsically feminine character of the masses will never be an effective speaker. Ask yourself, what does a woman expect from a man? Clearness, decision, power, and action... Like a woman, the masses fluctuate between extremes.' Women, he added, could wield useful influence – as bait: 'The Crowd is not only like a woman, but women constitute the most important element in the audience. The women usually lead, then follow the children and at last... follow the fathers.'[8]

His personal secretary Traudl Junge saw how completely Hitler gave himself to stage-management of the leader cult:

> Hitler didn't marry, he said himself, because he didn't want to lose his fascination for women. Obviously, an unmarried man is far more desirable than a boring husband... As a man, he didn't look attractive at all. It was more that he personified

power – that was his fascination. And also his presence. He had a way of looking at you with those eyes, which could really set you alight. And somehow he was a mythical figure for women. He was a saviour, and he gave off an aura of power, and that impressed women. Like a Messiah, perhaps.

Hitler knew this well – and used it. His demagogic powers, along with his contempt for women and the masses, were carefully honed. As he expressed it in *Mein Kampf*:

Like woman, whose mental state is governed less by consider- ations of abstract reason than by an indefinable emotional craving for complementary strength, and who, in conse- quence, would rather yield to a strong man than dominate a weak one, so the masses love a dominator better than a suppli- ant and feel inwardly more satisfied with a doctrine which tolerates no other beside itself than by the granting of liberal freedom. They have no idea what to do with it, as a rule, and even tend to feel that they have been abandoned.

Later, he elaborated to a colleague: 'The ordinary man in the street respects nothing but brute strength and ruthlessness... Women too, for that matter, women and children. The people need wholesome fear. They want to fear something. They want someone to frighten them and make them shudderingly submissive.'[9]

He also knew the value of the personal touch. Early on, when Hitler campaigned for votes, he moved among the crowds paying particular attention to women, shaking hands and even cuddling babies. His personal presence, Traudl Junge observed later, was almost unrecog- nizable in the yelling demagogue of his public appearances: 'The first time I met Hitler, what surprised me most was how different he was from the Hitler you knew officially. He had a soft gentle voice that was full of melody. It wasn't like a machine gun thundering away. And later I found him very charming in the way he behaved in private. And he had a sense of humour, I can't deny that... I never heard an impolite or angry word. He was always friendly and patient.'

Hitler's cultivation of women inspired their adulation. He was inundated with love letters from adoring fans. Women sent him presents – embroidered handkerchiefs, slippers stitched with the swastika and the rising sun, and cakes baked specially for him. 'Many of them were absurd,' Traudl Junge, who opened the presents and read the letters, recalled. Besotted women poured out their longing for him: 'To my beloved Führer! I think of you every day, every hour and every minute,' wrote Hanna G. of Elsflethersand. 'What I would really like to do is to come to Berlin and come to you! May I do that??? Whatever happens, my life belongs to you. I cannot work any more because I am always thinking of you, I can love no other as much as I love you. I hope my wish may be fulfilled.' Friedel S. of Hartmannsdorf declared that she wanted to have his child: 'Just the thought that you, of all people, should have no children gives me no peace. And so the result of my desire is this letter... Perhaps you think you have no time for a child, or you feel that you are too old for a child, and have dismissed this thought long ago. Despite all this, a child of yours must be born. This is my greatest wish, and I long for its fulfilment with my whole being.' A Frau Rosa was so smitten by Hitler that her marriage was destroyed: 'Because I have taken the great man into my heart, my husband has become a stranger to me. From the first moment when I heard of Adolf Hitler, he gave me a new faith, he brought me strength and power and love. He is my idol, and I will devote my life to him until I close my eyes forever, I will strive and struggle for him until my end.'[10]

At the political level, the early women converts to Nazism tended to be conservatives and nationalists who welcomed the Nazis' revival of esteem for traditional 'female' values. For them, women's emancipation had brought little benefit. Feminists – or 'New Women' – of the left, who called for equality and tried to imitate men, had undermined the value of motherhood and neglected their true maternal vocation. Hitler had a clear view on 'equality': 'Equal rights for women... means that they receive the esteem they deserve in the sphere nature has assigned to them.'[11] For ideologists, the 'emancipated woman' was seen as an agent of degeneracy, a tool of the 'Bolshevik–Jewish conspiracy' luring women into 'rational thinking', unrestrained individualism and an unhealthy preoccupation with sexuality.

The turmoil of the Depression, in a country where more married women had worked than in any other country in Europe, confirmed the 'mistake' of emancipation. For Paula Siber, a local Nazi leader in Düsseldorf: 'The women's movement of yesterday led thirty-six Parliamentarians into office and hundreds of thousands of German women out into the streets of the big city. It made one woman a ranking civil servant and produced thousands of wage slaves to the capitalist order.'[12] Another Nazi writer claimed: 'The woman has become a work machine... National Socialism will restore her to her true profession – motherhood.' Guida Diehl had a further complaint: the feminist movement had made women rootless and unstable: 'We women were cheated out of our right to womanly esteem, feminine nobility and maternal dignity, because, with our hands tied, we were compelled to witness every shamelessness and every manifestation of national debasement, down to and including complete cultural bolshevism and Godless propaganda.'[13]

The women who embraced the cause, and those who voted for Hitler, were prepared to barter political power in return for the privileges offered by the Nazis to women exclusively in their role as wives and mothers.

Enemies of the State

Women politicians were among the immediate casualties of Hitler's rise to power. The thirty-six parliamentary representatives in the Reichstag lost their positions. Most were in the parties of the left. Once Hitler had consolidated his power, he moved swiftly against the Opposition. Social Democrats and communists were rounded up in a massive purge against so-called 'enemies of the state', including thousands of women. Around eighty former members of the Reichstag – men and women – died as a result of Nazi persecution and over 160 went into exile.[14]

Elly Napp, aged nineteen, was a member of the Socialist Youth League. Almost all her friends were arrested: 'In 1933 I fell into a big black hole. [I lost] all my friends [in the Socialist Youth Group] – some of them disappeared, others didn't show up any more, and the others I couldn't see. We were banned, we couldn't hold meetings, and some of the leaders were sent to prison... And all my plans for a professional future were destroyed. Because of my former participation in the Socialist Youth Group I wasn't able to study any more.'

Her boyfriend and, later, husband, Kurt Napp, was active in the Social Democratic Party (SPD). Arrested in 1933, he served two years in prison for being a member of a banned party. He was brutally beaten. His eyes were damaged – on his release, his left eye had to be removed, while his right eye remained impaired. He was treated for severe head injuries and needed a new set of teeth after his were knocked out. 'My husband suffered greatly. He felt degraded, not because of his political ideas – that he didn't mind, but because he was treated like a criminal by that government. For a human being who hadn't committed any crimes, it was very hard to bear being treated like a criminal without any means of fighting against it. How could he do that? He had to keep quiet, he couldn't change the situation.'

Lotte Lasch was a member, with her boyfriend Walter, of the Communist Youth movement. Before 1933, she had been a frequent witness to brawls and street fights, often involving shootings, between her communist comrades and Nazi SA bands on the streets of Hamburg. On Hitler's rise to power, her father, treasurer of the local communist party branch, was arrested almost immediately, along with others: 'It was terrible. The SA people came and dragged our people out and hit them. The SA had a completely free hand. You couldn't call the police. Some people died.' As an act of resistance, she joined a five-strong communist cell and distributed an anti-Nazi pamphlet. One night, when she and Walter were on their way home, he left her in order to fetch something from his parents' house: 'I waited and waited and he didn't come, and finally he arrived with three men. He said, "I've just been arrested." And I said, "Well, what do I do?" and they said, "No, we want to take you too, we've already been to your parents."' She was taken to a prison, then a concentration camp, and interrogated, but never admitted to distributing the pamphlets and was kept in solitary confinement for three months of her sentence.

The purge was ruthless and swift. Of 300,000 Germans who belonged to the Communist Party in January 1933, half were in jails or concentration camps or dead a year later. Three million suspects were arrested for questioning during 1933, and 100,000 political prisoners were held in 'protective custody'. Around a fifth of those accused and found guilty of political crimes were women. By October, over 500 'enemies of the state' – women and men – had been killed.[15]

Opposition groups were overwhelmed by the speed with which the Nazis took hold, and the unpredictability of the terror unleashed against them. A combination of intimidation and punishment left little room for effective organized resistance. Only a few persevered; and they landed up in prison, were executed or escaped into exile. Minna Cammens was distributing Social Democrat pamphlets one Sunday in March 1933 in Bremen, as she had always done, when she was arrested. A few days later her husband received her ashes in a cigarette case.[16] Many women fled abroad. Former Socialist Reichstag deputy Maria Juchacz escaped to France where she helped German refugees, and survived despite Gestapo and Vichy surveillance. Johanna Kirchner provided shelter for refugees in Alsace, and edited a clandestine newspaper. After the invasion of France, she was arrested, sent to a concentration camp and eventually executed in 1944.

Many others gave up hope: 'Open conversations became exceedingly rare... The possibility of meeting without consequences diminished. Hopelessness cast a pall over us like death. As if everyone pulled their heads in.'[17] Even so, small groups of women banded together in trust with the aim of spreading disillusion in their daily lives. It was a way of keeping the faith, through silent refusal to co-operate with the regime.

The consequences of not conforming to the state ideology were well known. Part of Nazi intimidation was to publicize the penalties. Thousands of political prisoners were incarcerated in concentration camps, along with Jehovah's Witnesses, gypsies, homosexuals and others deemed 'enemies of the state'. An estimated million anti-Nazis served sentences between 1933 and 1939. On release, they were sworn not to talk about their experiences. But information spread. After an escapee from Oranienberg published details of atrocious conditions there, the commandant responded by claiming that he was re-educating 'brothers who have only forgotten they are Germans'. Cameramen were brought in, and a sanitized film about the camp was shown in every cinema throughout Germany.

Those living near concentration camps were invariably drawn into the economy of the camps. Helga Lohniger's father was the baker in the village of Dachau, near Munich. Nearby, Hitler had built one of his first concentration camps to hold mainly political prisoners. It was the beginning of a terror regime that would eventually engulf Germany but, in the village, it was part of everyday life.

The baker supplied bread to the SS guards in their barracks and to the camp prisoners. Clearly it was a lucrative contract. In their house, Helga's family had white porcelain candlesticks made in the camp, and they bought food from the camp vegetable plots. Prisoners worked in the bakery. As a child, Helga remembers them coming in their striped uniforms with armed guards on horse-drawn carriages: 'All of them were political prisoners with that red triangle on their arm... We were always really happy when they came with the horses and carriage because the little ones, my brother and sister, could be lifted up on the horses... For us it was just ordinary people who came to work. It was a normal relationship just like with anyone else. We talked to them. We knew them by their Christian names.' Helga never went inside the camp. But for these and many other children and their parents, living alongside Hitler's terror machine was a perfectly normal facet of life in the Third Reich.

Doubters were soon forced into at least outward conformity. Liselotte Katscher, later a Lutheran nurse, was mocking at first. She remembers 'walking down the streets after January 1933 and suddenly in the main street in every shop there were little swastika flags and pictures of Hitler. I laughed at the Hitler salute. It looked so silly, all these people sticking up their right hand in the air. And in school, suddenly all our teachers claimed they'd been National Socialists for a long time. We laughed because we knew they hadn't been, so we didn't respect them for that.'

But soon she too was swept up in the mood:

I heard that Hitler was at the Hotel Rosa, the best hotel in Wiesbaden. I was curious... I got there just at the end of Hitler's speech, so I didn't really hear him speak. I was standing at the back. There was a huge crowd singing the 'Deutschland' anthem and the Horst Wessel song. Until then I had always laughed at the Hitler salute, but when they sang the Horst Wessel song, I suddenly realized I was raising my arm. Much later, I thought, that's what they call mass suggestion. In my youthful innocence I thought that if all these people were so enthralled and enthusiastic about it, then there must be something in it. So I tried to do something myself for this new movement.

Liselotte Katscher joined the League of German Girls, the girls' branch of the Hitler Youth, and later, in 1935, the Nazi Party.

Women's Natural Sphere

The Nazi takeover infiltrated all aspects of life. It was their deliberate policy to Nazify the nation's life and institutions through 'co-ordination' (*Gleichschaltung*). By this process, all existing leaders in any sphere were replaced by Nazi activists, and all organizations were absorbed by the Nazis and forced to adopt Nazi programmes. In most occupations – and especially the government civil service, including teaching – Party members took over posts occupied by non-Party people, a measure authorized by law in April 1933 which allowed for dismissal on the grounds of 'political unreliability'.[18] Business contracts were awarded according to Party allegiance. Party membership climbed.

Women were steadily excluded from areas of public life. If married, they were sacked from civil service jobs. Promotion was closed to all women, and in education they were removed from the higher echelons of the school system.[19] Women judges and lawyers were dismissed, women were debarred from practising as barristers and solicitors, and the Women Lawyers Association was dissolved.

During the Weimar years, women had made substantial inroads into higher education. They made up 16–17 per cent of the student population. Even then, suspicion of highly educated women was widespread among men. The Nazis stigmatized the educated woman as a 'Jewish-intellectual ideal', insisting that women's natural sphere was domestic, not that of the intellect, and their education should be directed towards that goal. In December 1933, a quota was imposed by law restricting women's entrance to university to 10 per cent of the total. Despite this, their numbers did rise slightly (to 11.2 per cent) through the 1930s.

But the shift in subjects studied showed how effective this discrimination had been in orienting women towards more 'feminine' areas. The numbers of females studying medicine, dentistry, law, political science, liberal arts and natural sciences dropped substantially after 1933, as they shifted to pharmacy, journalism and physical education. In the latter subject, by 1939 half the students were female (up from under a quarter in 1933).[20]

Women were targeted in the drive to cut down unemployment, running at 6 million in 1932. They were to be removed from the workplace and returned to the home. This was a not uncommon reaction in other European countries during the Depression, but the Nazis were more directed and thorough. They mounted a sustained campaign against 'double earners' – families in which both partners worked – which vilified married women workers on the grounds that they were failing to carry out their womanly duty to the *Volk* and depriving men of jobs.

In June 1933, as part of legislation to curb unemployment, State marriage loans were offered to women who married, on condition that they left the workplace. This gave couples an interest-free loan of 1000 Reichsmarks (around a fifth of the average yearly take-home pay) to be paid (to the husband) in the form of vouchers for household furniture and other goods. This had the incidental advantage of boosting consumer industries. With each child, a quarter of the loan was deemed to be paid off; by the fourth child, no further repayment was necessary. The scheme was funded by a 2.5 per cent increase in income tax on single people and childless couples.

In a show of loyalty, mass weddings were arranged, accompanied by celebrations with the full Nazi paraphernalia of swastikas and Hitler salutes. In Berlin in 1933, forty-seven brides from the Lutheran Church were solemnly marched down the main street to the sound of brass bands and Nazi salutes from a surging crowd of enthusiastic supporters. They were all married that day. A 'shining example' of loyalty, according to the official Party organ, the *Völkischer Boebachter*, was the Reemtsma cigarette company. In November 1933, 122 women workers were married in a single mass ceremony. The company demonstrated their support of the marriage loan scheme by replacing the women, who immediately left work, with men, and gave every departing female employee a substantial cash payment. The Party newspaper praised this initiative and hoped many others would follow their example.[21] Later, the Reemtsma company donated 1 million marks per year to the Göring household to support their opulent lifestyle, which boasted lavish entertainment and expensive art treasures.

To obtain the loan, ever more stringent conditions were imposed. Applicants had to conform to the rigorous racial and social standards of the Nazi state. A Certificate of Fitness to Marry was introduced in 1935, which required both partners to submit themselves to medical examination to show that they and their families were 'racially pure'. They must also be free from 'hereditary disease' or 'eugenic flaws', and show no signs of 'asocial' defects – behaviour that did not conform to Nazi norms. Health authorities could be co-opted to trace the family's medical history, and welfare workers reported on 'asocial' behaviour. If the applicants showed any sign of 'defects', permission to marry was refused.

The aims of the marriage loan scheme – to remove women from the workplace, to encourage marriage and to provide inducements to have large families – had uneven success. The measures appeared to reduce female employment. By the end of 1934, around 360,000 women had given up work. Their proportion of the industrial labour force, around 30 per cent in 1933, was reduced to 25 per cent by the end of 1934. But there was a simultaneous rise in the overall number of women employed, since they continued to work in less depressed areas, such as consumer goods and service industries. Removing women from the workplace, except where they were in direct competition with men, made very little impact on unemployment statistics.

As the economy improved with the rearmament drive from 1935, women were tempted back to work. In 1937, the marriage loan condition that they left work was rescinded. The temporary fall in women's employment was not sustained, and by 1939 the number of women, including married women, working had risen above the 1933 figures. By 1939, 35 per cent of married women were combining home and family duties with full employment (compared with 32 per cent in 1933). As a labour shortage in the late thirties demanded more and more women in the workforce, concern for their welfare and physical wellbeing as future child-bearers, or their role as wives and mothers, took second place to the demands of an economy gearing up for war.

Nor did the marriage loan scheme substantially boost the marriage rate. There was a temporary increase in marriages in the first year, and then the rate settled at above the 1932 level. But barely a third of marriages in 1933 received loans, going down to a quarter, then up again in 1939 to almost half. Many couples may have been deterred from applying because they knew they would have to pass the stringent racial and medical conditions. The amount of the loan was not thought sufficient to cover the costs of the children who were expected from the union. The obligation to accept a free copy of *Mein Kampf* on pledging their vows probably didn't count either way.

Public approbation for marriage was everywhere. When Hermann Göring married the acclaimed classical actress Emmy Sonnemann in 1935, it was the occasion for a huge public celebration and grand display of party loyalty. Hitler was the solicitous best man, thereby associating himself with the family even though he had no intention of going down that route himself. Eight orchestras played during the pre-wedding party. A thousand guests danced the night away. On the wedding day, the streets of Berlin were decorated with swastikas, and cheering crowds joined the 30,000 soldiers who lined the route to the church. Journalists compared it to the marriage of the Kaiser. The day after, the couple opened their wedding presents, including paintings donated by Berlin museums, in public. Emmy gave up her acting career, but the couple had to wait three years – amid rumours that Hermann was impotent – before they produced their first and only child. The christening was accompanied by similar pomp. Hitler was filmed tickling and cooing over the child as she played with his moustache.

Motherhood

The main objective of marriage was to increase the birth rate. As in other European countries, a declining birth rate was a cause of national anxiety, particularly in France, where benefits were offered to encourage large families. But Nazi policy was not only about replenishment. It was directed towards creating a 'racially pure' nation of Aryans. German women's bodies were instruments for achieving this aim. Marriage was not primarily for the benefit of the partners, but for the propagation of the race. It was the cornerstone in building the Thousand Year Reich. Women's bodies belonged to the nation. 'Your body does not belong to you, but to your blood brethren and your... Volk', Nazi pamphlets declared.[22]

Motherhood was the apex of women's achievement in the Third Reich. This was women's true and ultimate destiny as well as their duty to the nation. Early women supporters praised the Party for elevating the status of motherhood and the sanctity of family life. The family, they believed, was the 'germ cell' or 'nucleus' of the nation. The years of turmoil and uncertainty during the Weimar years, it was argued, had pushed the family to the brink of crisis, as middle-class families lost their savings, working-class men lost their jobs and women claimed new rights. The Nazis capitalized on these fears with promises to restore social order – which included family stability.

In their idealized family, men and women had clearly demarcated roles. Men were warriors defending the home and nation from external threat. Women were building the new Germany as the 'warriors on the battlefield of childbirth'. They defended their natural domain of instinct, emotion and nurture. 'What the man sacrifices in fighting for his people,' declaimed Hitler, 'the woman sacrifices in fighting to maintain his people. The man shows heroism on the battlefield, the woman shows it in eternal patient devotion, in ever patient sorrow and endurance. Each child that she brings into the world is a battle that she fights for the existence or non-existence of her people.'

But by their zealous demand that individuals sacrifice their lives for the state, the Nazis invaded and destroyed the family as a place of safety and refuge from the outside world. And they infiltrated to the heart of women's private lives. Far from buttressing the ideal family, they used the family as an instrument for the realization of their political, racial and later military goals.

Nazi propaganda was carefully designed to elevate women's role. Motherhood was glorified. In posters, paintings and sculptures of variable quality and sickliness, mothers were portrayed as the pivot of an idealized National Socialist family. The breastfeeding mother appeared on sometimes graphically deplorable posters and was sculpted for placing in public spaces. Painters depicted mothers surrounded by their families in warm, soft-toned agricultural settings, intended to invoke the peasant rural idyll within which the Nazi fantasy of ideal family life was framed.

Motherhood was sanctified. 'Every mother of good blood should be holy to us,' pronounced Heinrich Himmler, head of the SS. German mothers were 'the protectors of the most holy source of blood and life that renews our nation every day'.[23] Early women supporters saw the political advantage of elevating the status of motherhood, and its appeal for women. It was the area where women could assert their power and worth within the national community: 'Woman is sacred to us in her predestined natural role, and every man reveres her calling. She is the guardian of the German race...' echoed prominent Nazi convert Guida Diehl.[24] Other activists used the terminology of maternal nurture and sacrifice in their appeals to women. Irene Seydel recalled her experience of:

> Women who have responded to our appeal... because they discovered they could once again serve the nation. Women had something to offer their people – the purity of their hearts and the power of their spirits! Women long to hear that politics emanates from love and that love means sacrifice. The German woman's talents wither at the sound of commands barked by north-eastern [Prussian] trumpets, But she is eager to work for someone who sends a friendly ray of sunshine her way.[25]

Motherhood was also rewarded. In 1934, Mother's Day became an official holiday. This had already been established during the Weimar years at the initiative of the German florist industry. It acquired new significance under the Nazis when it was changed to the date of Hitler's mother's birthday. From 1938, to encourage the others, *kinderreich* women – mothers who had four or more children – were rewarded with the Mother's Honour Cross, to be worn around their necks or pinned to their blouses. The honour came in three grades: bronze for four children, silver for six and gold for eight or more. Ever eager for gestures of militarism, members of the Hitler Youth were required to salute the recipients with 'Heil Hitler' in the street. Mother's Honour Crosses were first awarded on Mother's Day in May 1939, in ceremonies held nationwide, to 3 million, mostly older, women with four or more children. In addition to a supplement to their pension, they were promised preferential treatment in public – civil servants would treat them quickly and with respect, ticket collectors should offer them the best seats on the bus, and they got preferential seating at Party events. Mothers with three or more children were also rewarded with benefits – 'honour cards' meant that they could jump queues in shops, and they were allowed rebates of rent and public utility bills.[26]

In the interests of increasing the birth rate, the State intervened steadily further into the sphere of women's individual choice. Contraception was banned for Aryan women. The few birth control centres that had been set up during the Weimar years by pioneering women's groups were closed down, and birth control organizations, mostly linked to the Communist Party, were banned on the grounds that they were 'Marxist'. Contraceptive use clearly continued illegally, since the birth rate rose only very slowly. In 1941, the police under Heinrich Himmler cracked down further. In wartime, with mounting soldier casualties, he banned both the production and distribution of contraceptives.[27]

Abortion was outlawed, as it was in most western countries at the time. The penalties were more severe in Germany, where it was viewed as an unacceptable exercise of individual choice and a threat to the future of the race. Women who caused themselves to abort and those who helped procure an abortion were liable for five years' imprisonment, and later, after 1943, could be executed for impairing the 'vitality of the German *Volk*'. However, this law was subject to the overriding ideology of race. Abortion was legal, indeed encouraged, for Jews after 1938, and from 1935 it could be compulsorily applied to those deemed 'eugenically unfit'.

Prohibition did not stop women risking abortion, especially in the absence of contraception. The annual number of arrests or convictions for performing or aiding abortion more than doubled between 1932 and

1938 (up by 65 per cent). Estimates of the number of abortions are hazardous but, in Gisela Bock's study, a gynaecologist in 1939 estimated that of 220,000 miscarriages in hospital, 120,000 were abortions. In secret documents in 1937, Heinrich Himmler, who controlled the SS and the police forces as well as population policies, concluded there were between 400,000 and 800,000 abortions a year.[28]

Most of those convicted were women, since gynaecology was an area where women physicians could continue to operate. Some women took the risk of doing it themselves. Lotte Lasch, a former member of the Communist Youth movement, refused to have her private decisions forced on her by the state. 'I never used anybody else. I always did it myself. It turned out that I only carried through every third pregnancy. That's how it worked out. So, Stefan was actually the sixth child, and Bina the ninth. I didn't want to have a child forced on me. I wanted to really want to have the child. That was my point of view.'

Control over women became even more draconian when, after 1935, doctors and midwives were required to notify every case of miscarriage to the health authorities, who then handed the information over to the police for investigation as a possible abortion. The nexus of medical, health, welfare and police authorities, each under obligation to report to the other, formed an efficient web of control over women's domestic and private lives.

Official concern about the birth rate never translated into the hoped-for harvest of births, despite propaganda drives and inducements, including welfare benefits, for 'worthy' *kinderreich* families. The Europe-wide fall in the birth rate – which halved between 1901 and 1932 – was reflected in Germany. Couples preferred smaller families. The welfare inducements were not matched with improved housing that could accommodate larger families; marriage loans were inadequate to cater for more children. Even with an improved economy, the birth rate rose slightly above the 1933 figure. The number of large families dropped: in 1939 only a fifth of families had up to four children – in 1933 it had been a quarter.[29]

Among the racial elite of the SS, who underwent even more stringent vetting for marriage than the average, and were under greater obligation to propagate the master race, the SS members managed by 1939 to produce on average only 1.1 children, and the SS leaders a mere 1.4 children – far short of the four required by the State. Despite endless exhortation, moreover, three-quarters of SS leaders were married but well under half (43 per cent) of SS members were not.[30] Plans for the super-race were clearly falling short of expectation.

Political Schooling

Education in the duties of marriage and motherhood was a central feature of girls' and women's lives. Being a housewife and mother was professionalized. On courses throughout Germany, women were schooled in domestic science and to be skilled managers of the home.

The SS set up their own elite Bridal Schools to mould the wives of the future master race and strengthen their allegiance to the ideals of motherhood on which the Thousand Year Reich was to be built. By 1939, five schools had been set up, offering six-week courses. In very pleasant leafy and secluded surroundings, brides were taught what had now been elevated to the science of home management and mothercare. Following Nazi guidelines, they learnt the practice of home cooking and the theory of nutrition, with emphasis on fresh fruit and vegetables to retain vitamins and minerals (Hitler was a vegetarian), and the importance of fresh air and exercise. Each morning began with a jog or a swim before the parade and raising of the swastika flag. Students learnt about home decorating and design and colour combinations, about washing and ironing and health and hygiene. And they were instructed in the duties of being a wife and companion to their husbands.

At first, entrance was restricted to SS brides. But during the war, when Gertrud Draber was planning to marry an Army officer, she was accepted on a course at an elite bridal school at Schwanenwerder, near Berlin.

> I wanted to be a perfect housewife. And I wanted to do something different with my life, not just be a working girl in an office. I also wanted to spend time among other young women. None of us had a clue about running a household. So we were taught everything that was necessary to be a woman: housekeeping, being a mother, and being a good wife... My main aim

as a woman was above all, and as soon as possible, and against
all the odds, to become a mother. That was my main ambition.

'Racial training' was included on the course: 'We were quite certain that
we had to look for an Aryan man, so that we had Aryan children. You
were always hearing the word "Aryan", it was around all the time. And
there was great concern for German history and tradition.'

The women at the SS Bridal Schools were trained to qualify in the
profession of 'Master Housewife', and awarded a diploma at the end. But
the bulk of this kind of women's training was carried out by the newly
Nazified women's organizations.

Before Hitler came to power, women had been organized into
networks of local groups and federations under religious, political and
social banners. The Nazification policy of 'co-ordination' (*Gleischaltung*)
was immediately applied to the organization of women. After 1933, all
women's associations were required to submerge themselves under the
overall control of the Nazi women's organization. All non-Nazi organizations, even those nationalist and conservative bodies whose views
coincided with the Nazis', were forced to submit. If they resisted, as did
some Protestant groups, they were dissolved or eliminated. All leaders
had to prove their allegiance to the State, and non-Party leaders were
purged. Jewish women were immediately expelled or, if politeness still
counted, given no choice but to resign. The Reich Association for
Housewives, an independent lobby for the family and against the
suffrage, had included hundreds of Jewish women as members and
leaders. Sections tried initially to invent euphemisms, such as 'all
members must be Christian and nationally oriented' to cloak the naked
anti-Semitism that was forcing them to expel active and valued
members. Even so, they caved in with little struggle.[31]

The 'co-ordination' was not achieved without acrimony. Even
among Nazi women, differences had caused dispute. Though united in
their support of the family, and their opposition to leftism, Bolshevism
and the 'emancipated woman', Nazi women disagreed over, for
instance, the necessity that women's organizations be run by women,
over women's rights to work and to enlarge their educational and professional opportunities, and even over women's access to the ballot.

After a power struggle among leading women, the position of Reich Women's Leader (Reichsfrauenführerin) went to a thirty-two-year-old mother of five, widowed when her husband had died of a heart attack during a Nazi rally. Gertrud Scholtz-Klink was thought to have all the qualifications of the Nazi 'ideal woman'. Trim and neat, her blonde hair braided in plaits, without make-up, a *kinderreich* mother, she proceeded to educate women in their proper duties to the state, transforming women's groups into agents of indoctrination in Nazi ideology.

Though the Nazi women's organization claimed it had autonomy, its power was severely restricted. The Frauenschaft (Women's Bureau) was overseen by Hitler's director of national welfare, Erich Hilgenfeldt, whose first pronouncement was that women's job in the Third Reich 'was to leave all policy-making to men'.[32] He held ultimate responsibility for the direction, policy and activities of the women's organizations. Similarly, all matters relating to women's employment came under the control of Robert Ley, who ran the male Labour Front.

By 1938, Scholtz-Klink was complaining that she 'had not once had the chance to discuss women's affairs in person with the Führer'.[33] This was hardly surprising in view of the women leaders' conviction, echoing Hitler, that formal politics was the domain of men. Women's politics was something different, as the Nazi Mother Service, a branch of the women's organization, explained: 'The purpose of the National Mother Service is political schooling. Political schooling for the woman is not a transmission of political knowledge, nor the learning of Party programmes. Rather, political schooling is shaping to a certain attitude, an attitude that out of inner necessity affirms the measures of the State, takes them into women's life, carries them out and causes them to grow and be further transmitted.'[34]

To this end, organizations dealing with all aspects of women's lives – welfare, work, motherhood – proliferated. Women had to pay subscriptions to join. Though membership was not compulsory, pressure was put on women who did not sign up in the form of visits from local Party officials demanding an explanation. National schemes like the Winter Help Fund (*Winterhilf*), under which each Sunday during the winter months families ate vegetable soup instead of the Sunday roast and donated the savings to the fund to help the needy, were all but compulsory. Refusal to participate laid people open to accusations of failing in their duty to the Reich, which carried potentially serious penalties.

As well as providing support and welfare services, for instance maternity, crèche and kindergarten facilities, maternity support programmes, home help for large families and vacations for mothers, the women's organizations held training courses. These were ideal arenas for 'political schooling'. 'Mother Schools' were set up nationwide. Like the SS Bridal School courses, but shorter and cheaper, these gave instruction in the profession of home management and mothercare, health and hygiene. Much care was taken to link women's role to the national destiny, and stress the duty of service to the community and to their menfolk.

They learned how to cook cheaply with foodstuffs available in Germany and not use imported goods. They learned about nutrition and food values to ensure the health of the master race. The German housewife was educated to make meals from leftovers, as this would save 1 billion Reichsmarks a year. She was to make her own clothes, and dress in the German style, forgoing foreign fashion and imported clothes. She must know how to furnish her house on a small budget and to make toys and furniture as this would ease the pressure on German industry (which from 1936 was switching resources from consumer goods to war-related products and armaments). She should recycle unwanted goods rather than letting them go to waste.

This education had a wider political purpose. Women were being mobilized as key players in Hitler's Four Year Plan to make Germany self-sufficient. They were to help safeguard the economic independence of the Third Reich as well as its future. Reducing the demand for imported goods would boost German industry. The savings made by millions of housewives would thus assist in the national goal of building up Germany's defence and war capability. This training also equipped women to cope better with the shortages that would be the inevitable consequence of war.

And war was always part of the equation. In Nazi ideology, the major task of mothers was to breed the next generation of soldier heroes who would defend the Reich against danger from hostile neighbours – those neighbours who, as every schoolgirl knew, had so humiliated Germany at the Versailles Treaty and who still posed a threat to the nation's security. The sacrifice demanded of mothers was not only in surrendering their will to the greater cause of the State, but in willingly and proudly sacrificing their sons for the Führer and the nation's cause.

The proud warrior hero was the ultimate icon of Nazi manliness. 'The reward which National Socialism bestows on women in return for her labour,' Hitler proclaimed to thousands of uniformed young men at the 1935 Nuremberg Party Rally, 'is that it once more rears men, real men, decent men who stand erect, who are courageous, who love honour. I believe that, having watched the marching columns of the last few days, these stalwart and splendid youth from the Labour Service, our healthy and unspoiled womanhood must say to themselves, "What a robust and glorious generation is growing up here!"'[35]

As national leaders moulded men, the women's organizations backed official propaganda to mould an ideal New Woman, who fitted the leaders' vision of feminine perfection. Aryan, blonde and blue-eyed, she would conform to the sunny image of wholesomeness and strength that appeared in the mostly second-rate paintings, posters and sculpture approved during the period. In her own sphere, feminine grace and beauty was the aim to be achieved, along with dignity. At the very least, women should be pretty.

Edicts were delivered and disseminated on appropriate behaviour for the 'German woman'. She did not smoke, or drink, paint her face or indulge in fashionable fripperies. Hitler, a fanatical non-smoker and mostly a non-drinker, as well as a vegetarian, usually objected to both smoking and drinking in his presence. But other leaders who indulged in both were eager to extend the prohibition to women. The message filtered down. The young Hedwig Ertl, an active member of the League of German Girls (BDM), the girls' branch of the Hitler Youth, got the picture: 'The German woman must be faithful. She must not wear make-up and she should not smoke. She must be industrious and honest and she must want to have lots of children and be motherly.'

Apart from health considerations, both smoking and drinking were associated with 'degenerate' foreign Europeans (especially the French) and the dreaded Jewish-inspired 'emancipated woman'. But it was also thought incompatible with German duty. Police chiefs in some towns insisted that restaurants display notices stating that females were forbidden to smoke. In Erfurt, the police commissioner called on inhabitants to 'remind women whom they meet smoking on the streets of their duties as wives and mothers'.[36]

Make-up and nail varnish were also frowned upon, especially if they were foreign. Ninety-nine out of a hundred German women had no need of make-up, declared Hugo Kaiser, editor of *Notes for German girls who plan to become housewives and mothers*. In particular, they didn't need French cosmetic products because the German chemical industry could equal their quality and 'it was a crime against German resources' that 8 million Reichsmarks were paid to France for what they could get at home.[37]

However, it did not stop women using make-up or smoking. Eva Braun, Hitler's mistress, wore lipstick in his presence and smoked in private, but it did cause difficulties for others. The young Ilse Schmidt 'always put on make-up, and the other women said, "That looks nice." I was always very careful putting on powder so that my father didn't notice it, because my sister, who was four years younger than me, was totally against using make-up and she would tell on me – "Ilse put some powder on." And my father would take the powder and flush it down the sink. It made me furious.'

Traudl Junge was aware of an ideal who was 'naturally beautiful, sporty and healthy, and giving her leader a lot of children', but she paid little attention: 'It didn't touch me or my friends very much... We were interested in dancing and ballet, and I didn't care much for politics. But basically women should be natural, and, in particular, there was no eroticism then. Women were to be beautiful and look after themselves, but there was no sense of eroticism.' Those Nazi women held up as ideals made very little impact on her. 'The Führerin Gertrud Scholtz-Klink was the type we did not like at all. She was just bourgeois and she was so ugly and wasn't fashionable at all. So that was why we didn't bother about joining her organization.'

Health was women's duty, for their bodies were the receptacles for the future fitness of the race. Women were enjoined to take regular exercise and regular rest, sleep with the window open, and look after their bodies. Gymnastics became a national pastime. This was encouraged in private, but was usually done in groups. At huge public displays, women in flowing skirts, or trim short tunics, performed synchronized movements with hoops or balls or other apparatus. These demonstrated the participants' fitness and grace, but also their discipline.

Fashion, too, was subject to national edict. Wearing German regional costume was particularly lauded and encouraged. It celebrated the deep traditions of German rural culture which the Nazis held in special esteem, and which they cultivated in the masses through the 'Blood and Soil' movement. In their glorification of the pre-industrial rural peasant idyll in films, fresh-faced young girls in peasant costume were forever toiling in fields framed against a sunny sky, or dressed in colourful dirndls sitting on carts singing and waving ribbons in celebration of the harvest.

Nationalism played a part. Foreign women who dressed ostentatiously were derided. German men, claimed the author of the *ABC of National Socialism* (1933), wanted 'not an irresponsible toy, which superficially aspires to pleasure alone, adorns itself with baubles and finery and resembles a glittering husk whose interior is void and bare'. Women should dress modestly but elegantly in German-made textiles to German designs – even when they were making the clothes themselves. This they were also required to do, as otherwise they would drain the supply of textiles to uniforms – a rapidly expanding feature of the increasingly regimented state.

That Parisians should dictate fashion to the noble, naturally refined German woman was beyond the pale. Puritans railed against garish colours that made women look like 'whores'; others warned against giving support to Jewish clothing manufacturers. Mainly it went against the national interest. The pernicious element of fashion was that it kept changing, placing increased demand on textile resources for merely frivolous purposes, which could be better spent on the national good.

In 1939 Robert Ley, the Reich Director of Organization, opened the 'House of Beauty and Culture' in Berlin. He stressed the difference between elegant beauty, and novelty. Constantly changing fashion was detrimental to economic planning at a time when Germany was striving for self-sufficiency and diverting resources to armaments.

The official organ of the SS, *Das Schwarze Korps*, weighed in against lipstick, powder and silk stockings: 'as soon as they begin to stifle a woman's worth, these beauty aids – which are far from objectionable in themselves – create a danger that emphases will be wrongly distributed and real values take second place to a materialistic veneer.' But demand for cosmetics did not wane. After the occupation of France, that country's beauty products were the most highly valued presents sent home from soldiers at the front. After Goebbels declared 'total war' in 1943 and, astonishingly – considering the priorities – proposed an attack on 'beauty culture', Hitler, in one of the few statements that could be called broadly sane on the subject of women, warned his Propaganda Minister: 'Lift a finger against beauty culture and you make an enemy of her.'[38] Eva Braun may have played a part in this. Society woman Elisabeth von Stahlenberg recorded in her diary on 23 February 1943: 'Eva Braun telephoned and asked me to have lunch with her in the Osteria. We had a quiet table. She was more het-up than I've seen her – about the ban on cosmetics production. She is going to speak to "Adolf" about it: "I've never interfered with anything before, but this time I am going to have my say."'[39] Beauty parlours were among the few luxuries to escape restrictions during the war, bombing permitting. 'There is no need for a young woman to make herself look ugly,' Goebbels now decreed.[40]

The Nazis may have drawn the line at intrusion into women's lives in the matter of beauty in wartime, but they had little compunction about invading their private space in almost every other way.

NOTES

1 Picker, Henry, *Hitler's Table Talk,* Weidenfeld and Nicolson, London, 1953, p. 124
2 Cited Koonz, Claudia, *Mothers in the Fatherland: Women, the Family and Nazi Politics,* St Martin's Press, New York, 1987, p. 54
3 Cited Koonz, ibid., p. 54
4 Manvell, Roger, and Heinrich Fraenkel, *Heinrich Himmler*, Heinemann, London, 1965, p. 7
5 Lochner, Louis, *What About Germany?*, Dodd, Mead, New York, 1942, p. 22
6 Thomas, Katharine, *Women in Nazi Germany*, Gollancz, London, 1943, p. 31
7 Diehl, Guida, *Die Deutsche Frau und der Nationalsozialismus*, Neuland, Eisenbach, 1933, p. 42
8 Langer, Walter, *The Mind of Adolf Hitler: The Secret Wartime Report*, Putnams, New York, 1972, p. 72
9 Rauschning, Hermann, *Hitler Speaks*, Thornton Butterworth, London, 1939 p. 99
10 Ulshöfer, Helmut (ed.), *Liebesbriefe an Adolf Hitler: Briefe an den Tod*, VAS, Frankfurt, 1994, p. 43, 52, 59

11 Domarus, Max, *Hitler. Reden und Proklamationen 1932–1945*, Süddeutscher Verlag, Munich, 1965, p. 531

12 Cited Koonz, *Mothers in the Fatherland*, p. 75

13 Diehl, Guida, *Die Deutsche Frau und der Nationalsozialismus*, p. 76

14 Burleigh, Michael, *The Third Reich: A New History*, Macmillan, London, 2000, p. 155

15 Cited Koonz, *Mothers in the Fatherland*, pp. 334, 315; Burleigh, ibid., p. 198

16 Elling, Hannah, *Frauen im deutschen Widerstand, 1933–1945*, Röderberg, Frankfurt, 1981, p. 54

17 Cited Koonz, *Mothers in the Fatherland*, p. 330

18 Stephenson, Jill, *Women in Nazi Society*, Croom Helm, London, 1975, p. 29

19 Schoenbaum, David, *Hitler's Social Revolution: Class and Status in Nazi Germany 1933–1939*, W.W. Norton, New York, 1980, p. 189

20 ibid., p. 189

21 Stephenson, *Women in Nazi Society*, p. 88

22 Cited Koonz, *Mothers in the Fatherland*, p. 149

23 Pine, Lisa, *Nazi Family Policy, 1933–1945*, Berg, Oxford, 1997, p. 44

24 Diehl, *Die Deutsche Frau und der Nationalsozialismus*, p. 74

25 Quoted Koonz, *Mothers in the Fatherland*, p. 87

26 Clay, Catrine, and Michael Leapman, *Master Race: The Lebensborn Experiment in Nazi Germany*, Coronet Books, London, 1996, p. 55

27 Pine, *Nazi Family Policy*, p. 19

28 Bock, Gisela, 'Racism and Sexism in Nazi Germany: Motherhood, Compulsory Sterilisation, and the State', in (ed.) Renate Bridenthal, Atina Grossmann, Marion Kaplan, *When Biology Became Destiny: Women in Weimar and Nazi Germany*, Monthly Review Press, New York, 1984, p. 276

29 ibid., p. 277

30 Pine, *Nazi Family Policy*, p. 46

31 Cited Koonz, *Mothers in the Fatherland*, pp. 161–2

32 ibid., p. 168

33 Burleigh, Michael, and Wolfgang Wippermann, *The Racial State: Germany 1933–45*, Cambridge University Press, Cambridge, 1991, p. 249

34 Kirkpatrick, Clifford, *Women in Nazi Germany*, Jarrolds, [place?] 1939, p. 69

35 Domarus, *Hitler*, p. 531

36 Bleuel, Hans Peter, *Strength Through Joy: Sex and Society in Nazi Germany*, Secker & Warburg, London, 1973, p. 79

37 ibid., p. 81

38 Goebbels, Joseph, *The Early Goebbels Diaries*, (ed.) Helmut Heiber, Weidenfeld and Nicolson, London, 1962, p. 317

39 von Stahlenberg, Elisabeth, *Nazi Lady: The Diaries of Elisabeth von Stahlenberg*, Blond and Briggs, London, 1976

40 Goebbels (ed. Heiber), p. 317

7

THE RACIAL STATE

For those women included in the 'national community', welfare benefits and State privileges followed. But at the very core of the Nazi ideology was a pseudo-science of race that barred whole categories of Germans from inclusion in the New Germany. Since women's duty was to breed the new master race, they were the object of vetting on race, and also eugenic, grounds at the key points in their lives. By their behaviour, they could shift from being 'racially valuable' to being 'unworthy' human beings – with severe consequences in their private lives.

Education in 'racial awareness' began at school and, from then on, women were constantly reminded of their racial duties to the 'national community'. A ceaseless tide of anti-Semitic propaganda flowed from the official organs of the Nazi Party. In schools the range of subjects studied by girls narrowed as domestic subjects and those preparing them for motherhood took precedence over academic study. Biology, along with political education, was compulsory. Here, the Nazi pseudo-science of race was taught. Girls learnt about 'worthy' and 'unworthy' races, about breeding and hereditary disease. They measured their heads with tape measures, checked the colour of their eyes and texture of their hair against charts of Aryan or Nordic 'types', and constructed their own family trees to establish their biological, not historical, ancestry. School textbooks asked, 'Do you know what kind of blood runs through your veins?' as part of education in awareness of the Aryan 'blood community'. They also expanded on the racial inferiority of the Jews, along with Slavs, gypsies and other non-Nordic races, and vilified the allegedly sinister threat of the 'Jewish conspiracy' in national life.

Hedwig Ertl, an enthusiastic member of the BDM – the girls' branch of the Hitler Youth and a primary fount of indoctrination – remembers: 'We were told all the time that first the Jews are a lower kind of human being, and then the Poles are inferior, and anyone who wasn't Nordic was worthless. So any sense of injustice had gone.' Education glorified the German master race.

Schooling in 'racial awareness' was relentless. Another branch of propaganda, the Nazi Racial Policy Bureau, published ten rules to be observed when considering a marriage partner. Accompanied by explanatory notes, they were aimed at adolescents:

1   Remember that you are German! [The notes attached stressed that you owe what you are to the nation, not your individual merits, and your first allegiance is to the nation.]
2   Remain pure in mind and spirit!
3   Keep your body pure! [Only thus could you avert 'pleasures of the moment' which might threaten the nation's racial heritage.]
4   If hereditarily fit, do not remain single!
5   Marry only for love!
6   Being a German, only choose a spouse of similar or related blood!
7   When choosing your spouse, inquire into his or her forebears! [Note: you also marry his or her forefathers and clan; once human stock is 'tainted', your offspring are suspect.]
8   Health is essential to outward beauty as well!
9   Seek a companion in marriage, not a playmate!
10 Hope for as many children as possible! [Note: Your duty is to produce at least four offspring in order to ensure the future of the national stock.][1]

Any benefits from marriage and inducements to increase the birth rate applied only to those deemed 'racially valuable' and 'worthy'. Permission to marry at all was subject to conditions of racial 'purity'. Prospective brides and their husbands had to prove their families were 'Jew-free' for two generations. Documentation of ancestry – birth, death and medical certificates – was needed before permission was granted.

For prospective brides of the SS, the vetting was especially stringent. Heinrich Himmler, a fanatical exponent of race theory, envisaged the SS as the elite of the new master race. SS members from 1931 had to obtain a certificate of 'marriage authorization' (introduced after it was found that far too many of them had been marrying 'unsuitable', including 'racially inferior' women). To prove their hereditary fitness, prospective brides had to produce health certificates and documents of births and marriages going back to the great, great, great grandparents, as far back as 1750. This could add up to as many as 186 documents, all of which were sent to the SS Racial Bureau to be processed before permission to marry was granted. In addition, they had to prove their absolute allegiance to the Nazi ideology.

Luise Berner, a post office worker in Dachau, was preparing to marry Waffen SS member Karl Bierbaumer in 1935. Karl, originally Austrian, was recruited to the Waffen SS when he was unemployed. He was tall – 6ft 3in (1.9m) – with piercing blue eyes, and he played a musical instrument so, his wife recalls, he was inducted into the music corps in 1934.

To get permission to marry, she set about tracing the required documents. 'It wasn't that easy. The registry offices hadn't been in existence for that long. But they wanted us to go far back into the family tree. So I had to go to all the parish churches. And that took a very long time... When I had got it all together it had to go to the Race Bureau in Berlin and I never saw it again.' This vetting was necessary, she recalled, because 'there was so much talk at the time: we are the master race, and they wanted an absolutely pure master race... I myself didn't care that much about it. But it was important that an SS man married a girl who was of Aryan blood.'

Once she had the marriage permit, she was awarded a marriage loan of 3000 Reichsmarks (the usual sum was RM1000) and bought household furniture, including an extra long bed to accommodate her tall husband.

'Blood Purity'

The drive for 'blood purity' was enshrined in law when in 1935 the Law for the Protection of German Blood and Honour (one of the Nuremberg Laws) specifically prohibited marriage and sexual contact between Jews and non-Jews. It also forbade Jews to hire German women under the age of thirty-five as domestic help (presumably in the expectation that sexual contact, or 'race defilement', might occur). For the new crime of 'race defilement' (*Rassenschande*), penalties were severe. Prison terms of up to fifteen years could be handed down to both 'German-blooded' and Jewish men but, in practice, penalties were more severe for Jewish men. Jewish women were also prosecuted. After 1937, offenders, including women, could be sent to concentration camps. Their treatment at the hands of the Gestapo often involved lengthy interrogation including graphic and detailed descriptions of their sexual acts, which suggests a degree of Gestapo prurience in addition to any cruelty they might have meted out.[2]

In Krefeld alone, according to Eric Johnson in *The Nazi Terror*, in the first year there were 266 cases of 'race defilement'. In 1939, Ruth W., a sixteen-year-old Jewish housemaid, was picked up by the Gestapo after an anonymous communication revealed she was having a sexual relationship with a twenty-year-old Aryan worker, Joseph F. Called in to testify, he revealed in detail the course of their sexual relationship since 1937, ending with the claim that it was all her fault and he had tried to break off the relationship several times. Even before the girl was called in, the Gestapo officer concluded that she was 'ethically and morally on a low level', she 'creates a great danger for the folk-community and therefore the application of educational measures appears to be absolutely necessary'. When Ruth W. was called in, she at first denied having sex with Joseph F. but, after a night in a Gestapo cell, announced that she would tell the whole truth. She was put in 'protective custody' – a euphemism for unlimited sentence – and then sent to Lichtenburg concentration camp for nearly three months. After that she emigrated to Holland. Joseph F. was let free but had to stand trial and received a one-year jail sentence, its leniency justified by the judges who noted that he was extremely young and had been seduced by a 'Jewess'.[3]

For those already in mixed marriages, the laws were also draconian. In 1933 just under half (44 per cent) of new Jewish marriages were mixed. In addition, those who had one Jewish grandparent or more were defined as *Mischlinge* and led a precarious existence. Couples in mixed marriages were usually deprived of benefits available to Aryan couples and subjected to official harassment. Jewish husbands lost their jobs when the Nazis, on coming to power, immediately purged Jews from the civil service and the legal profession. Jewish doctors were removed from their posts and by 1938 allowed to treat only Jewish patients, while professors were removed from university posts. If they had Aryan wives, the measures might be slightly less severe. Victor Klemperer, a professor at Leipzig University, who had converted to Protestantism, had a non-Jewish wife and believed himself to be German; he did not officially lose his job at first, but his classes were steadily reduced and his income dropped to near zero.

Verena Groth, interviewed by Alison Owings in *Frauen*, told how her Jewish father, a medical director (hence a civil servant), was thrown out of his job in April 1933. Until then, she had not known that she was Jewish. He had converted to Protestantism, their family had lived in Germany for 500 years, and he was a German nationalist. With his Christian wife they moved to a smaller apartment. He was shunned by colleagues and thrown out of his club and other organizations. He set up a private dental practice but was told in 1939 that he could have only Jewish patients. The young Verena found her father at his desk, 'sobbing like a child', after they removed his certificate to practise. But because of his non-Jewish wife, he was saved from Auschwitz. Verena decided to train as a gardener, but anticipated that a half-Jewish woman would have difficulty getting her apprenticeship papers. A bureaucrat relented, so she had work, and later her father also found a job as a gardener.[4]

In 1938, new divorce legislation enabled non-Jews to divorce their Jewish spouses, simply because they were Jews, and penalties on non-Jewish former wives were later extended. In 1942, the Party Chancellery memorandum announced the Führer's decision that: 'permission for a soldier to marry a woman formerly married to a Jew must be rejected in every case. A German woman who has lived in matrimony with a Jew has thereby displayed such a lack of racial instinct that her subsequent union with a soldier can no longer be countenanced.'[5]

Official harassment extended to the children of mixed marriages. Rita Kuhn, whose father was Jewish and her mother Lutheran Christian, had been registered as Jewish. After the principal of her regular school told her father she did not want Jewish children there any more, even before they were officially barred, she was transferred to a Jewish school. Her father, a financier, had already lost most of his money in the 1929 crash. In 1933 he lost his job at a bank, had his assets confiscated and could not get work for four years. The family of four survived, living first in a damp basement apartment where her mother contracted tuberculosis, and later in a single room, on family help and a Jewish welfare organization. Later Rita Kuhn and her father were inducted into forced labour, but saved from deportation because their mother was non-Jewish.[6]

There were many forms of harassment. Some attempts were made to 'rescue' offspring who, with proper training, stood a chance of being turned into good Nazis. For, despite the race laws, no drop of German blood was to go to waste in the New Germany. Ilse Köhn, daughter of a Jewish father and a non-Jewish mother with socialist backgrounds, was at her grandmother's one day after school when two women from the Women's Bureau turned up at the door: 'I faced what seemed to be a grey wall moving towards me. I had the nightmare feeling that it would come close, closer and crush me. It consisted of two huge women dressed in long, identical grey coats with big black handbags and laced boots. Ugly, flat black boots. They had pallid faces, and their hair was tied back so tightly they seemed bald.' They inspected her grandmother's house to ascertain its suitability for bringing up a child, and then initiated proceedings to make Ilse a ward of court so that she could be returned to her non-Jewish grandparents to be brought up as an Aryan.[7]

In the case of both Jewish and mixed families, Nazi policy, far from upholding the value of family life, was intended to systematically destroy it. The first signal of the coming economic persecution of the Jews came in April 1933 with the national boycott of Jewish shops. Allegedly in response to a threatened international Jewish boycott of

German goods, it was instigated by Hitler who declared 'he had to carry out the boycott and was no longer in a position to hold up history'. It was planned by Party committees nationwide and carried out by the SA.[8] Bands of uniformed SA thugs turned up in yelling groups on lorries, then stood threateningly outside Jewish shops attempting to prevent entry and bearing placards reading 'Germans, Defend Yourselves. Do Not Buy from Jews!' and 'The Jew is our Misfortune'. Crowds of bystanders joined in chanting the slogan 'Jews out!' In several towns, shops were looted.

The boycott had only partial success. Many people brushed past the SA men and continued shopping as usual. Martha Brixius told Alison Owings how her mother:

> ...always went into Jewish shops, even when the SA stood outside to see who entered. Once I went in with her. SA men in uniform stood outside. My mother really gave me courage. This Jewish merchant was someone from whom one could buy sewing needles and cloth and wool and scissors and so on. It was so terrible – such a very large store and completely empty. The owner came over to us. He was so thankful that someone came. My mother really had nothing to buy but wanted to show him, I'm still coming.[9]

The actions in 1933 persuaded many Jews to emigrate immediately. Nearly 40,000 of Germany's 537,000 Jews left that year,[10] and there was a steady exodus over the following years. But many remained, unable to believe that things could get so much worse, or unwilling to pick up their families and move away from their homeland into the unknown. Avraham Barkai wrote: 'Whoever had a family and children of school age, a shop or some other business, a house or other property found himself unable – unless he was immediately threatened – to arrive so easily at a decision to take leave of his homeland. After the first shock waves of the Nazi takeover and April boycott had passed, people began to get used to the situation.'[11]

Nevertheless, the boycott signalled alarm, and a gathering feeling of forced alienation from the surrounding community of which, up till then, they had been a part. From then on, for Inge Deutschkron, 'our home did not seem the same secure place as before'.[12] Edwin Landau 'was ashamed that I had once belonged to this [German] people. I was ashamed about the trust I had given to so many who now revealed themselves as my enemies... Suddenly the street, too, seemed alien to me; indeed the whole town had become alien to me.'[13]

Shortly afterwards, Jewish officials in the civil service were 'retired' by law; Jewish lawyers were barred from practising, judges were dismissed and public service employees lost their jobs. It became increasingly difficult to make a living. In addition, they were ostracized socially, 'encouraged' or forced to give up membership of clubs and societies, and became steadily isolated from the rest of the community. 'With each day of the Nazi regime, the abyss between us and our fellow citizens grew larger... How much our life changed in those days... we no longer visited our friends, nor did they come any more to see us,' Marta Appel recalled.[14] Later, as more restrictions were imposed, association between Jews and non-Jews became an area of potential criminality, which increased their social isolation.

Children, who were frequently ostracized in the playground, were also humiliated by Nazi teachers in the classroom. Aryan BDM girl Hedwig Ertl, by then thoroughly trained in 'race-consciousness', remembers: 'We had a history teacher who was a very committed National Socialist, and we had four Jewish pupils. And they had to stand up during the class, they weren't allowed to sit down. And one after the other they disappeared, until none were left, but nobody thought much about it. We were told they had moved.' Jewish girls were excluded from the life of the school, even from participating in Mother's Day celebrations. One mother relates how her children were told that 'since you are Jewish, you are not allowed to join in the songs'. When the children protested that they wanted to sing for their mother, 'the teacher rebuked their protest. "I know you have a mother, but she is only a Jewish mother." At that the girls had no reply... but seldom had they been so much disturbed.' She reflected: 'It required a great deal of strength, of love and inner harmony among Jewish families, to make our children strong enough to bear all that hatred and persecution. My heart was broken when I saw tears in my younger child's eyes when she had been sent home from school while all the others had been taken to a show.'[15] By 1938 girls were forbidden to attend regular schools and allowed to attend only Jewish schools.

The pressure on family life became intense. In 1935, after a wave of 'individual acts' of terrorism against Jews (almost all instigated by the Party), Hitler responded to radical pressures in the Party to 'solve the Jewish Question' by revoking the right of Jews to be citizens and making them 'subjects of the State'. When the Nazis, after denying people jobs and citizenship, began expropriation of Jewish savings and property, families who had suffered steady humiliation in every other area of their lives were faced with the near impossibility of making a living. From then on, the policy of 'aryanization' of the economy — excluding Jews from the economic life of the country — was gradually enacted.

The resulting impoverishment blurred the roles of men and women, creating what Lisa Pine calls a kind of equality. Men lost their status outside the home, and their authority inside the home, as they lost their means of making a living. Women gained increased powers of decision-making. As income dropped, and Jews were forced to sell up property and businesses at unjustly low prices, families were forced to move to smaller premises. Many families disintegrated as despair took over. Men could no longer protect their families, while women had not the means to provide for them. Many people committed suicide. 'When one's livelihood is gone, what remains? Worry, despair, unhappiness!' one woman declared, after they had had to sell the family business.[16] It was women who had to keep the family going, and cope with running a household on shrinking resources.

As Marion Kaplan points out, women's role as the nurturer and spiritual support at the centre of the family assumed new importance as the outside world became more menacing, and the home the only safe haven available. They were the ones who kept up the family spirits, comforted children and tried to give them strength, and continued to support their husbands, even though, with evictions and expropriations, the safety of the home was no longer by any means assured. Women learnt new skills of negotiation with bureaucracy to get through daily life. Many retrained and found work when their husbands had lost their jobs or businesses, and became the family breadwinners. And in many cases it was women who detected more clearly the drift of events and instigated the decision to emigrate.[17]

Social Exclusions

In the building of the master race, it was not only Jews who, along with Slavs and gypsies, were excluded. Hundreds of thousands of Aryan Germans fell short of the 'racial and eugenic standards' and were denied any privileges or rights, especially in the area of procreation. The State apparatus removed decision-making in marriage and childbearing from individuals, and vetted people to establish their 'moral worth' as well as their 'racial' value. The Aryan, eugenically sound, socially conformist wife and mother was the ideal woman. Those who did not match up to this were categorized as 'unworthy' – more chillingly as 'lives unworthy of life' – or 'asocial', and cordoned off from the 'national community'. While the State tried to impel the worthy to have more children, it also tried to compel the 'unworthy' to have fewer or none.

This was rationalized in the 'science' of eugenics, which was seen as an early solution to population control directed at arresting any decline in national 'fitness'. It would ensure that genetic and behaviour 'defects' were contained, and, by controlling reproduction, eventually eliminated from the life of the 'national community'.

At the point of marriage, couples were required, especially if they were applying for a marriage loan, to prove not only that they were 'racially pure' for two generations, but also that they were free from 'hereditary disease'. Health authorities were enlisted to provide the necessary medical certificates, and welfare bodies were entitled to investigate an applicant's social background.

Education in 'racial awareness' directed particularly at women was a prerequisite of marriage. Films issued from Goebbels's Propaganda Department and shown in all cinemas, such as *Victim of the Past* and *The Inheritance*, pummelled home the message that selective breeding to produce 'worthy human beings' was the purpose of marriage. Both provided gruelling illustration of the 'mistake' – and cost to the State – of supporting those with 'genetic defects'. In *Victim of the Past,* a doctor explains to a somewhat unctuous prospective bride ('You have such a wonderful profession, Herr Doktor!') that women were duty-bound to investigate their and their partners' ancestors 'to ensure that their genes are worthy to be passed on'.

Those whose genes were not 'worthy to be passed on' could be refused permission to marry. Eugenicists estimated that 10–20 million Germans, of a population of 80 million, fell into the category of those whose offspring was undesirable. In one district of Berlin, between 1934 and 1940, half of those wishing to marry were denied permission. If this was the average, around 200,000 couples nationwide would have been prohibited from marrying.[18]

The 'unworthy' were also denied the right to reproduce. Since 1933, compulsory sterilization had been legalized (Law for the Prevention of Hereditarily Diseased Offspring) for certain categories of the 'unworthy' and those suffering from 'hereditary disease', as well as Jews and gypsies. These categories were extraordinarily loose and gave wide leeway to doctors, psychiatrists and the eugenics courts (Hereditary Health Courts) set up to decide who should be allowed to procreate. Included in the list of those with 'congenital' illness were schizophrenics, manic depressives, people suffering from Huntington's chorea, people with hereditary blindness or deafness or 'serious physical deformities', chronic alcoholics, and the largest category – the 'congenitally feeble-minded', which encompassed a wide range of behaviour deemed incompatible with duty to the State. The 'feeble-minded' included people with criminal records (including prostitutes), shirkers, people with behaviour problems, spendthrifts or those on welfare, and people who failed to keep a tidy house or raise their children to be useful citizens. Two-thirds of those sterilized for 'feeble-mindedness' were women.[19]

If patients landed up in a psychiatric institute, after 1939 they could also be candidates for the euthanasia programme. This was the plan to get rid of up to 100,000 inmates of psychiatric institutions, including 5000–6000 children under sixteen, by systematically murdering them as 'useless eaters' who were draining the State's resources. Propaganda films such as *Erbkrank* (1936) prepared the ground for vilification of the mentally ill. Doctors explained to pretty female students the 'laws of nature' – 'Everything that is weak for life will ineluctably be destroyed.' Patients were depicted as a drain on national resources and their care as a sin against the laws of natural selection. From 1939, on Hitler's orders, the systematic murder of patients by gassing took place in several killing centres. Nurses – out of obedience, duty or desensitization – assisted in this process, either in administration of the means of death, or in lying to relatives about the actual cause of death. The programme was not stopped until 1941. After protest by the Catholic Bishop Clemens Galen of Münster, and a few other Church leaders, Hitler stopped the programme, but transferred the killing machines of the so-called T-4 programme, and a number of 'experts', to the extermination camps to carry on their work.

Referral for euthanasia, or sterilization – known as the *Hitlerschnitt* ('the Hitler cut') – was also made through a net of social and welfare bodies with access to details about private behaviour, as well as doctors and psychiatrists who were obliged to provide information about their patients to the health authorities. A few doctors refused to co-operate. Dr Margret Blersch, a trained neurologist and an anti-Nazi, was aware of the consequences of referral in the sterilization and euthanasia programmes. She had heard through the medical network about clinics where euthanasia patients were murdered by gassing, and she saw buses pass through her village near Freiburg with curtained windows. 'We knew they did not want the mentally ill to live,' she said. 'I stood by the people who had congenital diseases, and said, "You may not go to another doctor. You must stay here. That is, I won't report you."' When word spread, an increasing number of people, including schizophrenics who were also candidates for sterilisation, came to see her. 'If those people had gone to a clinic, they'd have been removed immediately and been gassed.' She gave schizophrenics injections in a form of shock therapy that altered their behaviour – 'They lost their crazy ideas... I treated them at their homes... Here in the village, I injected them. They came through. That's why so many people came, because they knew... we're not handing people over to the health ministry. We don't notify the State about them.'[20]

Others got caught up in the net. Liselotte Katscher, training to be a Lutheran nurse in 1934, was posted to a home for girls who had been sentenced by a youth court for petty juvenile offences and sent into care. As a religious nurse, she was already aware of the disparity between her calling and a nurse's duties in the Nazi State: 'The National Socialists only cared for those who were worthy. So-called "unworthy" life was not cared for, nor were people of the "lower races".'

As part of her training she had to make a lengthy report on one of the girls, a sixteen-year-old named Henny, who at the age of fifteen had such a furious argument with her farmer employer that she burned down his farm and was sentenced to care. Liselotte Katscher recalls with remorse:

Henny was examined by a doctor who diagnosed a slight feeble-mindedness – in my opinion it was only a slight feeble-mindedness, and they had decided that she should be sterilized... I thought about it a great deal at the time, and I felt sorry for the girl, but it was the law, and the doctors had decided. I personally took her to the maternity ward in the hospital where it took place... But I never got rid of the doubt in my mind that the decision was too harsh. I formed the impression when dealing with this young girl that she was perfectly capable of leading a normal life.

The tragedy, she reflects, 'was that this girl, who behaved really well, and was released very soon after this, then got a job and met a nice young man, and was now not allowed to marry him because of her sterilization'.

The victims of sterilization were given no choice, or even the opportunity to speak. Dorothea Buck, from a religious family, had at the age of nineteen gone through what she called a spiritual crisis. Propelled by impulse, she had gone to the sea 'in pursuit of the morning star' where she experienced a 'rebirthing'. She was found unconscious and naked in the sand-dunes, and was sent by her parents to a psychiatric nursing institute where she remained in treatment for nine months. 'The doctor came with his assistants and they shook our hand but they never talked to us. There was never one single conversation with the doctor in the whole of my nine months in Bethel... And despite the fact that he never talked to me, he diagnosed me as heavily schizophrenic.'

Her mother was not allowed to visit. When, after eleven weeks, she was told her mother was there, she rushed to the reception: 'I was expecting to find my mother, but there were two men sitting there poring over some papers. They were asking me questions, like why I had gone into the sea, and one or two other things. I just wanted to get to my mother, so I answered their questions very superficially. I had no idea that this was a Hereditary Court hearing, and it was about compulsory sterilization.' Nobody had talked to her about it, but they had talked to her mother, she learned later: 'My mother was given a choice to either agree to sterilization or have me put in an institution until I was forty-five years old. And she thought that being in an institution was worse.'

Dorothea Buck was transferred to an open ward:

One evening the nurse came and shaved off my pubic hair to prepare for an operation. I asked her, 'What is happening?' and she said, 'Just a small necessary operation.' But didn't explain any further. Then they wheeled me into the operating theatre, and after the operation, still nobody told me what had happened. Later on I was told, that with this forced steriliza-tion, I was unable to have children, and forbidden to marry a man who was not sterilized himself. I was in despair. I cut my hair short, I had long hair then. So that at least one thing was still growing, when everything else in my body, in my develop-ment, had come to a stand-still. I didn't feel like a woman any longer after this dreadful sterilization operation.

There were further penalties. She was forbidden to study in higher education, and was unable to practise in her chosen profession of chil-dren's nurse. Dorothea Buck became an accomplished sculptress. Her studio is filled with sculptures of the mother and child.

Sterilization was a planned programme. Experts had already made estimates of how many people should be sterilized to achieve its goals: some said between 5 and 30 per cent of the population. In 1933 the Minister of Interior, Wilhelm Frick, quoted experts who claimed that 20 per cent of the German population was 'racially undesirable': 'We must again have the courage to grade our people according to its genetic value,' he declared.[21] Up to 1939 around 320,000 people, or 1 in 200 of the population, were sterilized. A study by Gisela Bock shows that just over half (53 per cent) of these were for 'feeble-mindedness', of which two-thirds were women; a fifth were for 'schizophrenia'. Around 400 women and 80 men died in the course of the operation between 1934 and 1937.[22] Altogether, around 5000 people died through surgical complications, the majority of them women.

Other forms of control were extended to those branded 'unworthy'. 'Asocials' were denied welfare and State privileges. Large families, lauded and encouraged in women who conformed, were penalized among 'asocials'. Mothers were denied the Mother's Honour Cross, and they were excluded from the benefits and support services, including child allowances, awarded to *kinderreich* families. Experts believed that some 'asocials' could be trained and re-educated. But the vast number of those who fell into this category – through, for instance, frequent contact with the police for criminal behaviour, 'promiscuous' behaviour, being work-shy, alcoholic, spendthrift or failing to keep a tidy house – were judged, under the loose definitions applied by the Nazis, to be suffering from 'congenital defects' and so beyond 're-education'.

Further State intrusion into family life and private decisions came with the Divorce Act of 1938. Though this was an enabling rather than a coercive measure, it furthered the State's aims of family and population control. Divorce was made easier. The new 'irretrievable breakdown' clause, which removed the requirement to prove 'guilt' – a clause fought for in Britain for three decades which became law only in 1968 – became the grounds for divorce in the majority of cases. A three-year separation was proof of breakdown. Other clauses served the Nazi State, since the object was to dissolve those marriages that were of no value to the community. Non-Jews could divorce their Jewish spouses simply because they were Jewish, under clauses allowing divorce of 'racially undesirable' or 'genetically inferior' partners. Husbands could divorce wives who refused, or were unable, to have children since they were failing to carry out their duty to their husbands and the State. The major aim of increasing the birth rate would be advanced by this measure, it was argued, since racially valuable men could go off and find partners who would increase and preserve the race. Immorality, venereal disease, mental illness, 'racial incompatibility' and 'eugenic weakness' were all now available as grounds for spouses to untie the knot.

Divorce rates spiralled in the first year, and men benefited more than women. In 30,000 divorces under the new law, four-fifths were initiated by husbands wanting to leave their wives.[23] One-third of these were on the grounds of infertility or unwillingness to have children. In almost two-thirds (60 per cent) of cases, women, whose primary value in the Nazi state was as wives and mothers, were divorced against their will on the grounds of being infertile (this included 'premature infertility') or, in the vague terminology current at the time, being 'feeble-minded' or of 'hysterical behaviour'.

'Every Drop of German Blood'

Most European countries stigmatized unmarried mothers as a threat to the institution of marriage. In Nazi Germany, however, motherhood and procreation by women of 'good blood' were so valued that steps were taken to re-cast the image of the unmarried mother and illegitimate child – not in women's interests, however, but for the good of the *Volk*. This did not mean a general upgrading of illegitimacy. Most unmarried mothers had sunk into the category of 'asocial'. But the fanatical Heinrich Himmler was forever spinning plans to ensure that no drop of valuable blood went to waste, and to this end he set up the Lebensborn, or 'Fount of Life' organization.

Marriage, Himmler claimed, need not be a preliminary to motherhood as long as women were breeding thoroughbred Germans. The bourgeois concept of marriage and 'morality' was outmoded as far as Nazi population policy was concerned. Hitler concurred: 'Let's remember that after the Thirty Years' War polygamy was tolerated, so that it was thanks to the illegitimate child that the nation recovered its strength.' As long as there was an imbalance in the population, with an excess of women of childbearing age, 'we shall be forbidden to despise the child born out of wedlock'.[24] Loyal supporters echoed him: 'The National Socialist state no longer sees in the single mother the "degenerate"... it places the single mother who has given a child a life higher than the "lady" who has avoided having children in her marriage on egotistical grounds.'[25]

The status of unmarried mothers in this new hierarchy was revised. After 1937, they could call themselves 'Frau', previously the term reserved for married women, and in 1939 the ban on single mothers working in the civil service was lifted, but that was almost entirely connected with a shortage of labour in that sector at the time.[26]

Himmler translated belief into action, in private and in public. After having a child by his first wife, he had two illegitimate daughters by his mistress, an attractive young secretary on his staff called Hedwig Potthast. He set up, and took personal interest in, a chain of nine Lebensborn homes, the first in 1936 at Steinhöring outside Munich, the others dotted around the country. Most were donated by supporters and local or regional councils anxious to show their loyalty. Heim Pommern was presented by the municipality of Pölzen to the Führer, who passed it on to Himmler. Heim Weinerwald, on the other hand, had been expropriated from Jewish owners by Himmler's Gestapo.[27]

These maternity homes, founded under the SS Race and Resettlement Bureau, were intended primarily for the brides and wives of young SS men and secondarily for illegitimate mothers 'of good blood'. In quiet and secluded environments, 'valuable' women would be cared for before, during and after birth, away from the prying and critical eyes of relatives and neighbours. Women were advised about the correct diet – Himmler was keen to promote the virtues of porridge and wholemeal bread – and were given expert advice on home management and childcare.

Mothers of illegitimate children were given the option of keeping their babies, or sending them to be fostered by SS families who had failed to manage the expected quota of children on their own. Those who remained in their care were the responsibility of the Lebensborn organization, whose motto was 'Every mother of good blood is our sacred trust.' If a mother chose to keep her child, the SS made sure that the fathers provided financial support for it. Doctors swore an SS oath of silence. No photos remain of the mothers, because photographing them was forbidden. Births were not registered through the official civil registry offices, but covered by a special certificate confirming their racial purity.

The Lebensborn homes fired controversy. The Catholic Church opposed the very idea of the State condoning illegitimate births. Rumours went about that they were SS 'stud farms'. Not-so-loyal mothers warned their daughters to steer clear of SS men for fear that, among other ills that might befall them at SS hands, they would be spirited off to one of the homes and used for breeding. Nor did all the leaders support Himmler's radical policies. Some argued that it still undermined the family. A solid body of race and eugenics 'experts' were clear that all unmarried mothers were 'undesirable' and had, by their nature, 'moral defects', so should not be singled out for any special treatment.[28]

Many Nazi women, including those in welfare organizations, had worked to improve the legal and financial position of both unmarried mothers and their illegitimate offspring. But very few went as far as to condone single motherhood as socially acceptable, since this would undermine the family which was the kernel of Nazi women's value and strength. Auguste Reber-Gruber, a long-time Nazi installed at the Education Ministry, was deluged with protests from teachers, and was moved to criticize the leader's disregard for women. On the other hand, Jutta Rüdiger, head of the League of German Girls, pointed out: 'Before then, it was a very shameful thing to have a child if you were not married. Many women committed suicide. But here the women could have their child in peace and quiet and mother and child were looked after, and they may even be able to get a job where they could take the child with them.'

For Himmler, pure blood was all. He only admitted women who 'after careful research by the Race and Re-settlement Head Office into their families and the families of their children's fathers, can be expected to give birth to equally valuable children'.[29] Half the applicants were turned down.

Rumours that they were literally 'stud farms' have mostly been discounted, but the idea behind them – to safeguard the propagation of German blood regardless of marriage bonds – suggests a racial imperative leaving open all sorts of options. Himmler chose to portray the homes in a philanthropic light, as he told Felix Kersten, his masseur, in 1943:

> I have made it known privately that any young woman who is alone and longs for a child can turn to Lebensborn with perfect confidence. I would sponsor the child and provide for its education. I know this is a revolutionary step, because according to

the existing middle-class code an unmarried woman had no right to yearn for a child... Yet often she cannot find the right man or cannot marry because of her work, though her wish to have a child is compelling. I have therefore created the possibility for such women to have the child they crave. As you can imagine, we recommend only racially faultless men as 'conception assistants'.[30]

In September 1939 he issued an order to his 'racially faultless' SS members which encouraged them to produce children, if necessary outside marriage, and assured them that any valuable children thus produced would be taken care of in the event of their death.

What is clear from the often painful stories of Lebensborn children who later sought out their parents is that women who fell pregnant after short affairs or one-night stands with SS members could, as long as they were racially 'valuable', count on care at the homes. Helga Kahrau's parents met at a party in Berlin to celebrate the conquest of France in June 1940. Her mother had been a secretary in both Bormann's and Goebbels' offices. Her father was a pro-Nazi Army officer. Helga was born in a Lebensborn home after their one-night stand. She was farmed out to an SS family in Lodz in Poland, where her foster-father oversaw the gassing of thousands of Jews at the Chelmo concentration camp. Her mother brought her up after the war but never talked about her experiences. When Helga investigated her past, she was horrified to find that she 'grew up on the side of murderers'.[31]

Lebensborn had its part to play in war, as Himmler extended his population policies in the occupied territories. So fanatical were the Nazis to save every drop of German blood that, when they invaded the East, Himmler directed that all children with any trace of German ancestry in the occupied territories should be 'rescued' for the Reich. The authorities informed the leaders of German women's groups in Minsk in 1943 that Lebensborn maternity homes were available where 'births can be recorded without any need to notify the home authorities', and reminded them of 'how important every genetically sound child is to our future... everything must therefore be done to support the mother and child and guarantee their health and survival'.[32]

This care for mother and child contrasted starkly with Himmler's pronouncement on the treatment of children of mixed blood in the conquered lands: 'It is obvious that there will always be some racially good types in such a mixture of peoples. In these cases I consider it our duty to take the children and remove them from their environment, if necessary by abduction. Either we acquire any good blood we can use for ourselves and give it a place in our nation, or we destroy it.'[33] From Poland, Russia, Czechoslovakia and Yugoslavia, children were forcibly abducted from their parents, who were never consulted, nor knew their children's fate.

Hostels were set up in Germany under Lebensborn auspices where children were tested for racial 'purity' and prepared for Germanization. Those who failed the racial tests, or whose ancestry was suspect, were returned to their parents. The others were farmed out to foster-parents, had their names replaced with German ones, and became all but untraceable as they were absorbed into the German nation. This inhumane policy towards children and parents was one small contribution to Hitler's larger ambition – to expand the population of the Greater Reich by bringing 30 million people of German blood back 'home' – to make it, with a population of 120 million, the most powerful nation in Europe.

The need to preserve and procreate German blood became more urgent as the war progressed. German soldier-heroes were dying in larger numbers than anticipated. The end of the war would see a surplus of women over men, which to some leading Nazis presented a problem of national resources. Women's child-bearing capabilities would be going to waste on a vast scale if there were insufficient men to renew the race. The solution proposed by Himmler, among others, was polygamy. That this went against the whole rhetoric of support for the stable family as the 'germ cell' of the State, or the reverence they professed for wives and mothers, did not at first deter them. Racial priorities and national duty must, as always, override the individual's concerns.

The regime had already made it legal for men to divorce their wives for infertility in order that they could form another relationship that could prove more fecund. Illegitimacy had been tolerated as long as the racial requirements were fulfilled. Propaganda had exhorted young women to have a child for the Führer, regardless of their marital status, as a matter of duty. In December 1939, Deputy Führer Rudolf Hess staked his support for unwed mothers in response to a letter from a distraught woman of 'good Aryan blood' whose fiancé had died at the front, leaving her pregnant. She now faced social ostracism as a single mother. Hess bounded to her rescue with a new code of duty: 'What use is it if a nation achieves victory but, as a result of the sacrifices made to achieve it, dies out as a nation?' Women bearing children outside marriage were servicing the Reich and should be accorded due respect. It was but a short step to the more radical solutions proposed by Himmler and others.

Bigamy was a lively topic of conversation in the household of Gerda and Martin Bormann, Head of Hitler's Chancellery. Gerda, a model Nazi wife, bore her husband ten children. In October 1943, shortly after the birth of the tenth, he began an affair with Manja Behrens, an actress at the Dresden State Theatre, whom they had both known for some time. He described his conquest enthusiastically to his wife.

> You can't imagine how overjoyed I was. She attracted me immensely, and in spite of her resistance I kissed her without ado and set her afire with my burning delight. I fell madly in love with her... I arranged it so that I saw her again many times, and then I took her in spite of all her refusals. You know how determined I can be, and M. naturally couldn't hold out for long. Now she is mine, and I – lucky fellow! – am doubly and unbelievably happily married... Now I must be doubly careful to look after my health and keep up my strength.[34]

Gerda was more than conciliatory. In a reply (which her husband annotated), Gerda wrote in January 1944:

> I am so fond of M. myself that I cannot be angry with you, and the children love her very much, all of them... It is a thousand pities that fine girls like these... should be denied children. In the case of M. you will be able to alter this, but then you will have to see to it that one year M. has a child, and the next year I, so that you will always have a wife who is mobile. [*What a*

wild idea.] Then we'll put all the children together in the house on the lake, and live together, and the wife who is not having a child will always be able to come and stay with you in Obersalzberg or Berlin. [*That would never do even if the two women were the most intimate friends. Better each on her own. Visits, alright, but even that within limits.*]... That she shouldn't have a child is something which seems out of the question, you being you. [*You're stupendous.*]

Several days later, Gerda, having thought about it, wrote again:

Beloved, does she love you as a wedded wife should, and will she remain yours for good even if she cannot bear your name! [*Time alone will tell.*] It would be a good thing if a law were to be made at the end of this war, like the one at the end of the Thirty Years' War, which would entitle healthy, valuable men to have two wives. [*The Führer is thinking along similar lines!*] So frighteningly few valuable men survive this fateful struggle, so many valuable women are doomed to be barren because their destined mate was killed in battle – should that be? We need the children of these women too! [*Absolutely, for the struggles to come, which will decide the national destiny.*]

Bormann wrote ecstatically back 'My Darling Mummy! You are wonderful and I love you madly!'[35] Gerda went further. She drew up a contract for a National Emergency Marriage (*Volksnotehe*) to be signed by herself and Martin, in which a marriage to Martha would have the same validity in law as the ties uniting them.

Martha stayed at their residence near Hitler's at Obersalzberg for some time in spring 1944, and the two women in this *ménage à trois* got on well. After several months Bormann's affair with Martha petered out, and only the two women kept in touch.

Whatever the personal motives, especially the long-suffering Gerda's, Bormann seized on the opportunity to justify bigamy on the grounds of the national good. The Führer agreed wholeheartedly, according to a memorandum by Bormann on 29 January 1944. It was a question of 'the future of our people', he decided. After the war, there would be a surplus of 3 to 4 million women, leading to a drastic shortage of soldiers in the future: 'The drop in the birth rate resulting from that would be impossible to put up with... In twenty or thirty or forty or fifty years we will be lacking the divisions that we absolutely need if our people is not to perish.'

Hitler proposed several solutions: 'Good men with strong character, physically and psychically healthy, are the ones who should reproduce extra generously... Every healthy woman capable of doing so after war's end will have as many children as possible... Our women's organizations must perform the necessary job of enlightenment.' They must get a 'regular motherhood cult going and in it there must be no difference between women who are married... and women who have children by a man to whom they are bound in friendship'. Bigamy could be legalized: 'On special petition men should be able to enter a binding marital relationship not only with one woman, but also with another, who would then get his name without complications.' He went further – State aid should be given to these relationships, and all impediments removed. 'New novels, short stories, and stage plays based on marriage and divorce are no longer to be permitted', nor were 'poems, writings and motion pictures that treat the child born out of wedlock as of diminished worth'.[36]

Himmler, who loathed Catholic morals (declaring, 'the present form of marriage is a satanic achievement on the part of the Catholic Church'), had for some time favoured legalizing bigamy as a mark of distinction for war heroes holding various Crosses of Honour, thereby ensuring their fine physical qualities would be passed on. Moreover, it would satisfy men's natural urge to polygamy. Individual sensibilities need play no part in their considerations, for 'Who will inquire in 300 or 500 years' time if a certain Fräulein Müller or Schulze was unhappy?'[37]

Hitler foresaw that many women would see the 'appropriateness' of the New Order but – since 'want of logic is something they are born with – in the individual case, in their personal lives, they will frantically reject it'.[38] Women did reject it, though protest was muted. Jutta Rüdiger, Head of the BDM, was present at a meeting when Himmler addressed BDM girls.

> He said that in the war a lot of men would be killed and there-
> fore the nation needed more children, and it wouldn't be such
> a bad idea if a man, in addition to his wife, had a girlfriend who
> would also bear his children. And I must say, all my leaders
> were sitting there with their hair standing on end. And it went
> further than that. A soldier wrote to me from the front telling
> me why I should propagate an illegitimate child. And I said,
> 'What! I don't do that.'

Rumour about the proposals spread. Despite the Führer's support, not all leaders were enthusiastic. They did not, in the middle of a war that was going badly on all fronts, want to risk antagonizing women, illogical though the women's reaction seemed to Hitler.

Plans to increase the birth rate by sanctioning births out of wedlock had little effect. The illegitimacy rate actually went slightly down, rather than up, between 1939 and 1943,[39] and any increase thereafter was more likely to be the consequence of wartime condi-tions. The benefits to women themselves were minimal, partly because the main consideration was not women's welfare but the leaders' popu-lation policy. Though single mothers were able to use the term 'Frau', and treated equally in some maternity provisions including those of the party's Mother and Child organization, the appeal to single women to make yet another sacrifice for the State fell mostly on deaf ears.

It is hardly surprising that leading Nazis supported such a proposition. It legitimized both their inclinations and their private activities, and clothed them in the respectable garb of duty to the *Volk*. Few Nazis had any respect for bourgeois Christian morality, but they did proclaim the virtues of stable marriage as the foundation of the nation – the 'germ cell' of the Nazi state. Few leaders conformed to this in their private lives. Hitler courted the nation in the image of the lonely bachelor on his self-denying crusade, serving his nation, 'married' only to Germany, while his mistress Eva Braun was kept for thirteen years in the background, out of public view. Even so, careful to associate himself publicly with support for marriage, he was the chief witness at the weddings of almost every one of his leaders, and at the christenings of their children if possible.

His devoted assistant, Martin Bormann, was well known even before his affair with Manja Behrens for disappearing off into side rooms and bedrooms with young ladies, even on official occasions. Reichsführer Heinrich Himmler married a woman, Margarete Boden, eight years his senior, produced one child only – nowhere near SS standard requirements – and virtually abandoned her for his public duties, though she does seem to have retained a hold over him as he was often referred to as 'henpecked' (perhaps a reference to the chicken farm he had left her to run). He set up Hedwig Potthast, the secretary with whom he had an affair, in a separate household not far from Hitler at Berchtesgaden; this liaison produced two illegitimate children and, though he once thought of marrying her, he abandoned the idea.

Goebbels used his power and position as Propaganda Minister to satisfy his voracious lust. No attractive young woman was safe, especially if she was an actress, for he controlled the film industry and was as unscrupulous in private as he was in public. After he married Magda Quandt in 1931, his attempt at fidelity was extremely short-lived, though he did produce with her a family of six children, five girls and a boy, who were then lauded by his own propaganda organs as the model Nazi family. Goebbels did little to camouflage his extra-marital affairs: 'I have no need to bow down before false bourgeois morality,' he declared, not least because his activities did not damage his standing with Hitler, who took the view that the private lives of his ministers was irrelevant to their public positions – unless a scandal was brewing, in which case it could provide a useful excuse to get rid of a colleague who had fallen out of favour. When Magda threatened to divorce Goebbels as a result of his affair with actress Lida Baarova, which he flaunted publicly for some years to Magda's evident humiliation, Hitler refused to allow the divorce to go ahead. Goebbels declared his intention to marry Baarova and threatened to resign and take a post in Japan – a cunning move, since he knew his Führer could not possibly afford the rumpus, or the rupture to the Nazis' image as the supporters of family life. The pair were reconciled, Goebbels climbed back into Hitler's favour, and the propaganda of family life as the inviolate foundation of the Nazi 'national community' – with wives as loyal companions and well-trained children as the highest fulfilment of National Socialist life – continued unabated.

NOTES

1 Bleuel, *Strength Through Joy*, pp. 194–5
2 Johnson, Eric, *The Nazi Terror: Gestapo, Jews and Ordinary Germans*, John Murray, London, 1999, pp. 110–14
3 ibid., pp. 111–13
4 Owings, Alison, *Frauen: German Women Recall the Third Reich*, Penguin, London, 1995, pp. 104–5
5 Cited Bleuel, *Strength Through Joy*, p. 193
6 Owings, *Frauen*, pp. 452–6
7 Köhn, Ilse, *Mischling, Second Degree: My Childhood in Nazi Germany*, Greenwillow, New York, 1977, pp. 22–3
8 Cited Kershaw, *Hitler: Hubris*, pp. 473
9 Owings, *Frauen*, p. 199
10 Johnson, *The Nazi Terror*, p. 91
11 Barkai, Avraham, *From Boycott to Annihilation: The Economic Struggle of German Jews, 1933–43*, University Press of New England, Hanover N.H., 1989, p. 37
12 Cited Pine, *Nazi Family Policy 1933–1945*, p. 151
13 Edwin Landau, in Richardz, Monika (ed.), *Jewish Life in Germany: Memoirs from Three Centuries*, Indiana University Press, Indianapolis, 1991, p. 311
14 Marta Appel, in Richardz, ibid., p. 352
15 ibid., pp. 352–4
16 Cited Pine, *Nazi Family Policy 1933–1945*, p. 155
17 Kaplan, Marion, 'Keeping Calm and Weathering the Storm: Jewish Women's Responses to Daily Life in Nazi Germany, 1933–1939', in Dalia Ofer and Lenore J. Weitzman (ed.), *Women in the Holocaust*, Yale University Press, Connecticut, 1998, pp. 40–3
18 Heineman, Elizabeth D., *What Difference Does a Husband Make? Women and Marital Status in Nazi and Post War Germany*, University of California Press, California, 1999, pp. 17, 24–5
19 Bock, 'Racism and Sexism in Nazi Germany', p. 285
20 Owings, *Frauen*, pp. 372, 375
21 Burleigh and Wippermann, *The Racial State*, p. 253
22 Bock, 'Racism and Sexism in Nazi Germany', pp. 279–80
23 Koonz, *Mothers in the Fatherland*, p. 192
24 *Hitler's Table Talk 1941–1944*, p. 352
25 Cited Pine, *Nazi Family Policy 1933–1945*, p. 39
26 Clay and Leapman, *Master Race*, p. 57
27 Bleuel, *Strength Through Joy*, p. 162
28 Heinemann, *What Difference Does a Husband Make?*, pp. 32–3
29 Clay and Leapman, *Master Race*, p. 59

30 ibid., p. 71

31 Hammer, Joshua, 'Hitler's Children', in *Newsweek International*, 20 March 2000

32 Cited Bleuel, *Strength Through Joy*, p. 165

33 Manvell and Fraenkel, *Heinrich Himmler*, p. 92

34 Bormann, Martin, *The Bormann Letters*, Introduction by Hugh Trevor-Roper, Weidenfeld and Nicolson, London, 1954, pp. 39–40

35 ibid., pp. 42–6

36 'Note Re Safeguarding the Future of the German People', 29 January 1944, in von Lang, Jochen, *Bormann: The Man Who Manipulated Hitler*, Weidenfeld and Nicolson, London, 1979, pp. 406–10

37 Kersten, Felix, *The Kersten Memoir*, Hutchinson, London, 1956, pp. 176–7, 75

38 von Lang, *Bormann*, p. 407

39 Bleuel, *Strength Through Joy*, p. 173

Above: Adolf Hitler's mother, Klara, and father, Alois

Below: Hitler, aged ten, and as political agitator *c*1925

Left: Geli Raubal, Hitler's niece

Below: Hitler and Geli on a trip to the North Sea coast c1930...

Above: ...and on a picnic with friends

Below and right: Eva Braun

Below: Hitler and Eva at home

Above: Marriage of Magda Quandt and Joseph Goebbels, 1931, with Hitler, their best man, in the background

Below: Hitler and Winifred Wagner, an early supporter and Munich 'Mutti'

Above: Nazi kitsch — putting the finishing touches to busts of Hitler

Below: Propaganda posters promoting the BDM and the pure Aryan family

Hitler cultivating the allegiance of youth

Girls greeting their 'saviour' at a Nazi parade

Hitler, the idol, signing autographs for young women

Interviewees for *Nazi Women*:
(left, from top) Luise Bierbaumer,
Gertrud Draber, Susanne von der
Borch. (Right from top) Hedwig
Ertl, Elly Napp, Lilli Gentzen

Above: Magda Goebbels with five of the six children she poisoned in 1945

Below: Berlin — Women clearing the rubble after the war

8

THE 'GRAND SEDUCTION OF YOUTH'

For Nazis, the key to the future of the Thousand Year Reich was the allegiance of youth. Hitler professed particular concern for children. He made a point of being filmed with them – at the Berghof, where he played the role of 'Uncle Adolf' to the offspring of other leaders, looking unusually at ease as he chatted to them and cuddled them on his knee. It is a chilling picture. With children – and dogs – Hitler appeared relaxed. Other, more formal, photo-opportunities show him surrounded by uniformed young girls and boys, laughing as they look up adoringly at him. It was another aspect of stage-management of the leader cult.

The boys' Hitler Youth movement was set up in 1926 and the League of German Girls – the BDM (Bund Deutscher Mädel) – established in 1932. As soon as the Nazis came to power, they set about eliminating all other rival youth organizations, just as they Nazified the rest of German life. Within a short time, the Catholic Youth organization was the only group left with a rival claim to young people's loyalty. All existing religious political and other youth groups were taken over, disbanded or banned. In one year the Hitler Youth movement, including girls, had climbed from a membership of 108,000 to more than three and a half million.

The leadership immediately set about organizing youth into a coherent body of loyal supporters. Under Baldur von Schirach, himself only twenty-five at the time, the organization was to net all young people from ages ten to eighteen to be schooled in Nazi ideology and trained to be the future valuable members of the Reich. From the start, the Nazis pitched their appeal as the party of youth, building a New Germany. The leadership was fairly young itself, compared with the elderly, whiskery leaders of the Weimar Republic. Hitler was only forty-three in 1933, and his associates were even younger – Heinrich Himmler was thirty-two, Joseph Goebbels thirty-five and Hermann Göring forty. Hitler intended to inspire youth with a mission, appealing to their idealism and hope. 'Regardless of what we create and do, we shall pass away, but in Germany you will live on,' he declaimed at the 1934 Nuremberg Rally – the Rally of Youth, filmed by Leni Riefenstahl as *Triumph of the Will*. 'And I know it cannot be otherwise for you are the flesh of our flesh, blood of our blood, and your young minds are filled with the same will that dominates us... And when the great columns of our movement march through Germany today, I know that you will join these columns. And we know that Germany is before us, within us and behind us.'

At first, membership was not compulsory, but pressure was put on parents whose sons and daughters did not join. After 1936, 'The Year of the Jungvolk', when there was a massive drive by von Schirach to recruit all ten-year-olds, reluctant parents could be imprisoned; before then, they might be threatened with losing their jobs. Girls joined the Jungmädel from age ten to thirteen, and the BDM from fourteen to eighteen. Posters of fresh-faced, smiling young girls in uniform with swastikas in the background proclaimed 'All Ten-Year-Olds To Us' or, more menacingly – because this was the intention – 'All Ten-Year-Olds *Belong* To Us!' Young people were schooled in loyalty to the *Volk*, which excluded all other loyalties, including to the family.

Many parents were disturbed that their young daughters were being swept up in this movement. Hedwig Ertl recalled the evening of 30 January 1933 when Hitler came to power. She was aged ten: 'There was a lot of singing and shouting in the streets. I came home inspired by these events, with my copy of "Der Stürmer" in my hand. And I said to my father, "The Jews are our misfortune." He looked at me in horror and slapped me in the face. It was the first and only time he hit me. And

I didn't understand.' But later, when he would go to visit her mother's grave, which was near the Memorial to Nazi heroes, and rail under his breath against the Nazis, Hedwig could hardly conceal how ashamed she was of him. She felt that her father didn't understand the significance of this great movement. The BDM had started to alienate daughters from their fathers.

Susanne von der Borch's mother was thoroughly opposed, and tried to deter her daughter: 'My mother went early on, before Hitler was elected, to a political rally and she listened to him yelling. She was convinced that something terrible was happening to us. As a child, I could not judge. I was simply besotted by it... "Little Nazi", they called me.'

The main aim of the BDM was to produce a new generation of 'little Nazis', who were utterly loyal to the state regardless of their parents' views. They were to enrol in building a new Germany, a nation distinct from the past, and from their parents. 'All the time you were kept busy and interested, and you really believed you had to change the world,' Hedwig Ertl remembers. 'As a young person, you were taken seriously. You did things which were important... Your dependence on your parents was reduced, because all the time it was your work for the Hitler Youth that came first, and your parents came second.'

For many girls, joining the BDM was an act of rebellion against their parents. Susanne von der Borch was 'the ideal German girl' – tall, blonde-haired, blue-eyed and mad about sport: 'From the first day on, this was my world. It fitted my personality, because I had always been very sporty and I liked being with my friends. And I always wanted to get out of the house. So this was the best excuse for me, I couldn't be at home, because there was always something happening: I had to go riding, or skating, or summer camp. I was never at home.' Renate Finckh found consolation in the BDM when her parents became active Nazis: 'At home no one really had time for me.' She joined, aged ten, and 'finally found an emotional home, a safe refuge, and shortly thereafter a space in which I was valued'. The summons to girls – 'The Führer needs you!' – moved her: 'I was filled with pride and joy that someone needed me for a higher purpose.' Membership gave her life meaning.[1]

Not only home but school was put in second place, which suited Susanne von der Borch because she didn't have to bother about her schoolwork: 'I only managed to get to the end of the school year with the help of my classmates. I was a very bad pupil. I was only good at sport, biology and sketching, I was very bad at all the rest... And the school didn't dare do anything (it was a church school and they were cautious) so I had my freedom [competing in BDM sports] and didn't go to school if I didn't want to.' The BDM attracted other girls because they were let off school on Saturdays to attend BDM events. Teachers who objected to this were given short shrift.

The BDM leaders were clear about their goal – to mould a New Woman. Their leader Jutta Rüdiger decreed: 'We wanted the "New German Woman" to be the bearer of German culture and moral standards for the whole People. Our aim was that they should achieve health, self-discipline, courage, and later on with the gymnastics, gracefulness – in the sense of beautiful harmonious movement which also reflects a healthy mind and body.' Girls would carry Nazi values into the next generation.

It was German girls' duty to be healthy, for their bodies belonged to the nation. They must be fit in every way for their ultimate destiny: childbearing. Sport, along with physical training and exercise, was essential. Massive displays of formation dancing and group gymnastics were a regular feature of BDM life. Sport and domestic skills took precedence over intellectual pursuits, which the male leaders considered were against their 'nature'. All girls were trained in household subjects – the theory of nutrition and baby care and the practice of sewing, handicrafts, cooking, healthy eating, and the importance of fresh air and exercise and cleanliness. Rules on health were drawn up in 1939 – the 'Year of Hygienic Duty' – by the Reich Physician for Hitler Youth:

> Your body belongs to your nation, to which you owe your existence and for which you are responsible.

> Always keep yourself clean, tend and exercise your body. Light, air and water can help you in this.

> Look after your teeth. Strong and healthy teeth are a source of pride.

Eat plenty of raw fruit, uncooked greens and vegetables, first washing them thoroughly in clean water. Fruit contains valuable nutrients which cooking eliminates.

Drink fruit juice. Leave coffee to the coffee addicts.

Shun alcohol and nicotine: they are poisons which impair your development and capacity for work.

Take physical exercise. It will make you healthy and hardy. Sleep at least nine hours every night.

Practise first aid for use in accidents. It can help you save your comrades' lives.

All your activities are governed by the slogan: Your duty is to be healthy.[2]

Political indoctrination in Nazi values was not, it was claimed, directly political, but designed to internalize in girls the values of the state. Jutta Rüdiger, an early convert to Nazism, became the BDM's leader at the age of twenty-seven: 'We didn't really have a political education as such. It was part of everything. It was covered in the term "comradeship". We intended them to act politically in the sense that they knew what was good for the People. This might be part of a cooking lesson, where the future housewife learned how to shop cheaply, how to keep her larder well-stocked. It could be in all areas of daily life, where she is made responsible for the whole of her People.'

Even so, at the weekly *Heimabend*, or home evening, along with sport or needlework and singing, they learnt about the history of the Nazi movement, the 'time of struggle' and its heroes such as Horst Wessel, the Führer's successes in Germany's regeneration, the nation's struggle against Bolshevism and the international 'Jewish–Bolshevik conspiracy' and the necessary fight for *Lebensraum* (living space). They were encouraged to revere German folk traditions and the cultures of their regions. Annual summer camps were highly structured, with every minute organized for further indoctrination, flag raising and salut-ing as well as competitive sports, physical exercise and route marches.

Girls enjoyed it. They saw their horizons widening. They were doing things their mothers had never been allowed to do, they were valued, they could get away from home constraints, and some found it liberat-ing. As part of the training in discipline, they learnt to be leaders. It was a novelty for girls. Leaders 'had to be an example in everything', Jutta Rüdiger recalls. 'They had to be better than the girls they were leading. So they had to be two or three years older. The young ones were often very impressed by them, and they listened less to their parents and more to the *Führerin* [leader]. They were inspired by them.' It was, however, all part of the carefully designed strategy for capturing youth. 'The interesting thing was that when you give young people responsi-bility, they grow into it. And they will give their last drop to fulfil their new duties and show the adults how capable they are. You just have to give young people some responsibility, and then they will follow you.' Hedwig Ertl followed them, and was delighted: 'I was a leader of lower rank, and very proud of it. And the best thing was, when you marched through the streets singing, I didn't have to march in the row of three girls, but marched alone on the left, and the whole world could see, this is the "leader".'

The BDM succeeded in building a sense of comradeship among the girls, which they cherished: 'There was an incredible sense of comrade-ship there. We would never let each other down,' Hedwig Ertl remem-bers. For Renate Finckh, 'Beyond all else lay that comforting feeling we all longed for, the "We-consciousness". We Hitler girls belonged together, we formed an elite within the German *Volk* community.'[3] Jutta Rüdiger was proud that the BDM attracted girls from all classes, thereby fulfilling the 'socialist' part of National Socialism – a classless society pulling together for the good of the People: 'We had aristocrats, princesses, working-class children, they were all treated equally and we took this very seriously – the *Volksgemeinschaft* ['national commu-nity'].' There were more pragmatic considerations for Hedwig Ertl: 'There were no class differences. You went on trips together without paying for it, and you were given exactly the same amount of pocket money as those who had lots of money and now you could go riding and skating and so on, when before you couldn't afford it. You could go to the cinema for 30 pfennigs. We could never go to the cinema before, and suddenly things that had been impossible were there for us. That was incredible, those beautiful Nazi movies.'

BDM girls were also trained in 'racial awareness'. Jewish girls were excluded from membership from the start. Jutta Rüdiger provided the guidelines: 'A young girl once asked me, "Are the Jews actually bad people?" And I said, "No, they are not bad. They are just very different to us in their thinking and their behaviour, and that's why they shouldn't control politics and culture," because that is what they did then.' The subject of race, she says, was treated with great care: 'The *Führerin* were specially trained to deal with this subject and they didn't talk nonsense. We said that they should marry a German, or a European who was a relative of our race, not a foreigner, following the old Indian saying: "The white man is from God, the black man is from God, but the mixture is from the Devil."' She instructed her girls: 'Only the best German soldier is suitable for you, for it is your responsibility to keep the blood of the nation pure. I said, "German girl, your honour lies in being faithful to the blood of your race."'

The message got through. Hedwig Ertl has described how all sense of injustice was removed when she was constantly told of the inferiority of non-Nordic races. Susanne von der Borch was told in the BDM and at school that 'We are the master race... The world presented to us was filled only with beautiful people, master race people, full of sport and health. And, well, I was proud about that, and inspired by it. I would call this a grand seduction of youth.'

Along with political 'consciousness' came adulation of the Führer. Girls were besotted by him: 'We were so enthusiastic – we would have done anything for him. And if he'd said to us: "Cut off your right finger," we would have done it without a second thought,' says Hedwig Ertl. A Hitler Youth poem expressed adoration akin to religious fervour:

Führer, my Führer, given me by God,
Protect and preserve my life for ever.
You saved Germany in time of need,
I thank you for my daily bread.

Be with me always, do not leave me.
Führer, my Führer, my faith, my light,
Hail to the Führer!

Most activities involved first hoisting the swastika flag and saluting the leader. Like the Hitler Youth, the BDM was regimented. Discipline was demonstrated in regular marching in file and in uniform, singing patriotic songs such as 'Our Flag Is Guiding Us'. Popularized in the propaganda film *Hitler Youth Quex*, which celebrated the patriotic death of a young Hitler Youth member for his Führer, this became the anthem of the Hitler Youth and the BDM:

Our flag is guiding us.
Into the future we march side by side.
We are marching for Hitler through night and despair,
With our flag of youth, for freedom and bread.
Our flag guides us.
Our flag is the New Age,
Our flag guides us to eternity,
Our flag is more to us than death.

'To die for the Fatherland – there was no greater honour for us. We didn't feel it consciously – it became part of us, unconsciously. I don't know what would have happened if it had become a reality,' confesses Hedwig Ertl.

At all the parades in the Nazi calendar, girls were there in spotless uniform cheering, intoxicated by the atmosphere. For most, it was inspiring to feel part of a cause, a movement that appealed deliberately to their idealism. According to Inge Scholl, they were mesmerized by the 'mysterious power' of 'closed ranks of marching youths with banners waving, eyes fixed straight ahead, keeping time to drumbeat and song'. The sense of fellowship was 'overpowering' for they 'sensed that there was a role for them in a historic process, in a movement that was transforming the mass into a *Volk*'.[4]

Hitler took only a passing interest in BDM activities. Jutta Rüdiger met him just once at an official occasion to approve the BDM's new uniforms. Uniforms had attracted his attention in 1932, when he had been horrified at girls' appearance in the march-past on National Youth Day. Himmler had echoed his concern about the girls' attractiveness: 'I regard it as a catastrophe. If we continue to masculinize women in this way, it is only a matter of time before the difference between the genders, the polarity, completely disappears.'[5] The new uniform was acceptable and, at the reception afterwards, Hitler went over to join Jutta Rüdiger and her companion: 'He looked at Clementine and me, smiled, and said, "I have always told the Mercedes company that a good engine is not enough for a car, it needs a good body as well. But a good body is also not enough on its own." And he smiled and left us. And we were very proud that he had compared us to a Mercedes Benz car.'

Hitler left the direction of BDM activities to his Reichsjugendführer, Baldur von Schirach, who, according to Jutta Rüdiger, always used to say, 'You girls should be prettier.' He said, 'When I sometimes watch women getting off a bus – old puffed-up women – then I think you should be prettier women. Every girl should be pretty. She doesn't have to be a false, cosmetic and made-up beauty. But we want the beauty of graceful movement.' Goebbels expressed alarm that girls were showing too much 'masculine' vigour in their training. He complained to one of his department chiefs, Wilfried von Oven: 'I certainly don't object to girls taking part in gymnastics or sport within reasonable limits. But why should a future mother go route-marching with a pack on her back? She should be healthy and vigorous, graceful and easy on the eye. Sensible physical exercise can help her to become so, but she shouldn't have knots of muscle on her arms and legs and a step like a grenadier. Anyway, I won't let them turn our Berlin girls into he-men.'[6]

Hitler's view of the role ordained for girls was clear. Traudl Junge recalls: 'Hitler himself adored beautiful women. But he had the very primitive view that the greatest hero deserves the most beautiful woman. He couldn't imagine that a woman might have other qualities besides her beauty, like charm or intelligence. This didn't interest him. For him it was very simple: the most beautiful woman belongs to the greatest hero.' Girls were there, with soldier heroes, to propagate the master race.

By 1938, three and a half million of them were members of the BDM. At the Nuremberg Rally that year, 5000 girls paraded before the leader alongside 80,000 Hitler Youth members. In the main stadium, the BDM put on a huge display of dancing and gymnastics, demurely dressed in long white skirts and short coloured jackets. 'It was a grandiose spectacle,' Jutta Rüdiger remembers, fondly. 'And afterwards the Reichs sports leader came to me and said, "The Führer said that this is the first time in his life that he was able to forget all his worries."' Jutta glowed with pride. The Hitler Youth marched in formation and the boys performed military-style parade manoeuvres, ending in a grand finale spelling out the name Adolf Hitler.

By now, Hitler was arming for war. In the massive stadium, BDM girls joined the Hitler Youth as they took an oath of undying loyalty to their Führer. The young men and women were sworn to fight and die for Hitler. He told them: 'Our generation is selected to experience and build great things for our people. You are witnesses to great and unique historic changes. You are destined to be warriors for Greater Germany.'

The following year, BDM membership became compulsory for all girls up to the age of eighteen. Around four-fifths of male and female youth – 7.3 million in all – were signed up to the Hitler Youth movement. A law in March 1939 conscripted all remaining eligible – that is, racially valuable and 'worthy' – young people, amid warnings to parents that unless they enrolled, their children would be taken away and placed in orphanages. By then another organization, Faith and Beauty (Glaube und Schönheit), had been set up so that young women from the age of eighteen, when they left the BDM, to twenty-one, when they were expected to join the Women's Organization (Frauenschaft), could not slip through the net of Nazi control. Faith and Beauty elaborated on the 'gracefulness' so admired by von Schirach and Jutta Rüdiger, deepening women's sense of duty and, it was hoped, developing women's individual interests and skills – but only in the areas of sport, gymnastics and hygiene, care of the body, and baby-care. They were also expected to develop their social skills – ballroom dancing, riding and playing tennis, in line with Goebbels's view that they should be healthy, graceful and 'easy on the eye'.

Throughout their Hitler Youth training the motto for girls was 'Be Faithful, Be Pure, Be German!' The sexual division – male active, female passive – was reinforced at every level. Boys from the age of ten were told: 'Live Faithfully, Fight Bravely, and Die Laughing!' Their participation in the nation's cause did not prevent BDM girls being made objects of derision, and not just from leaders concerned they were losing their prettiness. The essential misogyny of Nazism was reflected on the street. Jokes ridiculed women and girls. BDM (Bund Deutscher Mädel) was made to stand for Bund Deutscher Milchkühe (League of German Milk-cows), Baldur Drück Mir (Baldur [von Schirach] Take Me), Bedarfsartikel Deutscher Männer (Useful Things for German Men), Brauch Deutsche Mädel (Make Use of German Girls) and Bald Deutsche Mütter (German mothers-to-be).

After 1934, girls were subject to a compulsory year of work duty to be served on the land, or in domestic service helping *kinderreich* mothers. This was intended to put girls in touch with their roots in the rural peasant community, teach them about practical child care, and enhance their sense of service. On the Land Year, urban girls were sent to help farmers' wives plough fields, look after animals and bring in the harvest, in order to learn about the true value of work. Despite propaganda showing pink-cheeked girls on hay wains extolling the joy and virtue of this return to 'Blood and Soil', girls tried to escape it in droves. Mothers did their best to arrange for their daughters to be sent to relatives in another part of the country for their domestic duty year (Household Year) or get friends of friends to place them in suitable, known locations in the country.

From 1936, the Reich Labour Service took over the running of the scheme, and in 1939 it was made compulsory. All young women up to the age of twenty-five had to complete a year with the Labour Service for Young Women before being allowed to take up paid employment. Nine out of ten young women were sent to farms where they lived in barrack-like accommodation under close supervision. By then it was seen as the female parallel to compulsory male military service, aimed at producing a trained labour force in the event of war. At a time of acute labour shortage in the agricultural sector, they were also a source of cheap labour; since the girls received only pocket money, the work was virtually unpaid – another part of the increasing regimentation of all levels of Nazi society.

NOTES

1   Cited Koonz, *Mothers in the Fatherland*, p. 195
2   Cited Bleuel, *Strength Through Joy*, pp. 137–8
3   Cited Koonz, *Mothers in the Fatherland*, p. 195
4   Rempel, Gerhard, *The Development of HJ and SS as Nazi Party Affiliates*, http://mars.wnec.edu/-grempel/curriculum/publications
5   Godl, Doris, 'Women's contributions to the political policies of National Socialism', in *Feminist Issues*, 1 January 1997
6   von Oven, Wilfried, *Mit Goebbels bis zum Ende*, Dürer-Verlag, Buenos Aires, 1949–50, p. 41

9
THE ROAD TO WAR

By 1936, Hitler's popularity was at its height. The economy was showing signs of improvement with the acceleration of rearmament after 1935. In defiance of the Versailles Treaty provisions, conscription was introduced in March 1935, and the Luftwaffe was brought back into existence. Only later did Hitler get acquiescence for this fait accompli from the other European powers. It was followed rapidly by an agreement with Britain to rebuild the German Navy (up to 35 per cent of the British strength – many British observers believed they had reached this already). When Hitler took the bold step of occupying the demilitarized zone of the Rhineland in 1936, his boast of tearing up the Versailles Treaty and restoring Germany's honour and dignity seemed on the way to fulfilment. Forceful and risk-taking diplomacy had paid off. Respect for Germany was matched by growing self-confidence in its people. Honour was being restored.

At the 1936 Olympic Games, Germany's international reputation was enhanced. Diplomats and representatives of all nations gathered in a Berlin draped in swastikas to be fêted in splendour by Nazi leaders and functionaries. Goebbels gave a huge party with an Italianate theme for 1000 people on Peacock Island, with a spectacular fireworks display. Göring, 'wreathed in smiles and orders and decorations', laid on a 'dazzling crowded function' at his palatial residence, where a *corps de ballet* danced in the moonlight, a floodlit procession of white horses, donkeys and peasants appeared from nowhere, and guests took rides on roundabouts and carousels in the specially erected Luna Park. According to the British Conservative MP, Sir Henry 'Chips' Channon: 'The music roared, the astonished guest[s] wandered about. "There has never been anything like this since the days of Louis Quatorze," somebody remarked. "Not since Nero," I retorted.'[1]

Foreign observers noted a new sense of purpose. As the Germans carried off thirty-three Olympic gold medals – more than any other country – their national pride swelled. Foreigners who had seen the darker side of Nazism began to revise their views, though an undercurrent of deep distrust still prevailed. An American observer noted that visitors would be 'inclined to dismiss all anti-German thought and action abroad as insipid and unjust. [The visitor] sees no Jewish heads being chopped off... The people smile, are polite and sing with gusto in beer gardens. Everything is terrifyingly clean and the visitor likes it all.'[2] The American journalist William Shirer noted: 'I'm afraid the Nazis have succeeded with their propaganda. First they have run the games on a lavish scale never before experienced, and this has appealed to the athletes. Second, they have put up a very good front for the general visitors, especially the big businessmen.'[3]

All signs of anti-Semitism were toned down. A wave of 'individual acts' of terror against Jews had been brought under control by the Party machine, as effectively as it had instigated them during 1935. The Nuremberg Laws removing Jews from citizenship of the Reich and banning marriage and relationships with Aryans had satisfied the Party radicals who called for action on the 'Jewish Question'. Now, for the Olympic Games, the face of the nation was cleaned up. 'Jews Not Welcome Here' signs were removed from towns countrywide, and the newspapers temporarily ceased their anti-Semitic tirades. Victor Klemperer, a Jew married to an Aryan, observed the events with increasing bitterness. The Olympic Games were 'wholly and entirely a political affair... It's incessantly drummed into the people and foreigners that here you can see the revival, the blossoming, the new spirit, the unity, the steadfastness, the glory, naturally too the peaceful spirit of the Third Reich lovingly embracing the whole world.'[4]

To outward appearances, Germany was in the midst of regeneration as one of the most modern and successful states in Europe. Germans appeared to have a higher standard of living than when Hitler came to power. Hitler took the credit. Much of this was due to the economy from 1935 gearing up for armaments production, the priority in the Nazi agenda. But the emphasis on armaments had led to a crisis in the consumer sector. It was not possible to maintain the level of imports of expensive materials for arms production, as well as the required level of food imports. In 1935 food shortages were the price paid for the drive to rearm. Fats, butter, eggs and later meat were in short supply. Housewives carried the burden: queuing for food became part of their daily round in most towns and cities, and the price of food went up. This was alleviated only after Security Reports showed a level of disgruntle-ment among the population that demanded some action. Berlin police reported 'a serious deterioration in the mood', there was anger among women queuing for food, and butter sales had to be watched over by the police. The mood in Berlin among a 'shockingly high percentage of the population' was judged to be 'directly negative towards State and Movement' by January 1936, and criticism was now moving into 'uncontrollable territory'.[5] A temporary diversion of resources from armaments into food imports was ordered by Hitler. This eased the situ-ation by 1936 and put off the need to introduce food rationing – a meas-ure which, they judged, would inflame further damaging social unrest.

Housewives bore the brunt of the measures, under the Four Year Plan, to make the economy self-sufficient. There was a renewed drive to train women in the virtues of careful household management, economi-cal cooking, thrift, making do, recycling – which would save the Reich millions of marks a year and reduce the nation's dependence on imports.

From 1937, the labour surplus of the early years was being transformed into a labour shortage. Married women were now needed in the labour market and increasingly returned to work. An industry-wide wage freeze made this more urgent. Families found it increasingly difficult to manage on one income. But women were also encouraged to get back to the workplace to speed up production in the burgeoning industrial sector, in which armaments production was the key to expansion. The strictures against married women working had been presented as concern for their health as mothers and their usefulness as wifely companions at home. These restrictions were cast aside as the new national goals changed. The condition for a marriage loan that women should return to the home was revoked in 1937, and the requirement that female civil servants be sacked on marriage was lifted. By 1939 the representation of married women in the workforce was up from 30 per cent in 1933 to almost 34 per cent in 1939.[6] Altogether there were more than half again as many women working as there had been in 1933; the biggest increase was in production goods industries – up by 83 per cent; but in consumer industries it also increased by 36 per cent.[7]

Educational priorities also changed. As it became apparent that skills would be needed in academic and scientific fields, the 10 per cent quota introduced earlier on university student entrance was gradually loosened. Though they were still encouraged to study in those areas that led to the caring professions, the numbers of women students climbed gradually to over 11 per cent in 1939.

Home as the place of sanctuary and refuge was steadily invaded. As the State demanded the participation of its members in service to the *Volk*, the authority of the family was eroded. Children were required to participate in Hitler Youth activities that patently challenged the parents' authority, and deliberately claimed their loyalty to the State and the Führer above their loyalty to their families. Conscription would take young men away from home into the maw of the military machine. Girls' work duty year separated them from their parents from the age they left school. Nazi Party organizations had the right to intrude into family life and coerce its members to participate in any number of activities in the name of duty to the State.

The net of control tightened at every level of society. Local festivals as well as national days of celebration were taken over as Nazi events. May Day, 1 May, became the Nazis' most important official holiday, celebrating the social achievements of the Nazis and the new 'solidarity' between workers and leaders. The rituals of local harvest festivals were transformed by Nazi paraphernalia; small children marched in line with swastika symbols garlanded with ribbons and flowers while the local Party members, the Hitler Youth and the BDM marched in uniform to the beat of drums. Nazi parades were a regular occurrence in every small town, augmenting the frequent shows of uniformed strength on the

streets of main cities, and the ultimate display of ritual and regimentation at the annual Nuremberg Party rallies.

At most of these events women, except the BDM girls, were
bystanders. BDM girls were required to turn up en masse and engage in
exultant cheering and saluting. The parades struck a chord. Ilse Schmidt,
who later worked at the Army front lines as a typist, was enthralled:

> When the soldiers were marching, especially in Berlin, on the
> big squares, that was brilliant. I really liked that. And I would
> run there to watch the uniforms. I loved it. And I still like them.
> I haven't got over this. But at the same time, because I read
> books about Frederick the Great, for example, and how he
> inspired his armies and how he sent his people to their deaths,
> I realized that music is necessary to get them there. Music to
> march into death. I experienced that later on personally. Music
> is necessary so that these young, innocent people – who
> know nothing – are fired up to go to war.

Home movies show how Nazism penetrated to the heart of family life.
Loyal fathers taught their children to greet them with 'Heil Hitler' each
morning at the breakfast table. Boys as young as four dressed up in SS
uniform and paraded in the back garden, waving swastikas. Playing
shops, a two-year-old child was caught on film greeting his brother with
a Hitler salute. Portraits of Hitler adorned the living rooms of homes
throughout Germany. ('The masses need an idol,' Hitler declared.)[8]
Children's dolls' houses were supplied with his portrait already in place
in their miniature living rooms. Postcard portraits of Hitler, like pin-ups,
were on sale at street corners. Shopkeepers designed window displays
with Hitler's portrait as their centrepiece, and hung the swastika over
their doors.

Allegiance to the Party became a requirement for promotion. Major
contracts were allocated to Party members, and keeping in with the
Party was the means to maintain a decent standard of living. Ilse
Schmidt's father joined the Party to further his business prospects:
'Economic reasons made my father join the Party. Because to receive
the very lucrative orders he wanted, he had to become a Party member.

He didn't have any choice. My father was always worried about the business, and all his worries disappeared once he became a member of the
Party. And our living standard improved as a result.'

Karma Rauhut came from an anti-Nazi family. Her father cultivated
Nazi connections to survive. In 1939 he watched the huge parade for
Hitler's birthday pass by the bank where he worked. All the employees
were crowded onto the balconies. Her father commented out loud: 'Well,
this guy will bring us to war yet. Look at that, what else is it there for?' And
naturally, Karma Rauhut recalled, someone immediately reported him:

> But because my father had a lot of connections and... also was
> very friendly with the 'appearance Nazis' [*Scheinnazis*], that
> is, who were very brown on the outside and had a completely
> different colour inside, he always could get off. That is, he had
> to go to the police and was imprisoned for two days. Then he
> was allowed to spend five thousand marks for something or
> other, for some kind of organization. He could get off with the
> money. But only through his connections. Suddenly the [tele-
> phone] lines hummed. 'Could you not help?' and so on. He
> could always bring it back 'to order', *nicht*? I know my father
> did it deliberately. He tried to get to know people who could
> help him in need, but also he helped many.[9]

Party membership also determined children's schooling. Wilhelmine
Haferkamp, a mother of ten children, refused to join the Party, but her
husband was a member. She told Alison Owings: 'If you went to high
school, the parents had to pay. And if you were in the NSDAP [Nazi
Party], everything was paid for.'[10]

Failure to conform could lead to loss of jobs, or downgrading. Ursula
Meyer-Semlies had been a loyal Party supporter as a schoolgirl in 1932,
wearing a silver swastika badge secretly concealed behind her lapel. An
enthusiast for Hitler, she was also a committed Christian. She became a
teacher and, after a lot of deliberation, joined the Party in 1938: 'I didn't
have that good a conscience any more. And I decided I will,' she told
Alison Owings. 'I later used it. I thought, as long as I'm in the Party, they
won't throw me out as a teacher so fast.' But in 1938 she was required,

with all the other teachers, to sign a declaration saying she would not teach religion in school. She refused to sign. The other teachers were flabbergasted. She was put under pressure, though her mother told her, 'You've done well. You won't sign it.' The issue went up to the regional authorities. By then two other teachers (out of 300) had refused to sign, and she became more intransigent. She was allowed to continue for a short time, then transferred to a one-room schoolhouse in a rural village, four kilometres from a bus stop. Her Party membership, which she saw as a badge of her 'political reliability', counted for nothing.[11]

Karma Rauhut managed to avoid joining the BDM at school – 'This odd jacket and scarf and this leather scarf holder and the shoes, I would have died rather than put it on.' She told them that she had joined at home in another district. But then she was moved to another 'Nazi-infested' school. Alison Owings recorded her story:

> One day the director called her to his office and said, 'Well, my dear child, I cannot give you your diploma. And I must tell you, you will never amount to anything. You are not in the BDM, you don't join the Party.' He told her she might 'become a worker, but you'll never be anything'. To that, 'I said, out of stupidity, "Well, the world is round. It revolves." And of course he then reported me.' She said she saw in her school file that he had done so, and had knocked her down a grade in every subject.[12]

Grumbling about the increasingly ostentatious lifestyle of some of the leaders was picked up in Security Reports, but its expression was muted. The leaders' extravagance was funded by 'grateful' public bodies and private companies, as well as Party funds. By then, Göring's opulence was legendary, his extensive art collection regularly augmented by presents and 'donations'. Their entertainment was lavish, with visitors eating off the finest porcelain. Goebbels had acquired six houses, including his official residence on Hermann-Göringstrasse in Berlin which he completely remodelled in 1938 at a cost to the Party of 3.5 million marks.[13] He called it a palace and furnished it with treasures from the State galleries and museums, paintings from the National Gallery and carpets from the Art History Museum. From 1934, he also possessed a country house at Schwanenwerder, on the Havel – a white house set on a wooded slope with coach house, garden house, offices, ponies for the children and a yacht called *Baldur* moored at his private landing stage. He shortly acquired the adjacent property and entertained important foreign visitors there. The City of Berlin then presented Goebbels with Schloss Lanke on the Bogensee as official residence for the Berlin Gauleiter (for life) and a weekend retreat. But it was too small, so he built a larger modern building opposite, with air conditioning, central heating, advanced technical gadgetry and a film viewing theatre, at a cost of around 2 million marks. When the Finance Minister refused to pay for it, the film industry stepped in with a donation of 1.5 million marks.

Martin Bormann's base was at Berchtesgaden where, after 1936, he organized the refurbishment of the Berghof and the forcible removal of all those living inconveniently within range of the Führer's residence. Farmers were bought out or evicted and their land registered in Bormann's name. He built himself a suitably grand residence, large enough to accommodate his brood of ten children, and, since he controlled Hitler's finances, managed to cream off a great deal for his own use. Co-operation from local officials in this enterprise was suitably rewarded, while resistance was met with force.

Obedience and fear kept people in line, and mostly it kept them silent, not criticizing. It was well known that dissent could land people in concentration camps or 'protective custody'. The Gestapo had an effective network of spies who reported on those who did not conform. Individuals voluntarily reported on others who they claimed were failing in their duty to the State, or just because they had a grudge against a neighbour. Ilse Schmidt 'always had a sense of fear. I couldn't exactly locate it. The fear that you might lose out on things. Or that someone might talk about you behind your back. Or report you, even. You couldn't put your finger on it.'

Trust among neighbours was destroyed. Karma Rauhut said: 'It was like you were in a spider web and the spider always noticed if something vibrated somewhere and did not ring true... the organizations were everywhere and the human beings reported each other and one watched the other.'[14] Families could be divided. Rita Kuhn's mother was Aryan, her father Jewish. When her cousin on her mother's side joined the Hitler Youth, Rita argued with him about Hitler. Afterwards, her mother told her: '"Never do that again. Never talk to him again." Like that. I said, "Why not?" "Because you can't trust him."' Her mother told her not to talk to her aunt either, because, even though she was not a Hitler supporter, she would defend her son.[15] The atmosphere meant people could not be certain that a family member would not betray them.

The fear of denunciation by neighbours, work-mates or even friends was ever-present. Failing to make the 'Heil Hitler' salute in the street or shop, comments hostile to the leaders overheard by informers, listening to foreign broadcasts – all carried penalties, ranging from fines, to imprisonment, or incarceration in a concentration camp. Informers were everywhere, hoping to gain favour by being seen to 'do their duty'. In blocks of flats, it was the task of the local Party organizer to keep watch on the inhabitants.

The only opposition possible was daily acts of non-co-operation with the regime. Karma Rauhut remembers: 'One could create a certain free space for oneself. I don't know if you understand what I mean. In one's mind and in one's style of living, one could create a free space if one had enough connections and a little bit of money... You didn't want to stand out. You only wanted to carry on with your style of life without selling yourself.'[16] People voiced their criticism only among friends who were absolutely trusted.

By 1938, Hitler was still proclaiming himself a man of peace, even as he was steadily putting in place his plans for expansion. Though the shortages of foodstuffs affecting households three years earlier had been alleviated, the economic outlook was uncertain, and Hitler needed a national success. In March 1938, he moved into Austria. Portrayed as an *Anschluss*, a joining-together of all German-speaking peoples, rather than the takeover of a neighbouring country, it was welcomed as another bold move. As newsreel cameras filmed the crowds gathered to welcome Hitler in Vienna, it was ecstatic women who appeared in the foreground, cheering and weeping. 'Our Führer has pulled it off without bloodshed'[17] was one relieved response to his triumph on the road to the acquisition of *Lebensraum* – 'living space' – for the German people. It was another plank in building the Thousand Year Reich, and the western powers had made no response. But there was unease as well as celebration over Hitler's actively expansionist policy.

Anxiety intensified with Hitler's next step, the takeover of the Sudetenland region of Czechoslovakia. Justified as the legitimate demand to bring 'home to the Reich' the ethnic German population who were allegedly being 'oppressed' by the Czechs, it was another move to tear up the Versailles Treaty. Hitler had drawn up plans for a full-scale military aggression against the Czechoslovak Republic. His expansionist ambitions were stalled when the western powers initially intervened. Tensions rose as the prospect of war loomed. American journalist William Shirer noted the widespread opinion in Berlin that 'Hitler has made up his mind for war if it is necessary to get back his Sudetens'. He doubted it would come to that, because: 'First, the German army is not ready; secondly, the people are dead against war.'[18] Goebbels assessed: 'The war psychosis is growing... A gloomy mood lies over the land. Everyone awaits what is coming.'[19] Police Security Reports revealed a depressed mood: 'There exists in the broadest section of the population the earnest concern that in the long or short run a war will put an end to economic prosperity and have a terrible end for Germany.'[20] But at vast public meetings addressed by Hitler, crowds of loyal supporters were worked up into a frenzy of righteous indignation against the Czechs' treatment of Sudeten Germans and in support of Hitler's action to incorporate these Germans, by force if necessary, into the Greater Reich. Crowds of men, with some women, had clapped, applauded and finally chanted, 'Führer, command, and we will follow.'

Last-minute negotiations with Britain, France and Italy produced the 'Munich Agreement', which left Hitler to do exactly what he had intended: to occupy the Sudetenland – the first step in the takeover and then elimination of Czechoslovakia, a state brought into being by the Versailles Treaty. The Sudetenland also had the advantage of being the most industrialized region of Czechoslovakia, with raw materials that could now be plundered for the benefit of the Greater Reich and supply German industry, particularly the armaments industries, with significant new resources.

On Hitler's triumphant entry into the territory, the newsreel cameras again focused on women cheering and ecstatic as they garlanded the Army columns marching beside him with flowers and kisses. Hitler was praised in the twisted logic of propaganda for having preserved the peace. Once more, he had 'pulled off' his expansionist goal without bloodshed. But his preparations for war were now unmistakable. In 1939, all young men were conscripted into the Wehrmacht. Armaments production was stepped up. Propaganda against the enemies of the Reich was intensified as Hitler's successes were glorified – bringing Germans home to the Greater Reich, disregarding the Versailles Treaty, restoring national honour and dignity, and now putting into action his promises of *Lebensraum*. Women were constantly reminded of their duty as housewives to conserve national resources, and of their duty as mothers to sacrifice their sons and husbands in war in defence of the Fatherland and the *Volk*.

'The Enemy in Our Midst'

As Hitler strutted the international stage, plans were laid to tackle the 'Jewish Question'. Goebbels kept up vitriolic propaganda against the Jewish 'enemy in our midst'. 'Individual' terror actions had increased during the summer of 1938, but the leadership had distanced itself from an all-out terror campaign. Ilse Schmidt remembers one such attack in Berlin:

> I was on the Bluecherplatz and suddenly I heard screams, and a Jew came running out of a shop screaming. There was a huge sign on his window saying 'Don't Buy from the Jews'. He had his hands above his head because he was being hit on the head by an SA man. We were all standing there totally at a loss what to do. It was embarrassing, we were helpless. We looked at each other and didn't know what to say. It was embarrassing, the Jew screaming, the man hitting him, the screams of the Jew as he ran across the street and disappeared into a house. It was terrible... I was scared. I was afraid that I would be hit by the SA man in the same way as the Jew if I interfered. And it continued that you were always afraid. And later on, wherever I went, I had to keep silent about everything I saw or heard.

The clamp of legal measures tightened steadily. All Jewish lawyers and doctors were forbidden to practise except for Jewish clients. Goebbels put forward new plans for discrimination including special identity cards, and a ban on Jews using public parks, or visiting restaurants or cinemas. The main drive was to 'Aryanize' the economy. This was achieved through the steady expropriation of Jewish businesses and property, an action that directly profited non-Jewish interests. By April 1938, more than 60 per cent of Jewish firms had been liquidated or 'Aryanized'. By the multiplying discriminatory measures over the previous years, the Jewish presence in public life was steadily diminishing.

In November 1938 the full force of the State's brutality was revealed. On Kristallnacht (Crystal Night, the Night of Broken Glass, or the November Pogrom), all over Germany people witnessed the savagery lurking at the core of the regime. The excuse to endorse violence was provided by the assassination in Paris of a German Legation Secretary, Ernst von Rath, by a seventeen-year-old Polish Jew, Herschel Grynszpan. On the night of 9 November, at the instigation of the Party leadership, Nazi terror squads roamed the streets of towns and cities throughout Germany burning and looting Jewish shops, houses and synagogues. Allegedly a popular uprising in revenge against the assassination of a German by a Jew, the action was in fact co-ordinated at national and local level by leaders, who seized the opportunity to unleash terror against Jews.

Susanne von der Borch's mother was one of those who refused to stand by. Susanne, aged fifteen and a loyal BDM girl living in a suburb of Munich, was woken in the middle of the night:

My mother was at the window. I sat up and saw the house opposite in flames. I heard someone screaming, 'Help! Why doesn't anyone help us?' and I asked my mother, 'Why is the house burning, where are the fire brigades, why are the people screaming?' And she just said, 'Stay in bed.'

And she left the house with my older sister. I woke up my younger brother who was two years younger. And we sat on the stairs and waited for a long time. It was very ghostly, because we heard these screams and saw the flames.

After a long time, my mother came back. She had fifteen people with her. I was shocked because they were in nightgowns and slippers, or just a light coat. And I could see they were all our Jewish neighbours. She took them into the music room and my brother and I were told, 'Be quiet and don't move.'

My mother was very strict, so we didn't move. And we heard our mother phoning people up, and my sister was sent here and there to get drinks for them. Then these people were driven away by our chauffeur to relatives or friends.

And my mother told us afterwards that one of her neighbours, Frau Bach, was standing in front of her house without shoes in her nightgown, and my mother had a pile of coats and shoes and things, but Frau Bach said to her, 'Well, at least I have my husband.' And at that moment a car arrived with the SA, and they took Herr Bach into the car and he was driven to Dachau. But he was freed after a few weeks. He came back and they escaped to England, then America.

It was a shocking experience for me, and it did make me think more about the whole movement.

The next day she met up with friends from the Hitler Youth at the Prinzregentenplatz, beside Hitler's apartment, where they usually got together.

A few of the Hitler Youth leaders were there, who I normally liked a lot. And they were standing there telling us how they had spent the night. They said they had been at a shop, the Eichengrün in Munich, and they'd smashed the windows, and they'd got hold of one Jew and shaved the hair on his head. And I said, 'You horrible pigs!' And I thought, I have to find out the truth, what was really going on. And that was when I really started to ask serious questions.

Like thousands of other German women, Maria von Lingen witnessed the events on the street. She worked as a secretary in the technical division of the Opel AG in Rüsselsheim (a factory producing military goods). That evening, she went out to post a letter:

> I saw an enormous crowd on the streets, and on the most elegant street of Wiesbaden. It's a long wide street with very elegant shops. They were almost all Jewish owned. The synagogues were burning. And the SA was everywhere, and a crowd of human beings and cries and wailing and they were pushed together. I saw it! An SA man grabbed my arm and told me, 'Fräulein, get away, there's nothing here for you.' And I ran back home with my letter and never mailed it. I was completely in shock, completely in shock.
>
> The next day one heard that it was the anger of the *Volk*. It was the SA that did it all. I saw the SA men on the streets, how they pushed the Jews together and how they threw stones through the panes of glass, and destroyed the store, tore everything out and threw it in the street. Went up in their homes, threw all the furniture out the windows and took the Jews away.
>
> It was horrible. One thought, 'For God's sake, what is going on? What kind of government is it that we have? It's impossible! One cannot do that in a civilized country!'[21]

Lilli Gentzen, a ten-year-old schoolgirl, was travelling in a tram: 'I saw all the broken shop windows. Among the people sitting in the tram there was a quiet silence, and everyone felt subdued. Everyone was staring out, yet another window shattered, and nobody said a word. I remember it as a terrible experience.'

Ursula Meyer Semlies expressed the widespread mixed feeling of revulsion about the 'uncivilized' nature of the acts, but not necessarily hostility to their objective: 'We did not find it good, the way and means of how they did it. Of course we thought, "Jews out" was always the phrase. Well, such expressions and refrains were sometimes...' (she tailed off in the interview with Alison Owings). 'But I thought the methods, well, they should do it another way, but not with force... most of all not in such a criminal way.'[22] Rita Kuhn, who was half-Jewish, remembers, aged ten, walking to school and passing broken shop windows. Classmates told her their synagogue was on fire. Rita turned to passers-by telling them, 'Our synagogue is burning!' She remembered them looking away from her, as if they were 'ashamed and embarrassed. They said nothing.'[23]

Following Kristallnacht, almost 30,000 Jewish men were rounded up, arrested and sent to concentration camps. In the mayhem and wanton savagery of the night, over ninety Jews were murdered. Many others committed suicide. Fear swept the Jewish community. One newly-wed remembers:

> My terrified father-in-law had opened the door to two SA men who entered our bedroom, telling my husband to dress to be taken to the local prison... I helped him to put warm clothing on. We did not speak, although I could feel myself and my husband trembling. In less than two minutes both Günther (my husband) and his sixty-eight-year-old father had been taken away in the police van... while I tried to comfort my aged mother-in-law, who was crying uncontrollably.[24]

Her husband was sent to Sachsenhausen concentration camp.

Margaret Czellitzer returned to her house next day and found: 'my radio broken at the garden door, my lovely china smashed into pieces, the paintings as well as all the other valuables stolen... We were all heartbroken... we [had] spent the happiest time in our lives [there].'[25] Many children saw their fathers cry for the first time in their lives. Lore Gang-Saalheimar returned from Nuremberg and was met off the train by her parents: 'I don't think I realized how bad things were until I got home. My parents were on the platform. My mother was in a sweater and a skirt, no make-up, no jewellery, no anything. My father looked awful... It was the first time I really felt a feeling of oppression and persecution... This was a quantum step. This was the real thing.'[26] Elisabeth Petuchowski's grandfather committed suicide a few days after Kristallnacht, when his two sons had been taken to a concentration camp and his shop and warehouse completely destroyed. 'Unable to accept a future not resembling his past, he put himself to sleep forever,' his granddaughter related. 'During those November days, no Jew dared leave his house. So there we were... at 5.00am, the time set by the police for his funeral... we were horror-stricken. Not at his death – what more could now happen to him? – but at our nightmare.'[27]

Few believed the propaganda that it was a spontaneous outburst – most knew that the Party was behind it. Many ordinary Germans had joined in with hurling abuse at Jews as they were ejected from their homes and taken into custody. Most Jews were released later after humiliating treatment in concentration camps; 80,000 emigrated – or tried to emigrate, since restrictions were already being imposed on immigration quotas in other countries, so many just fled. To add to the humiliation, Göring decreed that Jews would be responsible for paying for the damage to their own property, and imposed a billion mark 'atonement fine' on them. It was a further step in his longer-term aim of 'Aryanizing' the economy, by excluding Jews from the nation's economic life. The remaining Jewish families sank further into helplessness, social exclusion and poverty.

The campaign of vitriol against the Jews was pursued relentlessly. In January 1939, Hitler added threat to the tirades of hatred when he addressed the Reichstag to celebrate the sixth anniversary of his taking power:

> In my life I have often been a prophet, and I have mostly been laughed at. At the time of my struggle for power, it was mostly the Jewish people who laughed at the prophecy that one day I would attain in Germany the leadership of the state and therewith of the entire nation, and that among other problems I would also solve the Jewish one. I think that the uproarious laughter of that time has in the meantime remained stuck in German Jewry's throat. Today I want to be a prophet again: If

international Jewry inside and outside Europe again succeeds in precipitating the nations into a world war, the result will not be the Bolshevization of the earth, and with it the victory of Jewry, but the annihilation of the Jewish race in Europe.

Expansion

As rearmament was stepped up, Hitler concentrated on his plans for expansion, and the conquest of *Lebensraum*. The pressure to rearm was diverting resources away from consumer industries, leading to threats of shortages, especially of foodstuffs. Labour was in short supply, especially in the agricultural sector. The decree that young women must spend their Labour Duty Year working on the land and that Hitler Youth should help out with harvests had only a marginal effect on the situation, though it added to young women's sense that they were playing a useful part in the nation's destiny. Their mothers, meanwhile, were being encouraged to return to work in industry to help stem the shortages there, including in the armaments factories.

The atmosphere was becoming increasingly uncertain. Though Hitler still masqueraded as a man of peace, he was in private telling Wehrmacht officers that Germany had a glorious future based on the heroic values of the past, which included 'brutality, meaning the sword, if all other methods fail', and that the future depended on the acquisition of 'living space'. The invasion of Prague in March was a clear signal of his future intentions. He gained more valuable resources, including the buoyant Czechoslovak armaments industry, which helped ease the German economic situation, and he accrued more credit for another bold triumph. He was greeted with wild cheering from the Party faithful on his return from Prague.

But there was nervousness that his policies were bordering on the reckless, that his justification for the use of force was specious and that he was bringing Germany closer to war. Hitler's declaration that Bohemian and Moravian lands 'had belonged to the living space of the Germans for a thousand years' was less than compelling to people whose main concern was to shore up the economic gains since 1933, and who had also noted with relief Hitler's declaration that the

Sudetenland was his 'last territorial demand'. 'Can't he get enough?' was the response of one mother, preoccupied with the daily round of making ends meet. Even so, Hitler's popularity increased, and faith in his leadership hardly wavered.[28] Goebbels's propaganda department trumpeted his success, while now launching a campaign of denigration of the Slavs who had come under the German yoke. Those who were anxious about war blamed his underlings, rather than their Führer, for taking risks.

Five months after the invasion of Prague, on 1 September, Hitler invaded Poland. The declaration of war that followed was greeted with widespread apprehension: 'There was no "hooray" atmosphere, like in the First World War,' Ilse Schmidt recalls. 'It was a subdued atmosphere. Very scared. Timid. Noiseless. All the older ones still had memories of the First World War. We were only schoolchildren, but the older ones still had the memories embedded in their minds.' Traudl Junge, later Hitler's secretary, was shocked: 'When suddenly the news came that war had started, we were all horrified. And I thought, this is the end of the world. I imagined something really dreadful. My heart was beating and I was in a terrible state of fear.' Liselotte Katscher's reaction was similar: 'When I heard that the war had started – I heard it on the radio by chance when I was tidying up, a special news announcement that the Germans had marched into Poland – I got such a shock. I was a child of the First World War, and was old enough to know what happened and I thought, "This is the end of the world, this is our damnation."' Even Nazi convert and BDM leader Jutta Rüdiger had doubts: 'As a child I experienced the First World War, and I thought, this is a very serious turn of events. This is not going to be an easy time ahead... We thought, well, whatever Hitler does is right. But we weren't happy.'

NOTES

1 Rhodes James, Robert (ed.), *Chips: The Diaries of Sir Henry Chips Channon*, Weidenfeld and Nicolson, London, 1967, p. 111

2 Lipstadt, Deborah E., *Beyond Belief: The American Press and the Coming of the Holocaust 1933–45*, Free Press, New York. 1986, p. 63

3 Shirer, William L., *Berlin Diary 1934–1941*, Sphere Books, London, 1970, p. 58 (16 August 1936)

4 Klemperer, Viktor, *I Will Bear Witness: A Diary of the Nazi Years, 1933–1941*, Random House, New York, 1998 (13 August, 1936)

5 Berlin Police Report, 6 March 1936, cited Kershaw, *Hitler: Hubris*, pp. 576–7

6 Heineman, *What Difference Does a Husband Make?*, p. 40

7 Schoenbaum, *Hitler's Social Revolution*, p. 185

8 Picker, *Hitler's Table Talk*, p. 30

9 Owings, *Frauen*, pp. 347–8

10 ibid., p. 19

11 ibid., pp. 60–2

12 ibid., pp. 345–6

13 Cited Bleuel, *Strength Through Joy*, p. 72

14 Owings, *Frauen*, p. 349

15 ibid., p. 456

16 ibid., p. 348

17 Kershaw, *Hitler: Nemesis 1936–1945*, Allen Lane, London, p. 86

18 Shirer, *Berlin Diary, 1934-1941*, p. 102

19 Goebbels, Joseph, *Die Tagebücher von Joseph Goebbels*, (ed.) Elke Fröhlich, Saur Verlag, Koblenz, Munich, 1987 (diaries dated 31 August 1938, 1 September 1938)

20 Report, Munich, 9 September 1938, cited Kershaw, *Hitler: Nemesis*, p. 108

21 Owings, *Frauen*, p. 121

22 ibid., p. 60

23 ibid., p. 456

24 Cited Pine, *Nazi Family Policy 1933–1945*, p. 162

25 ibid., p. 162

26 ibid., p. 161

27 ibid., p. 163

28 Cited Kershaw, *Hitler: Nemesis*, p. 173

10

CONQUEST

The outbreak of war brought little immediate change to women's lives. Traudl Junge recalled: 'At the beginning it was so calm, at home you didn't feel much. And then there were the victory parades, so slowly we were growing into the war, and getting used to it, I would say.' Nurse Liselotte Katscher agreed: 'I was surprised that life just went on as normal in the first weeks and months.'

Single women were moved into armaments industries to replace men who had been called up. As part of the recruitment drive, propaganda glamorized women who entered new occupations, such as tram and bus conducting and arms manufacture, and emphasized the 'feminine' virtues of selflessness and service. Wives were targeted. One poster showed a smiling wife working in an armaments factory: 'Earlier I buttered bread for him, now I paint grenades and think, this is for him.'

The potential 'reserve army' in 1939 amounted to 1 million single and 5.4 married but childless women. Attempts to mobilize married women were sluggish and ineffective. Calls to volunteer had little effect. By June 1940, only a quarter of a million women had been conscripted, and these were mainly transferred from one area, such as textiles, to another, such as defence, which was regarded as crucial to the war effort.[1] In one region of central Germany, 8000 women had been asked to respond to the Führer's call to contribute to industry, the war effort and the Fatherland. Only eight responded.[2] Women, especially middle-class women, had been persistently lauded as bearers of the future race from their power-base in the home, and were unresponsive to the about-face by the leadership in wartime. Nor was there any attempt to conscript the million and a half household servants.

Hitler opposed the idea of conscripting married women, arguing that this would threaten the birth rate and undermine Germany's racial strength. Despite his advisers' frequent pleas to take action, no coherent policy for deploying them was advanced until 1943. Moreover, existing policies actually deterred women from working. Wives were offered generous separation allowances – up to 85 per cent of their husbands' peacetime earnings. When they took on jobs, they lost up to 45 per cent of that allowance. Work conditions deteriorated, with longer hours and the removal of some protective legislation relating to women. Since they also had to shoulder domestic responsibilities and the daily grind of queues and shortages, women were inclined either to remain at home or, if working, to return there. Employers were reluctant to employ women who had no experience in their area. The number of employed married women consequently fell in the first two years of war. Overall, fewer than 200,000 additional women entered the workforce between 1939 and 1944.[3]

The ambiguity, or rather hypocrisy, of the Nazi position on women was exposed. Some measures for the protection of working women's health during pregnancy and childbirth were improved, and maternity and childcare facilities were expanded, but the previous restrictions on women's working hours were lifted. They were barred from being paid equally with men when doing men's jobs: 'Men, and in particular older men who are married and fathers, must be paid more than women... because they must make more sacrifices for the community; in the main, women simply have to look after themselves, whereas men have to care for their families and the national community.' Even if she was 'contributing to the national community', wage 'equality' should be achieved through child allowances or tax reductions. Equalization in wages 'would inevitably result in the tendency for an increase in male wages to occur'. Men who had worked in factories where 'typical' women's work was carried out, the Führer decreed, should be transferred 'to work which was more appropriate for them' – whatever that might mean. Women were paid on average 25 per cent less than men and in some cases only half men's wages.[4]

Women's organizations, meanwhile, continued to glorify women's role in wartime as child-bearers rather than workers. 'Today more than ever, the outcome depends on the quiet heroism of women. The willingness of men to die stands against the will of the woman for life,' declared the *Frauen Warte*, the Nazi magazine for women. 'The success or failure of the enemy's devilish plans depends on German women and mothers, on their will to sacrifice and on their love of their children... Our soldiers protect Germany and all that we have accomplished. But it is our women who are the foundation of Germany's future, who built it stone by stone through fine German children.'[5] No wonder, then, that many women resorted to pregnancy rather than volunteer for war work. In popular parlance, they became known as *Sauckelfrauen*, after Fritz Sauckel, the man in charge of mobilizing female labour.

Juggling domestic responsibilities with work became increasingly difficult. There were food shortages from the start. Ration cards had already been printed in 1937, and rationing of several basic daily items was introduced in August 1939. Housewives, long trained in thrift and stringent dietary habits, especially cutting down on imported fats and meat, were now exhorted to fight the war in their kitchens. 'The courage of the soldiers, the industry of the workers and the thrift of the German housewife guarantee victory!', posters declared. By 1940 there were shortages of fuel, shoes and most foodstuffs, including fruit, and meat was rationed. The women's organizations worked overtime to produce new recipes using whatever was available. The plunder of occupied territories, especially France, which brought to the market exotic vegetables such as fennel, chicory, aubergine and Jerusalem artichokes, alleviated the shortages only marginally. Rations were cut steadily throughout the war. Under-nourishment was rife even early on, adding to the housewife's burden of concerns.

Conquest

With the Army occupation of Poland completed when Warsaw surrendered on 29 September 1939, the leadership activated its policies of ethnic cleansing, subjugation and murder. Poland was designated as an area for 'colonization' by ethnic Germans, mostly from the East. Under

Heinrich Himmler, in his capacity as Reich Commissioner for the Consolidation of German Nationhood (RKF), up to 500,000 ethnic Germans, many living in territories in the Soviet sphere of influence, were to be brought 'home to the Reich'. This 'repatriation', partly carried out under a secret protocol agreed between the Nazi and Soviet governments, included ethnic Germans from the Baltic states, as well as those from Bessarabia, Volhynia, and Bukovina and Dobruja in Romania. They were offered land in the new 'colony' of the Warthegau of Central Poland. To make room for them, Poles and Jews were expelled from their homes, their land was expropriated and they were deported to the eastern areas of Poland (the General Government) or to ghettos and eventually concentration and death camps.

Ethnic German families arrived in large numbers at settlement camps, from where they were processed, given medical examinations, tested for racial and blood purity and, if suitable, awarded with certificates of German citizenship. Roughly 200,000 ethnic Germans were resettled between October 1939 and February 1940.[6] An increasing number had to wait around in the transit camps before the 130,000 Poles and Jews they were displacing were forcibly removed from the areas.[7]

Almost as soon as the military conquest was complete, young women were pressed into the nation's service. In the wake of the army, selected BDM leaders were sent, under SS control, to feminize and domesticate the conquest. Their task was to help the ethnic Germans settle into their new homes, and to 'Germanize' them, teaching German culture and customs to the families, many of whom didn't even speak the language. In BDM leader Jutta Rüdiger's words, they were to carry out Nazi women's role as the 'bearers of German tradition and culture'. To make way for the settlers, the Army and SS squads brutally evicted Polish and Jewish families, often with only a few hours' notice, sometimes clearing whole blocks of dwellings in a single night and loading the inhabitants on to open trucks to be transported south. One *Führerin*, Hedwig Ertl, who was recruited to be a teacher at a German school in the Warthegau, recalls: 'The Poles were told that they had a short time to get out and they could take with them a few possessions... I would say they were bitter, but I never experienced anyone who fought it, or threw stones or showed outrage. They went in silence.' Hedwig Ertl's racial indoctrination was complete: 'Looking back, I never had the feeling of doing something that wasn't right.'

After the Poles had left, she and other BDM girls 'went into the houses, cleaned them and painted the walls white. We put a tablecloth and flowers on the tables to welcome the incoming Bessarabian Germans and make them feel at home.' At the school where she taught, her task was 'to educate them as German children with German songs, German lessons and German reading books and things like that which they didn't have before'. She didn't teach Polish children – they 'only had four years at school, they weren't supposed to become clever'. Indeed, it was the leader's intention to eliminate the Polish intellectual class, as well as their political leaders, as a first priority in the conquest.

Susanne von der Borch also went to Poland, to a resettlement camp of 800 Bessarabian Germans near Lodz, which the Germans had renamed Litzmannstadt, to teach children art and woodwork. But first she faced her mother's opposition: 'I told my mother about it and she said to me, literally: "If you do that and if you go there, then I never want to speak to you again. And I don't want to see you ever again." And I thought, I have to risk that.' Susanne wanted to find out the truth of what was going on herself. But she understood her mother's fears: 'Imagine, I was seventeen years old. I was a blonde girl. My parents were writing me off. They knew the camps were run by the SS and they thought I was going to be drawn into their hands and that would be my fate.' She had first to report to the SS on her arrival, took an instant dislike to them, and avoided contact as far as possible.

Both she and Hedwig Ertl experienced at first hand the disillusion of the ethnic Germans, which contrasted with the portrayal in propaganda films of their joyous return to the Reich. In the transit camps, conditions deteriorated as the volume of settlers increased, leading to overcrowding. Susanne von der Borch recalls, 'Formerly they had been rich farmers, breeding sheep, and they were plunged into misery. They didn't have any ration cards, they were living in poverty in these camps.' Hedwig Ertl, working with families on their newly acquired farms, remembers: 'They didn't want to be resettled, they were really fed up, because they had very bad quality land and they couldn't get along with the people.' The young men were given no choice, but were immediately conscripted into the SS. Hedwig Ertl remembers going round grading the Poles into categories of how 'German' they were. She was instructed to encourage them to say they had some German blood, because the higher they were on the list, the more food stamps they got, and they might even get a German passport. 'But they realized that as soon as they were registered as *VolksDeutsch* [ethnic Germans] they would be called up into the [German] Army. So very few people asked to go higher up the list.'

While Poles were moved off their farms and land and into forced labour, Jews living in the incorporated territories had their property and possessions confiscated, were abducted for forced labour in territory further east, or evacuated to the ghetto at Lodz. Here they were joined by Jewish families forcibly deported from other parts of Poland and later from Germany. From May 1940 the ghetto, then with 163,000 inhabitants, was sealed off from the rest of the city. The numbers grew from then on.[8] Deprived of possessions or means of subsistence, they were thrown into squalor, overcrowding and destitution.

The pauperization of Jews was an integral part of the Nazi resettlement plan. Repatriation of ethnic Germans was to be paid for by the expropriation of Polish and Jewish property or, as the RKF main office reported in 1942, 'the uncompensated use of former alien property – that is, without utilizing Reich funds'.[9] When plans for the liquidation of the Lodz ghetto were delayed, the Germans set up factories and workshops producing profitable goods, such as textiles – including uniforms for the Nazis. The cost was minimal since the workers, mainly women, were slave labourers surviving on minimum rations.[10]

Enforced starvation was a deliberate part of German policy. 'The more that dies, the better,' declared Hans Frank, who ran the General Government area of occupied Poland. 'It's high time that this rabble is driven together in ghettos, and then plague will creep in and they'll croak,' Himmler decided.[11] Starvation preceded extermination. From 1942, families were deported from Lodz to the death camps.

Young BDM leaders working in the ethnic German resettlement programme were no longer shielded from the brutality of the regime, if they chose to seek the truth. Susanne von der Borch had heard in 1941 of the ghetto at nearby Lodz, and resolved to find out for herself what went on. She got a lift into the town, in temperatures of 30 degrees below zero, and boarded a tram:

> The windows were covered with paint so you couldn't see through. The tram doors were locked and then we drove through the ghetto. People had already scratched little peep holes in the paint. And I scratched a little more to see as much and as clearly as possible what was happening in the ghetto. Jewish children stood there, half-starved, wearing their Jewish stars, at the fence, this barbed wire fence. They were in a terrible state, dressed only in rags, like all the other people. What I saw – it was dreadful. It was worse than my worst fears... I saw one Jewish child, I couldn't see whether it was a boy or a girl, and he was there at the fence and he was looking out with huge eyes, starved eyes, in rags and obviously in despair... The ghetto was horrific and when I returned to the camp I was totally shattered.

On her return to Germany, she had to make a report for the BDM. She included 'everything that was important to me, I didn't keep silent about anything. I didn't gloss over anything.' Her group leaders were horrified; BDM reports were read out to the girls at the weekly home evenings. The leaders said: "'So you want that sent to Berlin?" And I said, yes. "And do you know what you're writing?" And I said, cheeky as I was, I said, "That's why I wrote it." And one of them turned round and said, "You know that concentration camps are there for young people too." And I said, "Yes, and I don't care."' The report was returned to her a few weeks later with her signature, 'but all the things that were important to me had been taken out. It was a beautiful trip and an exciting trip, and it was just a description of a trip. Somebody was playing my guardian angel.' Susanne von der Borch never went to another rally and distanced herself entirely from the BDM: 'For me personally, I drew the line and decided that this movement, which had been so very important, was now finished for me.'

Savagery

As the Wehrmacht advanced into Russia in June 1941, German savagery escalated. Murder squads – *Einsatzgruppen* – were enlisted to 'pacify' the population and remove 'subversive elements', by deportation, slaughter and executions on an increasingly random scale. Jews were the main target for liquidation, along with communist functionaries and the partisan resistance. On one day, 3 July, in Lusk in eastern Poland, 1160 Jewish men were shot; in Kaunas in Lithuania on 6 July, 2514 Jews were shot. Of 4400 executions over twenty days in July, the vast majority were Jewish men. With the advance further into Soviet territory, the massacre was extended to women and children. Einsatzkommando 3 murdered 56,459 Jews in September alone; 26,243 of them women and 15,112 children. The death toll continued to increase. An estimated half a million were killed by four Einsatzgruppen during the next four months,[12] as Himmler drafted in more men to assist in the 'pacification' of the conquered territories. The initial 3000 men directly involved in the killing units had swelled to eleven times that number by the end of 1941, and regular soldiers of the Wehrmacht were increasingly involved in the butchery. Eventually, between 2.6 and 2.9 million Soviet Jews were murdered in the areas under Nazi occupation.[13]

Felix Landau joined an Einsatzkommando in June 1941. An Austrian who had been imprisoned for his involvement in the murder of Austrian leader Engelbert Dolfuss in 1934, he had worked for the Security Police (SS) on his release, and was transferred to Radom in the Polish General Government in 1940. At Radom he had fallen in love with a typist, Gertrude, who was engaged to another man. From 1941 he kept a diary, written half for Gertrude, which includes his work with the Einsatzkommando. On 2 July 1941 he arrived at Lemberg: 'Shortly after our arrival the first Jews were shot by us. As usual a few of the new officers became megalomaniacs, they really enter into the role wholeheartedly.' On 3 July, he was interrupted while writing a letter to 'my Trude' with orders to get ready: '...with steel helmets, carbines, thirty rounds of ammunition. We have just come back. Five hundred Jews were lined up ready to be shot... I have little inclination to shoot defenceless people – even if they are only Jews. I would far rather good honest open combat. Now good night, my dear Hansi [bunny].'

His entry for one day, 5 July, records two Jews shot during his guard duty the previous night, and the discovery of a Wehrmacht guard who had been shot dead.

One hour later, at 5.00am, a further thirty-two Poles, members of the intelligentsia and the Resistance, were shot about 200 metres from our quarters after they had dug their own grave. One of them simply would not die. The first layer of sand had already been thrown on the first group when a hand emerged from out of the sand, waved and pointed to the place, presumably his heart. A couple more shots rang out, then someone shouted – in fact the Pole himself – 'Shoot faster!' ...What is a human being?... During the afternoon some 300 more Poles and Jews were finished off.

That evening he went into town:

There were hundreds of Jews walking along the street with blood pouring down their faces, holes in their heads, their hands broken and their eyes hanging out of their sockets. They were covered in blood... We went to the citadel; there we saw things that few people have ever seen. At the entrance of the citadel there were soldiers standing guard. They were holding clubs as thick as a man's wrist and were lashing out and hitting anyone who crossed their path. The Jews were pouring out of the entrance. There were rows of Jews lying one on top of the other like pigs whimpering horribly. The Jews kept streaming out of the citadel completely covered in blood. We stopped and tried to see who was in charge of the Kommando. 'Nobody'. Someone had let the Jews go. They were just being hit out of rage and hatred. Nothing against that – only they should not let the Jews walk about in such a state.

Later he relaxed at base: 'Our work is over for today. Camaraderie is still good for the time being. Crazy, beautiful, sensuous music playing on the radio again and my longing for you, the person who has hurt me so much, is growing and growing.' On 11 July he spends the whole night carrying out executions, 'mostly Jews but also some Ukrainians', and on 12 July he is woken at 6.00am to shoot twenty-three men and two women who had been assembled with shovels to dig their own graves: 'They are unbelievable. They even refused to accept a glass of water from us... As the women walked to the grave they were completely composed... Six of us had to shoot them... Strange, I am completely unmoved. No pity. Nothing.'[14]

The relatively few women working at the front lines, including 160,000 nurses, and typists and secretaries employed by the Wehrmacht administration witnessed the savagery of war at first hand. Ilse Schmidt was a typist with the Army Propaganda Department, posted first to Paris, then the Ukraine and Belgrade. In the Ukraine, she was assigned a maid called Klepka, who cleaned for her and her room-mate. 'She was Jewish. She was a very shy, very nice girl. My room-mate and I would always give something extra to her because Klepka was very skinny, and we felt that she probably didn't get enough to eat. We gave her bread, and some clothes.' One night, Ilse was woken up by loud noises outside her room:

I thought, what is this racket? People were throwing tin cans in the street, and from their clothes I could see that they were Jews. They were rounded up at night. I didn't know what was happening to them but I had a suspicion. These people wanted to attract attention to themselves: 'Look what is happening to us! Don't let it happen to us.' And I thought, 'Defend yourselves, don't let them do this to you.'... I found out later that there were many more guards than I saw that night. And later on I found out that in Rowno all Jews had been executed that night near the train station. I never saw Klepka again. This experience shattered me personally.

When she talked with her women colleagues afterwards, they responded with shock, tinged with pragmatism: 'Some of my room-mates said later,

"Why did they do this? We need the Jews as labourers." Klepka's father was a tailor, he had worked for the German Army. "We needed these labourers... These people had been helping us, our soldiers had been sent to the front to die, so we needed them to do all the other work... Why did it happen?" Everyone was really disgusted about it.' Ilse Schmidt's experiences at the front separated her from other women – but, trained in obedience, she kept silent: 'When I came home, I didn't dare to talk about the killing of the Jews, I didn't dare. I was afraid. At the back of my mind, the obligation that I had to be quiet about what I saw – it was like the oath of the soldiers.'

Ilse Schmidt was posted to Belgrade, where the 'pacification' programme involved the execution of partisans. She was working in the propaganda department: 'I had to open the post and I had no idea, I just opened this envelope, and then I saw to my horror how war reporters had photographed the executions of partisans. I didn't want to look at it, my first impulse was to get up and run away... And after that, whenever I thought there were photos in the envelopes, I just put them on the adjutant's desk unopened. He looked at me as if he wanted to say something, and then opened them himself.' Looking back, she was filled with shock and terror at the pictures – 'How on earth can you take pictures of an execution?' She wondered whether men felt differently from women: 'I think men think, it's either him or me. Before you shoot, I will shoot. Men do think differently.' But not all men:

> I was friendly with an army lawyer who had to attend executions and court-martials as a witness. He would always come back like an old man. His hair would be hanging down into his face, and he would always be smelling of sweat, he was so disgusted about it as well. He would say to me, 'I'm the son of a priest and I was brought up in the belief that you should not kill.' He was always sick afterwards, when he had to watch this. Especially later on, I had to distance myself from him because his depression made me even more depressed.

She also witnessed men strung up in the streets of Belgrade:

We were driving down from the old castle in Belgrade when we saw people hanging on the left and right from the lamp-posts – partisans. I still see them today. An older man, to stop his trousers falling down they had simply tied a knot in [them]. Young people and old people. Bunches of flowers had been placed beneath the hanged men. To their left and right, people were sitting in cafes, looking up at these hanged people... and I could feel their hatred, I could see the silent hate against us in the face of those onlookers.

Ilse Schmidt, working for the Wehrmacht, did not talk at the time about her experiences, but women on the home front heard some of what went on through letters from their soldiers at the front lines. Propaganda over years against the 'Jewish–Bolshevik conspiracy', with the constant reiteration of 'racial awareness' to the rising warrior class in the Hitler Youth, had prepared the ground for brutality in wartime – in men and women. The German 'right' to *Lebensraum* was as entrenched in the German consciousness as the natural inferiority of the non-Aryan peoples whom they were subjugating.

With the invasion of the Soviet Union, Goebbels's propaganda department rose to full volume in tirades against 'Jewish–Bolshevism' on the home front. Wehrmacht leaders whipped up hatred against the enemy among soldiers at the front lines, warning them to be merciless in their treatment of 'sub-humans', specifically Jews and partisans. 'The soldier in the eastern sphere is not only a fighter according to the rules of the art of warfare, but also the bearer of a pitiless racial [*völkish*] ideology and the avenger of all the bestialities which have been inflicted on the German and related ethnic nation,' Field Marshal Walter von Reichenau, Commander-in-Chief of the 6th Army, told his troops. 'The soldier must therefore have full understanding for the necessity of the severe but just atonement from the Jewish sub-humans... Only in this way will we fulfil our historic duty of liberating the German people from the Asiatic–Jewish threat once and for all.'[15]

Erich von Manstein, Commander-in-Chief of the 11th Army, echoed him: 'The Jewish Bolshevik system must be eradicated once and for all... Never again must it enter into our European living space.' The

German soldier's task was to smash 'the military means of power of this system'. He 'must show sympathy for the necessity of the hard atone- ment demanded of Jewry, the spiritual bearer of the Bolshevik terror'.[16] As partisan warfare spread, the leaders identified partisans with 'Jewish–Bolshevik' actions, which they used as further justification for barbarous reprisals against both. In March 1942, Goebbels wrote in his diary of partisans in the East: 'Their strength has increased in the past weeks. They conduct almost a guerrilla war. The brains behind this are the Political Commissars and the Jews. That's why it is necessary again to shoot Jews in increasing numbers. There will be no peace so long as the Jews are around in this area. Sentimentality has no place here' (Diary, 16 March 1942).

Soldiers absorbed the patriotic message of hate against the Russian Bolshevik and Jewish enemy. And in letters home, they revealed to mothers and wives some of what was happening at the front. Hugo Lapp, with a Panzer troop (Ersatz Abteilung 33 Ostfront) in Poland and Russia, wrote to his mother, praising her: 'You are a true soldier's mother, you found the right words for me. As a mother you can be proud that your three sons know how much they owe to the Fatherland.'[17] In August 1941, Lapp was just outside Kiev, full of opti- mism about German victory, and wrote to his mother: 'Each time that I look into the faces of the captured Russians, and I see the scum of their Asian vileness, then I am convinced over and over again that this battle is necessary to guarantee the survival of our homeland and culture.' From Dnjepr, he wrote on 5 September: 'The Jewish question is solved here completely and swiftly. As a retaliation for six of our comrades who had been buried alive by the Jews, we shot 250 of them in one village alone... My health is fine. The provisions here are excellent. Every day I have milk, honey and eggs for breakfast. For lunch we have meat almost every day, and for dinner, fruit and tea. All booty!'

Some mothers echoed the bellicose language of racial hatred in support of their sons. A few days after the invasion of Russia, one wrote: 'My dearest son, this is Bolshevism as we hate it, devious, cheating, brutal and without any compassion. I don't doubt for a single moment that we will be victorious over these inhumane beasts. The few days of war have shown that our brave soldiers are confronting the most beastly of enemies… I am praying that God will watch over you in this unholy country… I reach out to you and embrace you.'

SS Obersturmführer Karl Kretschmer, in fond letters home to his wife, affirmed the war as a struggle on behalf of mothers, wives and children for 'the survival or non-survival of our people'. His position in an SS Einsatzgruppe enabled him to support his family well. In September 1942, he wrote to her: 'After my experiences in Russia, my lovely home means more to me than anything else in the world. If I could pray, I would ask for you and the Homeland to be kept safe.' He was feeling 'in a very gloomy mood… The sight of the dead, including women and children, is not very cheering,' but it had to be done in the fight 'for the existence of our people. The enemy would do the same. I think that you understand me. As the war is in our opinion a Jewish war, the Jews are the first to feel it. Here in Russia, wherever the German soldier is, no Jew remains. You can imagine that at first I needed some time to get to grips with this.'[18]

Later, he enlarged to her on the theme of 'necessary' brutality: 'We have got to be tough here or else we will lose the war. There is no room for pity of any kind. You women and children back home could not expect any mercy or pity if the enemy got the upper hand. For that reason we are mopping up where necessary…' Occasionally he allowed himself to wonder about 'what we are doing in this country' but the argument of 'necessity' reassured him: '…it is a weakness not to be able to stand the sight of dead people; the best way of overcoming it is to do it more often. Then it becomes a habit,' he wrote. 'The more one thinks about the whole business the more one comes to the conclusion that it's the only thing we can do to safeguard unconditionally the security of our people and our future… Our faith in the Führer fulfils us and gives us the strength to carry out our difficult and thankless task. For everywhere we go we are looked upon with some degree of suspicion. That should not, however, divert us from the knowledge that what we are doing is necessary.' He reminded his wife to bring up the children to be obedient and self-disciplined, as befitted the master race: 'After all, fate permitting, we Germans are the people of the future. The future depends on how we bring up our children and their understanding that all those who were killed in battle did not die in vain. So teach Dagi that she must study hard and always obey her parents and her teachers. Only a person who has himself firmly under control can judge or rule over others.'[19]

The ruthlessness demanded of the soldier elite was spelled out by Heinrich Himmler to his officer troops in chilling detail. To defend their own homeland, their women and children with 'honour', they should ruthlessly abandon moral scruples in their treatment of everyone else, including women and children from other races:

The SS man is to be guided by one principle alone: honesty, decency, loyalty, and friendship towards those of our blood, and no one else... Whether other peoples live in plenty or starve to death interests me only insofar as we need them as slaves for our culture; for the rest it does not interest me. Whether 10,000 Russian women keel over from exhaustion in the construction of an anti-tank ditch interests me only insofar as the ditch for Germany gets finished. We will never be savage or heartless where we don't have to be; that is obvious. Germans are after all the only people in the world who treat animals decently... [But] if someone comes to me and tells me, 'I cannot dig these anti-tank ditches with children or with women, it is inhuman, they will die on the job,' I must say to him, 'You are a murderer of your own blood, because if the anti-tank ditch is not dug, German soldiers will die, and they are the sons of German mothers. They are our blood.'[20]

NOTES

1 Noakes, Jeremy, *Nazism 1914–1945*, vol 4, *The German Home Front in World War II: A Documentary Reader*, University of Exeter Press, Exeter, 1998, p. 312
2 Kitchen, Martin, *Nazi Germany at War*, Longman, London, 1995, p. 136
3 ibid., p. 139
4 Noakes, *Nazism 1914–1945*, p. 355; Kitchen, ibid., p. 150
5 *NS Frauen Warte*, No. 13, 1 January 1940
6 Aly, Götz, *'Final Solution': Nazi Population Policy and the Murder of European Jews*, Arnold, London, 1999, p. 108
7 Kershaw, *Hitler: Nemesis*, p. 318
8 ibid., pp. 319–20
9 Aly, *'Final Solution'*, p. 78
10 Unger, Michael, 'The Status and Plight of Women in the Lodz Ghetto', in (ed.) Dalia Ofer and Lenore J. Weitzman, *Women in the Holocaust*, Yale University Press, Connecticut, 1998, pp. 124, 130, 131
11 Burleigh, *The Third Reich*, p. 587
12 Kershaw, *Nemesis*, pp. 463, 468
13 Burleigh, *The Third Reich*, p. 629
14 Klee, Ernst, Willi Dressen and Volker Reiss, *Those Were the Days: The Holocaust through the Eyes of the Perpetrators and Bystanders*, Hamish Hamilton, London, 1991, pp. 88–97
15 Cited Kershaw, *Nemesis*, p. 465
16 ibid., p. 466
17 1 May 1940: Poland, Imperial War Museum Collection
18 27 September 1942; Klee, Dressen and Reiss, *Those Were the Days*, p. 163
19 19 October 1942; ibid., pp. 165, 171
20 4 October 1943; cited Fest, Joachim, *The Face of the Third Reich*, Penguin, Harmondsworth, 1972, p. 115

11

PLUNDER

After the first victories in the West, women had turned out in their thousands to cheer the conquering hero soldiers returning through the streets of Berlin, strewing flowers in their path and running forward to kiss the proud and grinning victors. With Poland subjugated, the mood was still buoyant, with the expectation that the war would soon be over, and the food shortages and daily anxieties of wartime life relieved. With each territorial advance, Germany plundered the occupied territories of raw materials, food and industrial goods.

They also plundered the populations. Poles and Russians, as well as Jews, were abducted into forced labour for the occupation authorities, chiefly as unskilled workers or servants. Prisoners of war and civilians from Poland, Russia and France were imported to the homeland to fill the acute shortage of manpower resulting from the conscription of German men. With Hitler refusing to authorize the conscription of the 'reserve army' of women despite entreaties from his ministers, and women reluctant to volunteer for work in war industries, the importation of foreign workers became an urgent necessity – although it had also been part of the expansion plan in the first place to use 'sub-human' races to service the master race. Already in 1941 there were over 3 million foreign labourers and prisoners of war working in the homeland, a figure that would rise to almost 8 million, of whom at least a million and a half were women.[1] Of the abducted Polish and Soviet workers, about half were women, with an average age of twenty.[2]

Almost all were forcibly deported from their countries. Polish, French, Belgian and Yugoslav prisoners of war were put to work mainly in construction and agriculture. When attempts to recruit civilian volunteers under the auspices of a Labour Procurement Agency failed in Eastern Europe, coercion was applied in the form of raids on towns and villages to round up men and women for transportation to the homeland. Mindful of the implications of importing 'racially inferior' Slavs, there was initial reluctance to deploy Russian prisoners of war in the homeland. By the end of 1941, 60 per cent of the almost three and a half million Soviet prisoners of war had died in captivity. As the labour shortage threatened a crisis, Göring agreed to use them in the workforce, after conceding that '"the Russian" could hump rocks and live off cats and dogs'. As Michael Burleigh points out, their deployment meant they could repatriate other foreign workers who 'ate more and produced less', and Russians could work on railways, in arms factories, construction, agriculture and the mines, and be herded into camps and work in groups 'with no disciplinary sanctions other than reduction of rations or execution'.[3]

Russian civilians were then coerced, though propaganda films made strenuous attempts to suggest that women and girls had come voluntarily after being offered attractive paid employment in the Reich. One Ukrainian woman described the process:

> It commenced with the arrival of a German called Graf Spreti in February 1942 who came to requisition labour. The Germans held a large meeting in a cinema. A crowd of people went along to see what was going on. Spreti said: 'I would like you citizens of Uman to go voluntarily to Germany to assist the German armed forces.' He promised us paradise. But we already knew what to make of such promises, and asked: 'What will happen if we don't want to go?' Graf Spreti replied: 'In that case we will politely demand despite this that you go.' That was on 10 February. Two days later they went from house to house and took away all the young people. They took us to a big school and at five o'clock in the morning to the station. There they shoved us into railway wagons, which were then bolted. The journey became a nightmare lasting several weeks.[4]

By the end of 1942, 1.7 million Russian civilians or prisoners of war were forced labourers in Germany.

Most foreign labourers lived in huts and camps, and were paid a pittance – if paid at all – to work on farms, in factories or as household servants. One recipient of foreign labour, Elisabeth von Stahlenberg, noted in her diary: 'It looks as if I am going to have a Slav *Dienstmädchen* [servant girl]. I have received the "conditions of work" leaflet which says they have no free time and can only go out if it is in connection with household tasks. They are not allowed to go to Church. I wonder how long before the actual slave follows the instructions on how to treat her.'[5]

Contact between foreign labourers and the German population was severely restricted, and amounted to a racial apartheid. Socialist Elly Napp recalls one encounter in Hamburg:

In a side street I was asked by a young woman, who I immediately recognized as a foreign worker by her snow-white headscarf, whether I could tell her where the Kieferstrasse was. And because I lived on the corner, I said, 'Well, it's on my way, just come along with me.' And she said to me in perfect German that I was not allowed to speak to her and certainly not walk with her because she was a Russian. And I said, 'That's ridiculous, it's rubbish.' I said, 'If you ask me for directions, then I have to show you the way, so just come along.' And she said that she had done her duty, she had told me what she had to say to me. And we had a very nice chat. I asked her where she had learnt her German and she said she had learnt it at school. And when I asked her whether she was here voluntarily, she said, no, she hadn't come there by choice. Lorries had arrived in the morning and picked up all the young people and driven them away. She hadn't even had a chance to say goodbye to her distraught mother.

Wilhelmine Haferkamp, a mother of ten living outside Aachen, refused to accept the sanctions against contact with the racial 'enemy'. She took pity on the foreign labourers who were set to work on a construction site digging draining ditches just outside her home. 'It was *cold* outside,' she told Alison Owings, 'and every day I cooked a big pot of milk soup for the children. Nice and hot. Got a lot of milk on the children's ration cards... And I looked out of the window and pointed to the "bandolios" [labourers] that I was putting something in the hallway. They were afraid to get out of the ditches and they wanted to eat it.' She went to the watchman and told him to turn a blind eye because 'it hurts me in my soul, I can't sleep the whole night if I have to pour away the soup and the men freeze there. He looked at me and said, "You are an obstinate dame. Go ahead and do what you have to but I have seen *nothing*." Then I made the soup... and put it in the hall with a ladling spoon and then I pointed to it. One by one they jumped out of the ditches and took the big ladling spoon.'

One day her husband got a card from the Party summoning him to the Party office. 'And they said, "Listen, your wife is doing fine things. How can she feed [the word was *füttern*, meaning to fodder, as in animals] our enemies?" "*Ja*, well, I can't do anything about it, I'm not always at home, I don't see it." When he returned he was furious: he really yelled at me, he said, "You will land me in the *devil's kitchen* if you keep doing that. And I am a Party member."' But Frau Haferkamp continued. 'They were so *cold,* so cold. They [the Nazis] came a couple of times and said to my husband, "Listen, Herr Haferkamp, if your wife keeps doing that, *ne*? Then she'll get a warning."' Frau Haferkamp was unfazed, and fed them something different each time.[6]

Among foreign workers there was a hierarchy of treatment. An eighteen-year-old French woman who volunteered for work in Germany was treated at the top end of the scale, but saw the inferior conditions for eastern workers. She worked at an IG Farben factory in Frankfurt Hoechst as a labourer, working a twelve-hour day starting with a march of several kilometres to the factory from the workers' camp, and supplied with only primitive work clothes. Everywhere she went there were signs saying 'Germans only' or 'Foreigners and dogs forbidden' and they were not allowed to sit in trams. Eastern workers were not allowed out at all. She was supposed to be paid the same as German workers, 'but the deductions were so large that, for example, I only got 8 RM for two weeks. And the eastern workers got nothing at all.' At every level distinctions were made. She got sheets on her bed 'to make it clear that we were treated as human beings'. The eastern workers got only straw and a blanket – 'they were considered to be sub-human'. When she found that the eastern workers were being fed rotten food, she complained and was sent to join them. They had the hardest work: 'We used to carry pieces of sulphur from one plant to another, often quite a distance. We only had gloves and had to press it to our chests which burned our skin.'[7]

Treatment of foreign workers depended largely on production demands. When need was greatest, rations were increased marginally to improve productivity rather than from any humanitarian impulse. To begin with, eastern women workers who became pregnant were despatched home, having ceased to have any productive value and to avoid the cost of caring for them. Some women got themselves pregnant in order to be sent home. In July 1943 Himmler reversed this directive, stating that they should now be sent back to work as soon as possible after the birth, due to 'the urgent priority for labour provision'. During the birth they must be segregated from German women, and their offspring cared for in 'infant care units of the simplest kind'; they must 'on no account be looked after in German institutions, be admitted to German children's homes, or otherwise grow up or be educated with German children'.[8] From 1943, abortion – illegal for Aryan women – was encouraged for Polish and Russian women. If it was too late, their children might be deposited in 'collection centres' where they were vulnerable to starvation or lethal medical injection. Those who were deemed 'racially valuable' were removed from their mothers and offered to German foster-parents, in the same way as 'racially valuable' children were abducted from parents in occupied territories under the Lebensborn programme.[9]

Fraternization with the German population brought increasing penalties, especially when it involved members of the opposite sex. Under a 1939 decree for safeguarding German military potential, unauthorized association with prisoners of war, specifically sexual intercourse, was made punishable by a heavy prison sentence. Arbitrary sanctions were used against women who had sexual relations with foreign workers. Women had their heads shaved by local townspeople and were publicly humiliated, often at the instigation of local Party activists. In Osnabrück in August 1940, an eighteen-year-old employed as a kitchen maid in the POW hospital at Lingen confessed to having sexual intercourse with Poles. 'On the instructions of the Kreisleiter, SA men cut off the kitchen-maid's hair in the Adolf-Hitler-Platz at Lingen, in the presence of a sizeable crowd. The girl was then handed over to the Gestapo.'[10] Similar incidents of public pillorying of women occurred all over Germany, though it decreased after the middle of the war when such contacts, especially with Europeans such as French and Dutch men, appeared less problematic. When the Gestapo took a hand, women who had erred from their 'racial instincts' were tried in Special Courts and sent to concentration camps. Up to 10,000 German women a year landed up in concentration camps for the crime of forbidden contact with foreign men, and they made up nearly a quarter of judgements for political crimes in 1940–41.[11] In Ravensbruck concentration camp, the women were known as 'bed politicals'.

The foreign men involved were punished by lynching, or summary shooting by the Gestapo, for having besmirched the purity of German blood. In a hamlet in the Bayerisches Wald, a peasant girl, Adeline G., became pregnant by a Polish former prisoner of war who had stayed on in the district. Two months after giving birth in February 1941, she was sentenced to ten months' imprisonment by a juvenile court. Her lover, Julian Majlca, was hanged by the Gestapo in a neighbouring wood, and his workmates forced to file past the corpse. A Polish agricultural labourer was removed from court custody and immediately strung up by the Gestapo, while another Pole, Jarek, who had relations with two girls, was hanged from a tree near the village in Bavaria and, on Himmler's personal orders, 119 Poles were ordered to file past the corpse.[12] By comparison, German men having sexual relations with foreign women suffered little more than official disapproval.

The penalties did not deter either men or women, who, out of loneliness or frustration or just mutual attraction, sought sexual pleasure and cared not a jot about 'racial infiltration'. The number of proceedings increased year by year, standing in 1942 at over 9000 cases known to the authorities.[13] Men and women thrown together in the workplace, and in the same household on farms, were vulnerable to temptation, especially when husbands and fathers were away. By 1944, almost half of agricultural work was done by foreign labourers. They were not supposed to eat or socialize with the farmer's household, but in rural areas this was more difficult to police than in urban areas, where labourers were segregated, though in Berlin and many cities around half of foreign labourers were housed in private homes.[14] By 1942, SD [Security Police] Reports were expressing alarm at the alleged suscep-tibility of German women to foreign, especially French and Polish, labourers and prisoners of war in every part of the Reich: 'The deploy-ment of millions of foreign workers has resulted in a steady increase in sexual relations with German women,' declared a report in January 1942, which expressed alarm that 'the threat of infiltration of German blood', and the estimated 20,000 illegitimate children who would be the consequence, was having 'a not inconsiderable negative effect on the mood of the people'.[15]

Farmers' wives were not immune to the temptation to form liaisons with male workers, who, some claimed in mitigation, had become essential to the running of the farm. The Stuttgart Public Prosecutor explained to the Reich Minister of Justice in 1943 that many employers, especially women, are afraid of foreigners who may threaten to with-draw their labour in the face of stricter discipline and, 'in order to please the foreigners, grant them various comforts, and, in spite of official prohibitions, let them eat at the same table, simply to prevent damage to their business'. Frequently, farmers' wives accused of prohibited sexual contact 'plead under questioning that they gave in to the prisoner of war so as not to lose his labour'.[16]

The plea of coercion was the most effective excuse for women accused of 'racial pollution', and the one used by a Silesian farmer's wife and member of the National Socialist Women's Association, a mother of two with her husband away at the front, who became pregnant by an East European employee who had since fled. 'Early in June he came to me and insisted that I have sexual intercourse with him or he would run off and leave me just at the busiest time of the year. He went on and on at me, and since I'm all alone with my sister-in-law on a 30-acre farm, and B. was a good worker, I allowed him to seduce me.'[17]

The morals of young German women and girls was a source of continuing anxiety. An SD Report in January 1942, assessing the racial implications of the epidemic of forbidden contact, concluded that 'one is often dealing with the less valuable part of the German population... often women with a pronounced sexuality, who find foreigners interesting and therefore make it easy for the latter to approach them'. They had observed 'a large number of German girls of unrestrained character, especially those working far from their home town, who throw themselves into the arms of foreigners'; and 'girls of German blood running after Czech workers'.[18] But they later conceded, 'They are by no means all of them women of loose morals. Among the accused there are respectable farmers' daughters from good families with no sexual experience, and wives of soldiers who have been happily married for many years, many of them women with several children. As soon as Frenchmen are found in more responsible positions, typists, housekeepers and members of the intelligentsia appear as the accused.' One case was cited of 'a 23-year-old telephonist from a bourgeois background', who made up to a French prisoner of war because he had 'dark hair and was a Latin type'.[19] Was something wrong with their 'racial training', or were blond Aryan males simply not up to scratch?

The issue exercised the leaders of the nation's youth. Jutta Rüdiger, the BDM leader, was concerned that in wartime, 'German girls tended to be attracted to the strange man, the foreigner. And von Schirach [head of the Hitler Youth] said to us once, "If there's a nice German boy standing next to her, and a horrible ugly Balkan man, she will turn towards the Balkan man." And we addressed ourselves to this, of course.' She amplified the propaganda: 'I said to them: "The only one for you to marry is the most brave, heroic German soldier, or the European man, who is the same type as us... Your honour lies in being faithful to the blood of your race."' By this time, the complex emotional exigencies of war were taking over from the simple slogans of race theory.

War Work

The use of foreign labour on a vast scale had saved married women from being conscripted into the workforce. It did not solve the labour shortage, however. By 1943, 11 million men had been called up; at this time Hitler was told by all his labour advisers that the situation was becoming critical. Single women had already been shifted from consumer to war-related industries. Voluntary recruitment of married women had been a marked failure; many women returned to the home when faced with juggling the reduction in their separation allowances and increased work hours with running a household, queuing for food and the daily aggravation of just getting by. The employment of women *decreased* by 540,000 between July 1939 and March 1940.[20] Most working-class women continued in employment out of financial need, but middle-class women resisted it. Hitler also knew that women's conscription to war work was unpopular among their men at the front as it was identified with a loss of status for their wives.

Despite fears about the possible damage to morale, in January Hitler caved in and decreed that all women between the ages of seventeen and forty-five were to register to be deployed in war work. The results were disappointing. A large number were exempted – pregnant women, women with two children under the age of fourteen, women working in agriculture and the civil service. Where possible, they opted for higher-paid desk jobs which did nothing to solve the crisis in industry. Of the 3 million who registered by June 1943, fewer than 500,000 additional women joined the workforce, and a substantial number of these had found reason to leave by the end of the year. By May 1944, only 1.2 per cent more women were working than before the war, compared to 50 per cent increases in both Britain and the USA in the same period.[21]

Young women had been compelled to do a Year of Duty since 1939; 336,000 women were tied into this scheme, effectively a draft, but it did little to solve the industrial labour shortage. They worked on farms, where there was also a labour shortfall, or on household assignments. With the introduction in 1941 of a compulsory six months' auxiliary war service (*Kriegshilfdienst*) for girls after the completion of their Year of Duty, 130,000 were conscripted for work in armaments factories, where they were paid a pittance and lived in barracks. Despite resistance, including from Hitler, to the 'militarization' of women, they began from 1942 to replace men in the armed forces where they were assigned to military duties as 'Female Wehrmacht Auxiliaries'. They were not required to wear uniform at first, since 'The "female soldier" does not accord with our National Socialist view of womanhood.'[22] This changed, as did so much of the National Socialist view of women in wartime. Gertrud Scholtz-Klink, the *Frauenschaft* leader, had opposed women serving in the army, declaring, 'I have sons in the war, I will protect my daughters.'[23] Jutta Rüdiger, head of the BDM, adamantly opposed the idea, proposed later by Bormann, to form women's battalions:

> I said simply, 'That is out of the question. Our girls can go right up to the front and help them there, and they can go every-where, but to have a women's battalion with weapons in their hands fighting on their own, that I do not support. It's out of the question. If the Wehrmacht can't win this war, then battal-ions of women won't help either.' And the Reich Youth Leader said to me, 'Well, that's your responsibility,' and I said indeed it was. I said women should give life and not take it. That's why we were born.

Rüdiger relented only at the end, when the Russians were advancing on Berlin, and she instructed BDM leaders to learn to use pistols for self-defence in emergencies.

Young Labour Service women were assigned increasingly to military duties, and soon put into uniform. Elisabeth L. worked for six months in a grenade factory and was paid one mark a day. She was then drafted into the army on the Soviet border, where she learnt to operate a telex, and later transferred to Berlin to be trained as a radio operator.[24] Some women volunteered as more jobs in the armed services opened up, because they saw it as an adventurous occupation. Elisabeth Techen had worked in her parents' shop until she saw a couple of women in Luftwaffe uniform in the street and enquired about joining. She was one of the few in 1942 selected to go on a training course, where she lived communally under Luftwaffe discipline with a mix of other women. To her surprise, she discovered she had an aptitude for languages, so was sent on an English language and then a typing course, and spent the rest of the war in a signals communications intelligence centre near the Dutch border, listening in to RAF pilots taking off for raids in Germany and translating such phrases as 'I-India to H-Harry – get down, old thing, will you? You're holding up the whole bloody show!' and 'Mayday, Mayday! We are about twenty miles out and going in now. I'll leave my key down so you can get a fix!' Elisabeth Techen recalls, 'I was very excited and in somewhat of a state as I listened in to this drama. I had no idea at all that I would be involved in such things.'[25]

As the war dragged on, more and more women were recruited for secretarial and communications work in the services, mainly on their Labour Year, which in 1944 was extended to eighteen months and then made indefinite. Those with nursing qualifications were directed to the Red Cross at home and work in field hospitals in the occupied territories. Women were also enlisted for searchlight duties and worked on anti-aircraft guns by the end of the war. Erna Tietz, aged twenty-two, was in early 1945 responsible for teams of young women anti-aircraft gunners (*Flakwaffenhilferin*) handling the powerful 'eighty-eight' gun. Her identification papers stated that she was on 'special assignment' because 'one wanted to avoid that the public learn that women were assigned to weapons. That, one wanted to veil.'[26] Women soldiers did not fit the Nazi view of women. Younger BDM girls had their work cut out, helping in the harvest, handing out food ration cards, collecting money for the Winter Relief Fund, helping soldiers with washing and mending clothes, looking after the wounded and tending soldiers' graves. They were also enlisted in a scheme to keep up the troops' morale by corresponding with soldiers at the front. Hedwig Ertl wrote to many soldiers: 'It was a very emotional thing. It didn't matter whether it was someone close to you. We were writing a lot of letters to unknown soldiers, soldiers who otherwise wouldn't receive letters from anyone else, soldiers who didn't have any relatives. And they would reply, and sometimes very beautiful relationships grew out of that. And most of them ended on the battlefield, but that was the way it was. The letters were very important.'

Deportation

From the beginning of the war, the position of the Jews remaining in Germany deteriorated rapidly. In September 1941, the pauperization of the Jewish population through expropriations and evictions, and the accumulating humiliations in daily life through the removal of all liberties, civil and otherwise, was compounded by the introduction of the compulsory

Yellow Star of David to be worn by all Jews. 'The Führer has allowed me to introduce a kind of marking for the Jews,' Goebbels reported jubilantly on 20 August 1941, writing in his diary: 'Every Jew will have to wear this sign. With this they are made visible and will be driven out of our cities pretty soon.' According to SD Reports, the measure met with general approval, though for some it did not go far enough – *Mischlinge* should be included as well as full Jews. But there were also signs of disapproval and some sympathy in the population. Inge Deutschkron, living in Berlin, was devastated at the discrimination signified by the Yellow Star, but also experienced small acts of kindness: 'There were people who looked at me with hate; there were others whose glances betrayed sympathy; and others again looked away spontaneously.'[27]

Before then, life for Jews had reached the edge of the endurable. Banned from restaurants, cinemas and other public places, deprived of driving licences, forbidden to use public telephones, most were confined to home. Here they faced regular, often daily Gestapo raids to check whether they had banned radio sets or forbidden foods, woollen clothing or furs or household pets – all banned to Jews since early 1942. They were denied clothing rations. Their food rations were reduced to half that of the rest of the population and, from 4 July 1940, they were allowed to purchase food only between 4 and 5 o'clock in the afternoon.

Lilli Gentzen, as a thirteen-year-old working in her father's butcher's shop, witnessed their plight.

The Jews could only shop between 4.00 and 5.00pm. They all wore the Yellow Star, and all their ration cards had 'Jew Jew Jew' printed over them. They only got half of the rations the others got. And we always asked ourselves, how can these people live on these rations? Because it was already so little food. Once a week we made sausages. The sausage was cooked in a huge pot, and the result was some nice sausage stock, and all the customers came to get it because there were a few fatty bits in it and it was free... And my mother always felt very sorry for the Jews. We always made potato salad for which you didn't need any ration cards, and we sold it in little paper bags, and the Jews would buy a lot of this salad.

The deportation of Jews from the Reich to the East was authorised by Hitler in September 1941. A few days later, Goebbels had recorded ecstatically in his diary for 20 August 1941:

> Furthermore the Führer has given the green light that I can deport Jews from Berlin to the new territories in the East as soon as the eastern campaign is over. Berlin will have to become a city clean of Jews. It is a scandal that there are still 78,000 Jews in the capital of the German people, parasites. They not only destroy the picturesque street life but they also create a bad mood. You can only stop it altogether by doing away with them. We have to sort out the Jewish problem without any sentimentality. [28]

In October, several thousand were sent from Berlin, Krefeld and other cities to Lodz, the preliminary to their eventual deportation to the death camps in Poland. From then on, the Jewish population lived in fear of 'evacuation'. The full enormity of their fate was barely comprehended. They were told they were being evacuated to 'settlements' in the East. A propaganda film showed Jewish 'settlers' in the new 'Jewish city' and 'cultural centre' of Theresienstadt, which boasted library facilities, concerts and theatre performances, pleasant airy streets and regular food, though the sleeping accommodation looked suspiciously like a crowded barracks. It was to be a staging post on the way to extermination.

In January 1942, Nazi leaders agreed on the 'Final Solution'. The comprehensive programme for the systematic killing of European Jewry was put into action. It was accompanied by a renewed blast of violent anti-Semitic propaganda. The killing began immediately in Belzec, Treblinka and Sobibor. In his diary for 27 March 1942, Goebbels reported that Hitler remained 'pitiless' regarding the 'Jewish Question':

> The Jews are now being deported to the east. A fairly barbaric procedure, not to be described in any greater detail, is being used here, and not much more remains of the Jews themselves. In general it can probably be established that 60 per cent of them must be liquidated, while only 40 per cent can be

put to work... No sentimentality can be allowed to prevail in these things. If we didn't fend them off, the Jews would annihilate us. It's a life-and-death struggle between the Aryan race and the Jewish bacillus. No other government and no other regime could produce the strength to solve this question generally. Here, too, the Führer is the unswerving champion and spokesman of a radical solution.

Transports began in July to the newly completed and largest camp at Auschwitz-Birkenau. The operation was top-secret, but the deportations were not. Gertrud Draber was among many who witnessed the forced removal of Jews. She worked at the Siemens factory in Berlin, which still employed Jewish women. One morning she arrived at work:

It was early in the morning before eight o'clock, before we started our shifts. People were flooding by, on their way to their offices. And I saw not one, at least two lorries had turned up and they were open, with no covers. Many women were there being herded towards the open trucks and pushed up – hauled – on to them. These women were wearing the Jewish Star.

They were yelling, and crying. And I heard all the women screaming for their children. 'I have to get back to my children!' 'I have to fetch my children!' 'I have to go home to my children!' They were packed like sardines on to these lorries, and they were crying and yelling and fighting it and they were in such pain and sorrow. But nobody in charge took any notice of them. For me, for all of us, it was horrific. We were so sad and disbelieving, you couldn't believe it could happen, that it was real. Then we were ordered, 'Keep walking!' 'Don't stand here!' That's how it was. And we had to walk on. Once you've seen it, you can't forget something like that. It burned itself into my mind.

Many others noted the disappearance of Jewish families from their neighbourhoods, but few asked where they had gone, beyond supposing they had emigrated, or gone to settle in the 'East'. This was the official version put out by the Propaganda department – even as it churned out the unceasing tide of hysterical vitriol against the Jews. Jewish professor Victor Klemperer noted in his diary the increase in transports, and gathered information from within the Jewish community and outside. On 28 November 1941, he received news of large-scale deportations from major cities: 'One knows nothing precisely, not who is to go [on them], not when and not where [they are going].' By March 1942, he had heard of Auschwitz – a camp with a reputation 'as the most dreadful concentration camp... Death after a few days'. By February 1943, Klemperer believed that 'from now on it is no longer to be expected that any Jews will return alive from Poland... After all, it has long been reported that many evacuees do not even arrive in Poland alive. They are gassed in cattle trucks during the trip.'[29] Rumours circulated. Among the non-Jewish population, many chose not to ask any further questions.

For Jewish families it was a period of intense fear and uncertainty: 'Now, one was no longer sure of one's life even for a minute within one's own four walls, and every meal could be the last,' Camilla Neumann remembered. When rumours were circulating in 1943 that the Nazis were rounding up Jews from factories, Camilla woke her husband to warn him not to go to the factory next day: 'And as always he tried to calm me and said, "Don't worry so much, it doesn't have to be exactly tomorrow they start." ...After a goodnight kiss I went to bed with a heavy heart. It was our last goodnight kiss.' He was rounded up next day. 'In a completely indescribable state I now walked the streets at random... Things were going round in my head and my only thought was Ludwig... I was considering how I might help Ludwig, but I saw that I was powerless. This powerlessness made me frantic with rage.'[30] Many people committed suicide.

Rita Kuhn was among the large number of Jews rounded up for forced labour in the Reich in 1942. She counted as Jewish although her mother was a Christian who had converted to Judaism on marriage. In February 1943 she was arrested from her workplace, an ammunitions factory, in the 'Factory Action', instigated by Goebbels to empty Berlin of the remaining Jews and declare it 'Jew-free'. It was ten minutes past seven in the morning. 'All of a sudden the whole place was full with SS men, rounding up the Jewish workers. They were shouting *"Juden raus!"* [Jews out!]' They were loaded on to trucks and driven to a build-ing with thousands of others where the women were separated from the men. 'I didn't care what happened to me. I really didn't care. I was numb. I knew that if I have to die, I am going to have to die... You need that inter-nal defence, or armour to put on... The only thing that troubled me was my parents. Also not knowing what happened to them. Being separated.'

Asked by Alison Owings if she knew she was going to certain death, she replied, 'Yes' – if not immediately, then eventually, and added: 'We really didn't know what was happening. [We] knew Jews were dying of disease and starvation.' But she 'did not know of crematoria or shoot-ings... until after the war.' She didn't know of gassings – 'not at all'.

In the building, they were kept waiting all day and into the night and then told to line up. A selection process was going on. Rows of SS men were checking papers, and sending people to the left or right. 'Most went to the left... That meant to the camp.' When her turn came, the SS asked about her mother: 'Is she Aryan? Do you live with her?' Because her mother was Aryan, she was released, but a week later, the Nazis arrested Rita, her father and her brother. Her mother had gone to get their ration cards and returned, saying that they had to fetch them themselves. Her father knew what this meant, and told them to put on an extra layer of clothes. When they arrived to fetch their ration cards, they were locked into a room. At one point Rita heard 'a woman crying outside wanting her children and not just wanting to see them, but "I want to *be* with them. I want to *go* with them." ...I didn't even recognize the voice. But my father said, "That is Mutti, our Mutti."' She was not allowed in. Then they were loaded on to trucks and Rita saw her mother. She 'just stood there. And we were on the truck. And there she was, wait-ing... I'll never forget my mother's face. Just white. And stony. By that time, everything had gone out of her. I mean, she couldn't even *say* anything to us. She could hardly wave. Anything.'[31]

They were taken again by lorry to a collection centre, but then, after a short time, released. She and her father were returned to forced labour on the railways. Their release was, she believes, connected to the only mass protest demonstration of the Third Reich, and the only protest against the deportation of the Jews. Aryan wives of Jewish husbands who had been rounded up for deportation took to the streets outside the

Rosenstrasse detention centre on 27 February 1943 and protested, shouting, 'We want our husbands back!' When they were ordered to disperse, they refused. Their courage grew. Other Germans joined them. When they were threatened with machine guns they stood firm as their ranks swelled to more than 1000 people, some now yelling, 'Murderer, murderer, murderer!' On 6 March Goebbels, Gauleiter of Berlin, caved in and ordered the release of the mixed-marriage men detained in Rosenstrasse. His concern, according to Eric Johnson in *The Nazi Terror*, was that women's morale might be affected. With an urgent need for female support, especially female labour, he wanted to avert public discussion of complaints and any grounds for unrest. It could open wider discussion of the deportations, which would also damage morale.[32]

Deportations continued, and Jews continued to work in slave labour factories. Vera Friedländer was arrested in 1943 as a teenager and forced to work in a shoe factory with Polish forced labourers. The workers did not produce anything. They repaired worn-out shoes. Nobody ever claimed them. Claudia Koonz recorded Vera's thoughts: 'What strange customers, she thought. They drop off their precious shoes before they are totally worn out – without tags, without instructions. How do they think they will ever get their shoes back in the midst of bombing raids? Vera asked herself, where are the clients? Only half-worn shoes, from all sorts of factories. Without quite saying it, Vera knew.'[33]

Jews record many deeds of kindness towards them, though there were also people, and not only zealous Party officials, denouncing them to the police for simple things like not wearing the Yellow Star. Some non-Jews helped Jews to hide. Alfred Meyerowitz was helped by a friend, Herr Sommer, who gave him the use of a small room on the top floor of his factory, where he had to observe total silence for fear of discovery by the Gestapo. When the Sommer family were bombed out and moved to the country, they took Alfred Meyerowitz and his wife with them and hid them in a summerhouse until the Russians arrived.

NOTES

1 Stephenson, Jill, 'Women, Motherhood and the Family in the Third Reich', in Michael Burleigh (ed.), *Confronting the Nazi Past: New Debates in German History*, Collins and Brown, London, 1996, p. 177

2 Kitchen, *Nazi Germany at War*, p. 153

3 Burleigh, *The Third Reich*, pp. 479, 551

4 ibid., p. 552

5 von Stahlenberg, *Nazi Lady*, diary entry 26 June 1942

6 Owings, *Frauen*, pp. 20–1

7 Noakes, 'Nazism and High Society', pp. 326–7

8 ibid., p. 327

9 Burleigh and Wippermann, *The Racial State*, p. 261

10 Bleuel, *Strength Through Joy*, p. 230

11 Heineman, *What Difference Does a Husband Make?*, pp. 57, 59

12 Bleuel, *Strength Through Joy*, p. 232

13 ibid., p. 233

14 Heineman, *What Difference Does a Husband Make?*, p. 56

15 Burleigh and Wippermann, *The Racial State*, p. 262

16 Stephenson, 'Women, Motherhood and the Family in the Third Reich', p. 180

17 Bleuel, *Strength Through Joy*, p. 235

18 Burleigh and Wippermann, *The Racial State*, pp. 262–3

19 ibid., p. 263

20 Heineman, *What Difference Does a Husband Make?*, p. 61

21 ibid., p. 63

22 Noakes, 'Nazism and High Society', p. 341 – OKW directive 22 June 1942

23 Cited Koonz, *Mothers in the Fatherland*, p. 398

24 Heineman, *What Difference Does a Husband Make?*, p. 65

25 Blandford, Edmund, *Under Hitler's Banner*, Airlife Publishing, Shrewsbury, p. 178

26 Owings, *Frauen*, p. 270

27 Kershaw, *Hitler: Nemesis*, p. 475

28 Goebbels, *Die Tagebücher von Joseph Goebbels*

29 Cited Johnson, *The Nazi Terror*, pp. 440–1

30 Camilla Neumann in Richardz (ed.), *Jewish Life in Germany*, pp. 436–43

31 Owings, *Frauen*, p. 461

32 Johnson, *The Nazi Terror*, pp. 423–5

33 Koonz, *Mothers in the Fatherland*, p. 382

12
BOMBED OUT

By the middle of 1942, optimism about an early end to the war was evaporating. The German offensive in Russia slowed down, casualties were mounting and it was increasingly clear to the leaders, and the population, that no end was in sight. Autumn counter-attacks by the Soviets at Stalingrad and by the Allies in North Africa successfully repulsed the German advances. In February 1943, after a crucifying struggle in appalling winter conditions, the German 6th Army at Stalingrad laid down its arms. The tide had turned, and the German people knew it. Attempts by Goebbels to massage the defeat as a strategic consolidation of forces were fruitless.

Morale had been at low ebb for some time, as food shortages, bombing raids and overwork bit into people's lives. Support for the Russian invasion had not been wholehearted even back in 1941. Goebbels had triumphantly proclaimed that the war would be over in eight weeks. Loyal Nazis believed him. But there was an undercurrent of dismay. Ilse Schmidt, then an Army typist, remembers her father's reaction when he heard the announcement of the invasion: 'He said spontaneously, "That's the end." He knew, as a soldier in the First World War, the huge vastness of Russia, the stone-hard earth where you couldn't even bury your dead, the earth was too hard. I was scared then.' According to SD Reports: 'Overworked and exhausted men and women do not see why the war must be carried further into Asia and Africa,' was the report from one region. People longed for a return to 'normality', not an extension of the conflict. The 'catastrophic state of provisions', anger at food shortages, high prices, wage conditions, and black market prof- iteering by Nazi officials were cited as reasons for discontent.[1]

As the casualty lists lengthened, anxiety about loved ones at the front increased. By March 1942, over a million of the 3.2 million troops who attacked the Soviet Union were either dead, captured or missing.[2] Very few indeed of the captured German soldiers survived. From autumn 1942, the situation at the front deteriorated rapidly. Soldiers' letters gave people at home a grim picture of horror and despair. Hitler insisted on overriding his generals' advice and refused to withdraw. In the intense cold of winter, supplies of food were running out, men were fighting hand to hand with Russians in the streets, starvation and disease were rife, and morale was at rock bottom. Emergency winter clothes donated through collections organized on the home front failed to get through. On 22 January, Field-Marshal Paulus, commander of the 6th Army, requested permission to surrender. Hitler rejected it. As a point of honour there could be no question of surrender. The Army was to stand fast 'to the last soldier and the last bullet'.[3]

Soldiers were given the opportunity in January to write last letters home. Most letters didn't reach the recipients as they were taken by the Army censors to be analysed for their attitude to the leadership. 'Please don't be sad and weep for me, when you receive this, my last letter,' one captain wrote to his wife. 'I'm standing here in an icy storm in a hopeless situation in the city of fate, Stalingrad. Encircled for months, we will tomorrow begin the last fight, man against man.' Another wrote: 'They're falling like flies, and no one bothers and buries them. Without arms and legs and without eyes, with stomachs ripped open, they lie around everywhere.' Soldiers did not hold back their feelings: 'I love you, and you love me, and so you should know the truth. It is in this letter. The truth is the knowledge of the hardest struggle in a hopeless situation. Misery, hunger, cold, resignation, doubt, despair and horrible dying... I'm not cowardly, just sad that I can give no greater proof of my bravery than to die for such pointlessness, not to say crime... Don't be so quick to forget me.'[4]

Soldiers were right in thinking: 'We're completely alone, without help from outside. Hitler has left us in the lurch' – and the leaders paid the price. The censors found only 2.1 per cent remained favourable to the leadership; 57 per cent rejected it; around 30 per cent were by then indifferent. A few tried to cling on to the faith, even as it was everywhere draining away. 'The Führer solidly promised to get us out of here. That's been read out to us and we firmly believed it. I still believe it today, because I have to believe in something... I have believed my entire life, or at least eight years of it, always in the Führer and his word. It's horrible how they're in doubt here, and shameful to hear words spoken that you can't contradict because they're in line with facts.'[5] At Stalingrad, 91,000 prisoners were taken; only 5000 survived the war.

Belief in Hitler himself was waning for the first time. SD reports found the nation 'deeply shaken' by the defeat. Doubts emerged 'about whether the leadership was fully capable of grasping the enormous problems created by the war and of mastering them'. Hitler was blamed. 'Hitler has lied to us for three months,' people fumed, remembering the optimistic reports then, compared with the present debacle. Many no longer believed the war could be won, despite Goebbels's bold pronouncements of 'Total War' and Hitler's now sometimes lacklustre speeches. The leaders' credibility had been critically undermined. Hitler was seen less and less in public. He spent his time at his headquarters at the 'Wolf's Lair' in East Prussia, or at his mountain retreat at the Berghof.

By November 1943, however, SD reports indicated an improvement. The public were making a clear distinction between Hitler and his subordinates in its assessment of professional performance and personal behaviour. 'Faith in the Führer is virtually unshaken', especially among women who took the line that he would definitely sort it out if he knew about it all. There was a marked decline of trust in the rest of the leadership due to 'the failure of promises and prophecies to be fulfilled', and the belief that they were not taking their share of the nation's sacrifice and, moreover, using their position to buy up land, and provide themselves with private air raid shelters; generally, 'they preach water but drink wine'. Faith in the media had suffered from their attempts 'to disguise the true picture when the situation was serious or to play down ominous developments, for example, by portraying withdrawal as a success'. More and more people were listening to 'news from neutral and enemy states', despite the risks.[6]

As the war continued to go badly, women's law morale was a cause for increasing concern. After Stalingrad, Hitler had reluctantly agreed to conscript women aged seventeen to forty-five to war work, despite fearing this would adversely affect morale. The actual damage stemmed from a multitude of causes. Women were 'calm, but quite depressed' by November 1943. Concern about heavy fighting and continual withdrawals in the east was one reason, especially among those who had relatives fighting in the field. Women supported the Führer, but criticized the other leaders. Young women showed little interest in the day-to-day events of the war, were anxious to avoid anything that reminded them of the war, and ignored radio programmes, newsreels and newspapers. All women were preoccupied with the daily practical issues, particularly shortages of food – potatoes and vegetables at that time – with mothers suffering sleepless nights because 'they often don't know what they are going to put on the table'.

Food shortages persisted through 1942 and 1943 with frequent ration cuts of basic essentials. Carrying on daily life became increasingly difficult. With different shopping hours, shortages of household goods and clothes, and unfriendly service in the shops, 'shopping is frequently like running the gauntlet' (18 November 1943). This was compounded by the overwhelming fact of women's lives – the chaos and destruction caused by bombing raids.

The war had come to the home front.

*　　*　　*

Allied bombing raids during 1941 had disrupted Germany's main cities, but on nothing like the scale that was to befall them later. The first major raid in the Allied campaign of mass bombing began over Lübeck on 28–29 March 1942. Around 8000 incendiaries were dropped as well as 'liquid bombs' made of petrol and rubber with high explosives. The population showed 'a really remarkable composure' despite the extreme destruction and loss of life, SD reports noted. The BDM, the Women's Welfare organization (NSV) and the Hitler Youth were praised for their 'tireless commitment' in providing food, clothing and care for the injured and homeless' (9 April 1942). Despite initial food shortages due to destruction of shops and restaurants, canteens were set up and food brought in from other cities. The next day, tradespeople opened up their shops and, on the Monday after the Saturday bombing, 70 per cent of employees turned up for work. But there was anger and annoyance. When the official communiqué stated there were 'some losses', angry Lübeck inhabitants declared their faith in the credibility of Wehrmacht communiqués had dropped to near zero.[7]

On 30 May 1942, the Allies targeted Cologne city centre with an arsenal of explosives: 100,000 inhabitants lost their homes, and the face of the city was transformed – though, miraculously, the cathedral remained standing. Munich, Bremen, Düsseldorf and Duisburg were next. Hitler's apartment in Munich was badly damaged. While he was pleased to share equally the experience of the Munich victims, he also thought it would have, in Ian Kershaw's words, 'a salutary effect in waking up the population to the realities of war'; moreover, he told Goebbels in August, destroying old buildings would make the postwar modernizing town planners' task all that easier.[8] Hitler never visited bombed-out cities to keep up morale; that task was left almost solely to Goebbels.

The bombs pounded German cities day and night with ever greater ferocity over the following years. Their target was civilian morale as much as Germany's industrial and war-making capacity. The Luftwaffe seemed unable to stem the damage, which further dented confidence in the leadership.

From 1943, women's lives were disrupted by the screech of air raid sirens and the rush to the air raid shelter, cellar or bunker at any time of the day or night. By March, all major cities were targets – forty-three cities were bombed between March and July – and the Allies' incendiary bombs were starting fires as well as destroying buildings. In Hamburg, Mathilde Wolff-Mönkeberg wrote: 'No one beds down for sleep these days. We sit stiffly on hard chairs, ready to jump up at a moment's notice, and superficial conversation barely hides the inner tension.'[9]

Ursula von Kardorff, passing buckets along a line in a Berlin street, noted that 1700 fires had been started across the city. Schoolgirl Lilli Gentzen remembers how, in Berlin, 'We didn't get dressed any more. We went to bed in our clothes, and we had everything packed in the so-called air-raid bag: a torch, biscuits, the passports and documents... Because I was young I had nerves of steel. I made everyone else nervous because I did my pearl embroidery. The others used to say, Miss Lilli, stop this, you are making us all nervous.' Her parents' house was bombed out when she was sheltering in the cellar: 'We heard an enormous bang. The lights started flickering, the plaster started to come down the walls and we simply put our heads down... When we came out of the cellar I thought I was dreaming. Just now there had been a four-storey house and suddenly it's just a heap of rubble. But the main thought was, we are alive. That was the most important thing. We didn't think about the things we had lost. That worry was for later.'

Sometimes there was more than one raid in one night. Lilli Gentzen was mad about films: 'I remember there was one film which I saw in three or four stages. Every time I sat down to watch it, there was an air raid and we had to go into the cellar. And then they let you back in to continue to watch the film.'

One mother in Cologne, Käthe Schlecter-Bonnesen, whose husband had been killed at the front, went into town and dropped her two children off at a kindergarten, where she thought they would be safer. There was an air raid, and she rushed back to them, to find a bomb had hit the kindergarten:

At first I looked in the bunker where the children went during an alarm, but I didn't find them. I saw other children, but I couldn't find my own two... Later, I heard that a whole group of people had been buried in a house in Nibelungen Street, including children from the kindergarten... More and more people were pulled out of the cellar of that hosue... My two children were pulled out dead. You could hardly see any injuries on them. They only had a small drop of blood on their noses and large bloody scrapes on the backs of their heads. I was in a state of total shock. I wanted to scream, right then and there I wanted to scream, 'You Nazis, you murderers!' A neighbour, who had only been released from a concentration camp a few days before, grabbed my arm and pulled me aside. He said, 'Do you want to get yourself arrested too?'[10]

The list of civilian casualties lengthened. Some 305,000 Germans were killed and 780,000 injured in air raids.[11] Firestorms in Hamburg, Berlin and later Dresden wreaked unimaginable slaughter. Hamburg had already been bombed on the three nights previous to 28 July 1943, when dry weather conditions combined with the incendiary onslaught to produce a firestorm that destroyed most of the city and left tens of thousands of its citizens dead. Some died asphyxiated in cellars, some from burns from phosphorous attached to their clothes, others as their bodies shrank from the extreme heat that engulfed the city. Hamburg's Police Chief reported: 'The cores of the most ferocious fire areas sucked the fires from the smaller areas towards them. As a result... fires in the smaller areas were pumped up as if by bellows, since the central suction effects of the largest... fires had the effect of pulling in the surrounding masses of fresh air. In consequence, all the fires grew into a single huge conflagration...' The raid covered an area 5.5 kilometres long and 4 kilometres wide. The action of fire-fighters was rendered all but useless. Everything was on fire. 'The destruction is so devastating that, in the case of many people, there is literally nothing left of them.' In one air raid shelter, doctors could only estimate the number of occupants – about 250–300 – on the basis of a large layer of ash. The report went on: 'The streets were covered with hundreds of corpses. Mothers with their children, men, old people, burnt, charred, unscathed and clothed, naked and pale like wax bodies in a shop window, they lay in every position, quiet and peaceful, or tense with the death throes written in the expression on their faces.'[12]

Elly Napp was in Dresden with her child on the night of the firestorm on 13–14 February 1945: 'I had my child on my lap. Opposite was a school, which was a burning inferno. I don't know whether you ever experienced a fire-storm. It was horrific. We didn't dare go out into the street, because we would be sucked into the fire-storm. And I sat there with my child on my lap, and thought, what do you do with this child when the fire starts here in the cellar?' Before the next raid, it was calmer, 'but we heard a train full of ammunition exploding, one wagon after another. And before we could get any rest, at 1.30am the next raid started and the whole of the old town was reduced to rubble and ashes.

All the bridges over the river were destroyed, and everything along the riverbank of the Elbe was alight with flames. It was dreadful.' In Dresden, 35–40,000 civilians died.

Millions left the cities after air raids. Hamburg was emptied of half its population after the firestorm in 1943. Mathilde Wolff-Mönckerberg described the aftermath in a letter to her children:

> There was no gas, no electricity, not a drop of water, neither the lift nor the telephone was working. It is hard to imagine the panic and chaos. Each one for himself, only one idea: flight... There were no trams, no underground, no rail traffic to the suburbs. Most people loaded some belongings on carts, bicycles, prams or carried things on their backs and started on foot just to get away, to escape... anything rather than stay in the catastrophic inferno of the city.[13]

After Dresden, Elly Napp collected a few possessions and, at seven o'clock next morning, fled the town with her daughter, mother and fifteen-year-old sister. They walked until lunch-time, when there was the third raid on Dresden, which they saw in the distance: 'and for us that was the first time we actually saw the burning town. A cellar where we took refuge was on a little hill, and the whole hill was shaking from the continuous bombing.' She had lost everything and, meanwhile, her husband Kurt had gone missing in action. But the experience induced unexpected feelings:

> Despite the loss, I had a feeling of great happiness. One morning, I had to get some bread, it was three-quarters of an hour to the nearest baker's, and I had to go through a little dell. There were flowers – forget-me-nots and the most beautiful cowslips, and the birch trees were just starting to turn green again. And in that moment I felt such intense happiness that I had survived the attack. And I had saved my family, those I was responsible for. I can hardly describe this feeling of happiness. I felt light at that moment and – just happy.

Plans were activated from 1942 for the evacuation of the towns and cities. Thousands of families were separated. Mothers and children were settled, often unsatisfactorily, in countryside lodgings, or children were sent by themselves, often to government-run establishments under the auspices of the Hitler Youth. There was a lot of friction. Complaints about the disparity of treatment between middle-class and working-class families were rife, and reflected growing unrest already expressed that sections of the population, and especially party functionaries' wives, were getting privileged treatment. Working-class women complained of having to take in children, or live in overcrowded conditions, while middle-class women and those with Party connections continued to live in their spacious accommodation, or in hotels. Or middle-class women could move their whole families to relative safety while working-class children were sent far away from their mothers, where visiting was difficult. Some parents at this stage were reluctant to place their children full-time in the hands of the Hitler Youth, or suspicious of religious organizations taking in evacuees, which might be an unwelcome influence on their growing children.

Husbands working at home in war industries while their wives and children were evacuated were particularly upset. Official reports found that 'men suffer from the separation since nobody is there to look after them' (18 November 1943), and a drop in productivity was the consequence of loss of morale and strength and increased strain. Wives also wanted to stay at home and look after them. There were fears of the 'sexual problem' and the danger of marriage break-up caused by separating husbands and wives for an indefinite period. Separation from children was the greatest burden and, with visits uncertain, there were fears that they would drift apart. Many women returned to the cities to face the hazards of bombing rather than the uncertainty of settling in a strange environment. When they did, they had their ration books withdrawn. In Dortmund (Witten) on 11 October 1943, around 300 angry women demonstrated to demand their ration books back. When police were called in to restore order, they refused to intervene, claiming the demand was rightful and the decision to withhold them was illegal. Crowds of women gathered in other towns and, in one, miners refused to go down the pit until they had secured the ration cards for their families (SD Reports, 18 November 1943). Abuse of officials who tried to coerce the women was widespread, along the lines of: 'They'd better keep out of my way. My children aren't going to be sent away and if I have nothing to eat then I can bloody well die with them.' Or: 'They might just as well send us to Russia and point machine guns at us and have done with it.'[14]

With morale plummeting, especially among women, the penalties for 'defeatism' were increased. This included any remark critical of the leaders, or which implied loss of faith in the nation's ability to win the war. The maximum penalty for 'malicious denigration' was the death sentence, and it was widely publicized. One result was that the Security Police were unable to tap the mood, for 'nobody is prepared any longer to say what they think'. People lived in renewed fear of denunciation by neighbours and acquaintances or just passers-by. 'People discuss what really concerns them only in the most intimate circle in which they feel free from denunciation,' the SD reported.[15] Special courts were instructed to be rigorous in the punishment they meted out, though in practice penalties varied. A diary entry or a passing comment that the war looked hopeless or could not be won might bring heavy penalties, the maximum the death sentence carried out by guillotine.

A former World War One officer and now a works supervisor predicted that Germany would soon be defending itself on the Brenner Pass and behind the Elbe (which was true), and criticized the leaders as incompetent – Göring a morphine addict, Goebbels syphilitic, Hitler a hysterical and choleric person and Keitel an old aunt. He was sentenced by a regular court to a year in prison.[16]

Fear of denunciation became a constant in people's lives. Elly Napp, as a socialist, though not an active one, was vulnerable. After her husband Kurt was killed in the East, she could not disguise her true feelings, and she dropped her caution:

A well-meaning neighbour came by to console me over the loss of my husband. She said: 'Don't worry, the Führer is developing the miracle weapons and that will be the turning-point.' At that moment I lost my temper and said, 'Are you so stupid that you believe in the miracle weapons?' She was taken aback and left. And I didn't sleep for several nights because this was a defeatist remark, and she could have done me real harm, if she'd reported me.

Liselotte Katscher worked as a nurse in a Lutheran hospital in Cottbus: 'I remember one scene when a nurse stood up in the middle of the ward, and she was angry about something the National Socialists had done, and she was a Party member herself. And we all gathered round her saying, "Please, please, Sister Hanna, be quiet! If someone overhears you, it will get you in real trouble." We were all very scared, especially in the last years of the war.' She also had to teach race theory to young women in the nursing school. A lot of young women were not Nazi supporters but, if they raised any criticism, 'I kept saying to them, "Please do me a favour, stay quiet. Because if you speak up about it, they'll close the nursing school down."'

Susanne von der Borch was living with her soldier husband in lodgings with a landlady:

We had two rooms. And there was a Hitler photograph in one, above the piano, and my husband said, 'Well, he has to go. I can't look at that any more.' I said, 'Don't do that.' He said, 'No, this picture has to go.' So he takes it away and puts it behind the piano. Two days later, he was summoned to the Army commandant who said, 'Well, there's been an accusation from the Party that you have removed a Hitler portrait. She said your wife has taken that Hitler portrait away.' And my husband said, 'No, that was me. My wife didn't do that.' He said, 'Never mind, either you or your wife was accused of doing it.' 'By whom?' He said, 'Well, your landlady.' And my husband said, 'Well, I just put it behind the piano.' And the commandant said, 'We'll let the matter drop, but you have to pay 500 marks.' And that was a huge amount of money, we couldn't afford it. My father gave it to us.

The penalties for listening to foreign broadcasts were stepped up. This had always been illegal, but more people resorted to it as faith in the media's credibility and the leadership waned. This too was cause for denunciation by disgruntled neighbours or merely loyal Nazis. Elly Napp listened regularly:

> Nobody had any excuse if they were caught listening, so, to be as safe as possible, the radio was wrapped in blankets and you only listened to it when you were by yourself. And you were very careful to never, even by accident, pass on the news you'd heard... They encouraged people to denounce other people if they heard that friends, family or neighbours were listening to these radio stations. And they did something which I think is really scandalous. They even told schoolchildren to denounce their parents if they listened to enemy stations. And my sister, who was at school in Dresden, came home one day and said, 'If you listen to the radio station I will have to denounce you.' She naturally wouldn't have done it, but it was a warning for us to be even more cautious, and after that I only listened after midnight.

One of her neighbours came round one day after an argument with the family who lived below, and said that she intended to denounce them for listening to the BBC. Frau Napp 'immediately realized it was probably my radio that she'd heard. I said, "I won't back it up. I don't know what the broadcast sounds like. I didn't hear it. But be careful. If you say that you've heard the enemy broadcast signal, then they will know that you recognize it, so that you must have been listening."' The woman turned round in silence and never mentioned it again.

People went to considerable lengths to conceal what they had heard on foreign radio stations. One family arranged a funeral cere-mony for their son who had been reported killed on his submarine, even though they had heard from BBC broadcasts that he was alive in a prisoner of war camp. Only afterwards were a few trusted friends told the truth.[17]

Though the Gestapo net was spread wide, the number of paid informers in the population was not large. In 1937, Duisburg had only twenty-eight paid informants, while Würzburg had twenty-two.[18] But there was a regular flow of voluntary denunciations from the population, which arose from malice and the desire to ingratiate with the authorities as well as from a sense of duty. According to Eric Johnson, the informants tended to be male, though a third were female; skilled workers made up the largest single group, with lower middle and middle-class people from a large number of occupations making up most of the rest. The majority were neighbours, acquaintances or co-workers of the accused; few were family members.[19] So many denunciations in the early years arose from personal matters or petty disputes between neighbours that the police had, in 1934, recommended the denouncers be penalized for wasting police time. In wartime, however, the situation was more critical and the penalties more severe.

Jokes directed against the regime or the leaders were particularly risky, especially when the mood turned sour after Stalingrad. Denunciations for irreverence towards the leadership were common, but jokes, as well as rumours, about the leadership, flourished, and most had a bitter edge. A Party Chancellery report for April (11–17) noted the 'number of political jokes which involve the Führer have increased sharply', while an SD Report in July deplored the increase in 'political' jokes told in cafés and factories, and regretted that even sections of the Party membership had lost the feeling that listening to political jokes 'is something which a decent German simply does not do'.[20] The report was concerned about jokes betraying 'defeatism', and listed examples such as: 'What's the difference between the sun and Hitler? The sun rises in the East, Hitler goes down in the East'; 'What's the difference between India and Germany? In India one person starves for everybody [Gandhi], in Germany everyone starves for one person'; 'Zara Leander [a popular singer] is summoned to the Führer's headquarters every day. Why? She has to sing "I know a miracle will happen one day".'

Telling jokes carried penalties. A lampoon of Hitler landed a shorthand typist from Frankfurt with two years' imprisonment in 1943:

He who rules in the Russian manner,
dresses his hair in the French style,

trims his moustache English-fashion
and wasn't born in Germany himself,
who teaches us the Roman salute,
asks our wives for lots of children
but can't produce any himself –
he is the leader of Germany.

A Catholic priest, Father Josef Müller, was sentenced to be hanged in July 1944 for telling a Hitler joke: 'On his deathbed a wounded soldier asked to see for one last time the people for whom he had laid down his life. The nurses brought a picture of the Führer and laid it on his right side. Then they brought a picture of Reischsmarschall Göring and laid it on his left. Then he said: "Now I can die like Jesus Christ, between two criminals."' Leaders were not spared the sharp edge of mockery of their hypocrisy, as in 'Mottoes of a true German':

Be prolific like Hitler
simple and unostentatious like Göring,
loyal like Hess,
silent like Goebbels
sober like Ley,
and beautiful like Scholtz-Klink!

A variation was: 'The perfect German? Blond as Hitler, slim as Göring, tall as Goebbels.' Göring, Head of the Luftwaffe and known for his ostentation, pomposity and love of uniforms, was a particular target, as in: 'A watermain bursts in the Air Ministry basement. Göring calls his secretary: "Fetch me my admiral's uniform immediately!"' And: 'One night Emmy Göring wakes up at an early hour and sees her husband with his back to her performing a strange dance with his baton. Asked by his wife what exactly he is doing, he replies: "I am promoting my underpants to overpants."'

Jokes, as Adam Lebor and Roger Boyes point out in *Surviving Hitler*, were 'a little bit of resistance'. But they also 'provided a snapshot of the level of popular awareness of the dangers posed by Hitler'. One circulated in 1940, at the height of optimism about Germany's military victories: 'Two friends are talking. "When the war is over," says one, "I plan to make a bicycle tour around Germany." The friend replies: "Fine, what will you do after lunch?"' Another dating from 1941 suggests widespread awareness of Hitler's plans for the ultimate destiny of the Jews: 'An SS man says to a Jew in a concentration camp: "You will die today but I will give you one last chance. I have a glass eye. If you can tell which one I will spare you." The Jew looks at the SS man and says: "It is the left one, Sir." "How did you guess?" The Jew replies: "It looked more human."'[21]

Fractured Lives

After Stalingrad, the war turned against Germany. The hospitals at home were filling up with the wounded. Long lists of the fallen and missing appeared daily in the newspapers. Millions of families mourned their dead, as they carried on the everyday round. Family life was fissured by war.

Women lived in constant anxiety about their menfolk at the front. Long separations were taking their toll on marriages. Mutual under-standing between partners was beginning to suffer. Women, whose role in the Nazi ideology was to support their warrior heroes at the front, were themselves suffering at home from deprivation, worry about chil-dren, and bombing of their homes. When couples were able to snatch time together on the husband's leave, they were finding a distance had developed between them. Soldiers on leave failed to understand the pressures at home. Wives were saying that 'having looked forward to being together again during their husbands' leave, the occasion is spoilt by frequent rows caused by mutual tensions' – even in marriages that were previously 'models of harmony'.[22] Women, too, were undergoing strains, and demanded emotional support from their husbands. And, as happened in other nations at war, women coping alone grew accus-tomed to managing their lives and families. They developed an inde-pendence that could lead to conflict with husbands who expected more submissive behaviour, and felt their authority was undermined.

The leadership, too, was concerned about the state of marriage, but mainly from the point of view of the birth rate. For, as the war claimed thousands more lives, the question of replenishment became urgent.

Himmler stepped in with the reminder to the SS troops that their duty was to reproduce at the earliest opportunity, and especially before dying. The strict conditions for a marriage permit were lifted, not least because the bureaucracy couldn't keep up with the paperwork, doctors were failing to examine people before permits were issued, and, anyway, the necessary certificates had often been lost in the chaos of bombing. The regional SS commander in Silesia complained to Himmler in 1943 that all sorts of riff-raff – epileptic wives, impotent SS men – were being granted leave to marry. Himmler was clear on the question of quality. In war, some concessions had to be made: 'The most important thing I am capable and desirous of achieving is that every SS man who can should have a child before he dies in battle. If this increases the total number of children, *I accept the runts* – in breeder's parlance – that will occur in the mass. Better a child than no child at all. Even the slightly inferior son of his father will be a German grenadier in twenty years' time, and his family will not have died out.'[23]

To ensure the safety of every drop of German blood, the penalties for abortion were increased. In February 1942, the Reich Ministry of Justice decided that the sentences imposed on self-abortion, and on those who assisted in abortion, were 'still too light'. Abortion was possible on 'racial grounds', but forbidden to Aryan women. The sentence for those doctors, midwives and quacks who impaired 'the vital energy of the people' – especially in wartime when the nation's blood was draining away in battle – was to be capital punishment.

By now, the leadership was encouraging the new attitude to 'racially valuable' illegitimate children. Hitler wanted to remove any stigma attached to the illegitimate child, and even to encourage women to have children outside marriage as a duty to the nation. This was interpreted widely as making it girls' duty to 'have a child for the Führer'. The issue gained urgency as it became clear that there would be a shortage of men after the war to father the future divisions to defend the Fatherland. Bigamy was proposed as the solution; the childbearing capacity of Germany's womanhood must not be allowed to go to waste. Men of good stock and proven heroism should be able to enter into contracts of second marriage with fecund women to keep up the birth rate. Though seriously proposed and widely supported among the leadership, it did little to raise morale among women and Church organizations, who greeted it with horror. The plans got no further.

Himmler's Lebensborn organization catered for single mothers of good racial stock by providing care facilities for the mothers during and after the birth, and if necessary, taking responsibility for the children, usually by farming them out to SS couples. Children deemed to be 'racially valuable' and capable of 'Germanization' were forcibly abducted from their parents in the occupied territories, and brought to Lebensborn homes in the Reich or those set up in countries such as Norway. These children, too, were given for adoption by suitable parents, had their names changed, not allowed to see their parents and disappeared into the maw of the Nazi State.

The Nazis promoted marriage at every opportunity. Strenuous attempts were made to maximize contact between single soldiers and unmarried women. 'The creation of a good social environment for the soldier on leave from the front is essential for reasons of population policy,' Bormann decreed in Circular 83/44. On soldiers' leave, women were imported to their clubs and places of entertainment to facilitate match-making. The BDM was asked to provide suitable girls with whom the men could 'strike up well-founded acquaintanceships'. By arranging social functions, the Party Chancellery (Bormann) decided, 'the Party will not only give the soldier on leave the chance to enjoy himself and meet girls with a view to choosing a companion in life, but also steer him back to the Party and its organizations'.[24] No aspect of private life was to be left free of Party edicts, especially in war.

Wartime marriages, often hurriedly contracted, were put under strain by almost immediate separation, with letters the only form of contact. Though wives benefited from their new married status, they were not entitled to receive the generous separation allowance for wives of serving soldiers unless they had been married for a year before his call-up. Consequently they had to make their own livings. They never experienced routine family life: 'We hadn't even really begun to lead a married life,' one woman recalled. 'We married in 1943. That was a so-called war marriage and our son came in '44. It wasn't exactly a broken-in marriage. Now we were actually together for the first time.'[25] Many marriages did not survive when partners met as relative strangers after the war.

Marriage was made easier, not only by the removal of restrictions requiring proof of genealogy and medical checks. 'Long-distance marriages' were introduced in November 1939. Couples made their vows and celebrated the union in separate locations, the men being usually at the front. Between September 1939 and April 1940, 40 per cent of marriages were conducted by this method. One particular Nazi invention was the 'post mortem' marriage – known as 'corpse' marriage – whereby women could marry already-fallen soldiers. Hitler in 1941 authorized 'the subsequent marriage of women with fallen military men... when serious intent to marry can be proven and no evidence is presented to indicate that this intent was abandoned before death'.[26] This held particular advantages for women who had already conceived, since it legitimized the offspring. It also entitled women to widows' rights, including pensions and property, as long as they fitted the profile of the socially acceptable Aryan woman. Although the most important factor was the presence or expectation of children, in fact marriages where proof of intent was obtained were usually approved.

Another scheme for ensuring the future of the race aimed to bring racially valuable, but severely wounded, men into contact with 'valuable' women. Introduced in 1943, it acknowledged that fertile men of good eugenic stock had reduced chances of marriage, but aimed to minimize their difficulties. Few marriages resulted from this initiative, since, according to Elizabeth Heineman, both veterans and women still wanted to exercise choice. Some women lost interest when they discovered the meaning of 'severely wounded'. In addition, 'Most female applicants had a relatively high-class background, performed pink- or white-collar work (the majority were in the female professions) and lived in cities. They had little desire to marry the farmers, small-time artisans, and labourers who made up the bulk of the male applicants. The wounded, for their part, did not want to settle for second best (that is, older, physically imperfect or uppity because of their class background) just because they were wounded.' Few war widows or young women showed any interest in the scheme.[27]

Adultery among soldiers' wives was a cause for rising concern. While only a few cases were reported in, for instance, Hamburg in 1940 of 'wives of military men [who] don't adhere very precisely to marital fidelity', by 1942 there was alarm at 'the increasing number of wives pregnant by men other than their husbands'. Some municipalities took the initiative of cutting or revoking separation allowances to wayward wives. This was endorsed by the Ministry of Interior when, in May 1942, separation allowances were denied to wives who engaged in 'dishonourable or immoral conduct' or who neglected their children. The same year, a new crime was introduced – 'insult of husbands at the front' – under which husbands could sue the third party only and not the wife as would have happened in divorce cases. Guidelines also discouraged any suit against either party, and husbands were encouraged to be lenient with their wives, because the overriding official view was that a marriage which may produce more children should be held together. Wives' adultery with non-Aryan foreign labourers came under the category of 'racial crime' and penalties could be more severe. A substantial proportion of the almost 10,000 women sent to concentration camps for 'forbidden contact' were married women.[28]

Young girls seemed to be getting out of hand. Social workers reported a rise in unruly behaviour, such as hanging around soldiers' quarters. A decree of March 1940 forbade 'endangered' minors from loitering after dark, visiting restaurants, movies or dance-halls, and smoking or drinking in public. Women students seen consorting with foreign colleagues were subject to censure, and the SD reported particular concern about girls seen with Turkish students, or appearing in bars at the Wannsee lido accompanied by Arabs. 'All sections of the public are urgently demanding that a move at last be made to deal with this unworthy behaviour. It is felt,' the report went on somewhat irrelevantly, 'that, however necessary they may sometimes have been in the past, considerations of foreign policy are out of place today...'[29]

There were growing reports of sexual laxity. Everywhere, girls were forgetting their training, and losing their heads to the hero warriors who for years had been held up as the ultimate focus of their destiny and duty. In Munich, in 1942, girls from the age of fourteen allegedly engaged unhesitatingly in sexual intercourse with soldiers and young men of the Labour Service. Hans Peter Bleuel found reports that 'After Hitler Youth parades, young people roamed the darkened streets, went to forbidden films and allowed themselves to be led astray by corrupt adults.' One fifteen-year-old girl was reproached by her mother for persistently associating with SS men and soldiers. The girl retorted that, 'if she got herself pregnant she'd be just what the Führer was always asking for – a German mother.'[30] The incidence of pregnancies and vene- real disease among the fourteen–eighteen age group in towns went up. Hamburg health authorities estimated that two-thirds of young women with sexually transmitted diseases had been infected by soldiers. [31]

The germ of opposition appeared in the form of bands of youths, including girls, who deliberately displayed their non-allegiance to the Nazi state by wearing their own kind of 'uniform', listening to American jazz and swing music, beating up Hitler Youth boys and daubing graffiti. They roamed in gangs, gave themselves names like 'Edelweiss Pirates' and 'Swing Youth', 'Snake Club', 'Bush Wolves' and 'Charlie Gang', and attracted the wrath of the police and Gestapo. Their opposition was rarely overtly political, though a few participated in distributing Allied leaflets and helping refugees, deserters and prisoners of war. They rejected the regimentation of the Hitler Youth and the values of Nazi society by establishing their own youth culture, with their own songs, forms of entertainment, music and dance styles – mainly swing and the jitterbug. Police reports stressed the prevalence of sexual licence, of under-age and group sex, stimulated by banned music: 'Twelve-year- olds exhibit the precocity of sixteen-year-olds and many sixteen-year- olds have the sexual maturity of twenty-one-year-olds' was their verdict. A report on 300 young people attending a jam session described 'degenerate and criminally inclined juveniles, some of mixed blood, who terrorized the healthy-minded public by their mode of behaviour and undignified musical excesses', and urged action against them.[32]

Large gatherings were banned after 1940. In one day, 7 December 1942, the Düsseldorf Gestapo broke up twenty-eight groups containing 739 adolescents from towns in the surrounding area. Later, in October 1944, Himmler cracked down with a decree on 'combating youth gangs'. In November, the leaders of the Cologne Edelweiss Pirates were publicly hanged.[33] Other leaders were recommended for 're-education' in the Labour Service, or forced labour in concentration camps.

NOTES

1   Cited Kershaw, *Hitler: Nemesis*, p. 423
2   ibid., p. 515
3   Domarus, *Hitler*, p. 1974
4   Cited Kershaw, *Hitler: Nemesis*, p. 547
5   ibid., p. 547
6   Noakes, *Nazism 1919–1945*, pp. 550–1
7   ibid., pp. 553–4
8   Goebbels, *Diaries* (29 September 1942; 20 August 1942)
9   Beck, Earl R., *Under the Bombs: The German Home Front, 1942–1945*, The University Press of Kentucky, Kentucky, 1986, p. 47)
10 Steinhoff, Johannes, Peter Pechel and Dennis Showalter (ed.), *Voices from the Third Reich: An Oral History*, Da Capo Press, New York, 1994, pp. 462–3
11 Noakes, *Nazism 1919–1945*, p. 552
12 ibid., pp. 555–7: Report of the Police President of Hamburg
13 ibid., pp. 554, 557
14 SD Report 18 November 1943; ibid., pp. 360–5
15 SD Report 27 November 1943; ibid., p. 552
16 Beck, *Under the Bombs*, p. 95
17 Lebor, Adam, and Roger Boyes, *Surviving Hitler: Choices, Corruption and Compromise in the Third Reich*, Simon & Schuster, London, 2000, p. 4
18 Ibid., p. 4
19 Johnson, *The Nazi Terror*, p. 272
20 SD Report 8 July 1943; Noakes, *Nazism 1919–1945*, p. 549
21 Lebor and Boyes, *Surviving Hitler*, pp. 35–6
22 SD Report 18 November 1943; Noakes, *Nazism 1919–1945*, p. 360
23 Bleuel, *Strength Through Joy*, p. 200
24 ibid., p. 169
25 Heineman, *What Difference Does a Husband Make?*, p. 47
26 ibid., p. 47
27 ibid., p. 49
28 ibid., pp. 54–6
29 Bleuel, *Strength Through Joy*, pp. 239–40
30 ibid., pp. 240–1
31 Heineman, *What Difference Does a Husband Make?*, p. 54
32 Bleuel, *Strength Through Joy*, p. 243
33 Peukert, Detlev, *Youth in the Third Reich*, in Richard Bessel (ed.), *Life in the Third Reich*, Oxford University Press, Oxford, p. 35

13

COLLAPSE

In August 1944, home front morale was perilously near collapse. For the citizens of Stuttgart, the question was not 'whether we can win the war – the vast majority are convinced the enemy powers will win – but rather how long this war will go on and whether we shall come under an Anglo-American or Russian protectorate'.[1] They noted 'the most serious aspect' – that 'most compatriots... have lost all faith in the Führer'. The German military outlook was grim, and showed little sign of improvement. Everywhere, the German armies were being pushed back. Between August and December 1944, almost a million and a quarter German soldiers were killed.

By the start of 1945, Hitler's empire was crumbling fast. The Allies advanced steadily in the West. The Russians had mounted a counter-offensive in the East which would soon break through into the German homeland. Though Hitler in his 1945 New Year's address to the nation insisted that the war would continue until final victory, the Wehrmacht High Command, on 15 January, conceded that 'the initiative in the area of the offensive has passed to the enemy'.[2] In early March, American troops reached the Rhine. Inhabitants in the path of the advance were hanging white flags of surrender on their houses even before the military authorities had conceded defeat. They were punished – the male head of each household was taken out and shot. Special courts handed out up to 500 death sentences a month for 'defeatism'.[3] Soldiers were deserting in large numbers when not surrendering. A third of all German forces in the West were lost – either captured, killed or wounded between early February and mid-March.[4]

Ilse Schmidt had worked with the Wehrmacht on the front lines. When the Russians advanced on Krakow, she fled with the rest of the German troops:

That was one of the most terrible experiences, fleeing from the Russians. We'd started to withdraw, and we could see the searchlights and hear the thunder of the guns nearby. I'll never forget, my boss didn't want to take me, you had to look after yourself, but another soldier helped me and we kept running from the Russians through these filthy streets. I was the only woman, and we were terrified that the Russians would get us. And then we were sitting packed tight into these trucks, and I was so scared I really flipped my lid. I screamed and screamed and I thought, 'You men, it's all your fault that the war happened,' though I did know I'd done my share as well. But I was beside myself, and I didn't care what the others said. We got away from the Russians and spent the night in a soldiers' camp, and I was so grateful to this Sister [nurse] who was there, because she said to me, 'You can sleep in my bed.' She treated me like a patient after I had gone berserk like that.

In the East, the Russian advance was rapid and brutal. Liselotte Katscher worked in a hospital at Cottbus:

When the eastern front came nearer to us, the home-front hospitals were turned into real front-line field hospitals and we got all the wounded directly from the dressing stations on the battlefield. I remember one night – it's a horrific memory. We got a huge sports hall, with all kinds of training facilities which we emptied out and just put mattresses on the floor, we had run out of space. And then for a whole night I just carried wounded soldiers, still in their bloodied uniforms, just putting them on the mattresses on the floor. We just had to nurse them there, lying on the ground in the hall.'

As the Russians swept though East Prussia, Pomerania and Silesia, thousands of refugees, a vast number of them women, picked up their belongings and fled. One report described the scene:

> The roads are full of refugees, carts, and pedestrians. Now and then cars packed with people and suitcases go by, followed by envious looks from those on foot... People are gripped by panic as the cry goes up: 'The Russians are close!' People look at each other. That can't be possible. Then a man comes on horseback shouting in a loud voice: 'Save yourselves, you who can. The Russians will be here in half an hour.' We're overcome by a paralysing fear.[5]

As the refugees fled westwards, they passed long lines of dejected and demoralized German prisoners of war, freezing in the winter conditions, heading for the East. Those who deserted risked death. A boy refugee on a train from Poland observed the bodies of German soldiers lying at the roadside, and others who had been hanged, with notices round their necks denouncing them as cowards and deserters.[6]

Hitler remained adamant that Germany would fight to the last man. On 19 March he issued the 'Nero Decree', which would have compelled the armies to destroy anything that might be used by the enemy on Reich territory to their advantage, including all military transport, communications, industrial and supplies installations and material assets. It was a scorched earth policy in retreat and was never implemented. Albert Speer, Armaments Minister, intervened to persuade the Gauleiters and eventually Hitler of the folly of the decree. It was a sign that Hitler's power was faltering. Goebbels observed: 'We're giving out orders in Berlin that in practice no longer arrive lower down, let alone can be implemented... I see in that a danger of an extraordinary dwindling of authority' (Diary, 28 March 1945).

The chaos in the eastern territories of the Reich worsened. Countess Maria von Lingen lived in a castle in Silesia. When the Russians were twenty-five miles away, she was inundated with refugees after the evacuation of nearby Breslau:

All the streets were stopped up with treks, people with hand-carts, people with bicycles, with baby carriages, people on foot. It was completely ghastly. And it was twenty-five [degrees Celsius] below zero. It was insane. There were people whose children had died in their arms. The old people died, and one had laid them in the street ditches. The minister came and said, 'For God's sake, where shall we bury the people?' The earth was frozen hard as stone. I had straw thrown everywhere for the refugees so they could sleep somewhere or lie down. Then came the trek with very proper people, Count Garnier-Turava and others. I had to put them up in the guest rooms.

She recounted to Alison Owings how she had planned to get out with her young son: 'Every day I went to the train station. But you could not get on a single train. People hung from the running boards, from the roofs, between the cars, on the buffers. Then their hands froze and they fell to the ground.' She was not allowed to leave, anyway, until the local Ortsgruppenleiter gave the order – and he waited until the last moment.

She had already decided what to do when the Russians came: 'I had a Walthers police pistol and diligently practised skeet shooting with our forester. I was completely decided they would not get me alive, me or my son. First I'll shoot him and then myself. That was certain.'[7] A German officer came to her rescue, offering to take her and her son with him to the nearby town. Eventually, with the help of a series of officers, a military pass she had obtained, and her aristocratic name, she travelled – despite bombs falling – by trains and lorries across Germany to her home in Schweinfurt, only to be strafed by the Americans for five days before the local Gauleiter surrendered.

Twelve years of relentless propaganda against the 'sub-human' Slavs and Bolsheviks had given notice of what women could expect of the Russians. Hitler was explicit in his final speech to the soldiers, aimed at bolstering their determination to fight on: '[The Jewish–Bolshevik mortal enemy] is attempting to demolish Germany and to exterminate our people. You soldiers from the east know yourselves in large measure what fate threatens above all German women, girls and children. While old men and children are murdered, women and girls are denigrated to barrack-whores. The rest are marched off to Siberia.' Women knew that they could expect rape, plunder and killing with the conquest, and were terrified. One 'careful' estimate put the incidence of rape in the eastern territories at 1.4 million women – 18 per cent of the female population there – and in East Prussia it may have been higher.[8]

Liselotte Katscher remembers when the Russians first came on the hospital:

> The hospital was in an old school building. We kept the gates of the school yard closed, so we were living in a kind of oasis. We had a head doctor who spoke fluent Russian, but even our head doctor couldn't prevent the Russians breaking into our courtyard. He got to them very quickly and spoke to them in Russian. I don't know how this young girl from the house got into the yard, but one Russian officer grabbed her and raped her in front of all of us. The doctor was horrified and spoke to him and he just turned round and said very coolly, 'Well, this is what you did to my wife.'

She had already witnessed the brutality of the invasion: 'I still remember the long lines of German prisoners going through Cottbus to the east. In the villages and towns there were mostly women and children and they were helpless in the face of the invading Russians. There was an incredible number of rapes, and a lot of young women took their own lives, or tried to take their own lives... [They] were scared of being raped, especially the young women, and because they were scared, they tried to cut their wrists.' Many refugees were in an appalling condition: 'One older woman had been found on a path in the forest, and they brought her to us. She had false teeth, and when she took them out in the washroom, I suddenly saw all these ants, which had already been rummaging in this poor woman's mouth.'

The nurses tried to treat them in the hospital: 'These women didn't feel like talking. They were withdrawn. We cared for them and tried to bring them back to normality and health as far as we were able, but we had nothing to eat for these people. Food was very scarce. They were lacking protein and they had oedema and we couldn't help them because we didn't have anything to eat.' The help the nurses could give was limited by their own circumstances: 'We nurses were also sick. I was sick. I looked in the mirror and I thought, "Oh my God, the patients must think I eat so much," because I had such swollen cheeks. And then my director came in and he said, "Put your finger on your forehead," and there was a big dent. The dent remained. It wasn't fat.'

By then Liselotte Katscher had been through so much that she had all but erased her feelings. 'I had seen so much destroyed through bombing, I had been sitting in so many cellars with debris tumbling around me, the hospital had been bombed out. The house in which my mother lived was totally destroyed – she luckily survived. I don't want to say I was numbed, but I couldn't afford to have so many emotions any more.'

Regina Frankenfeld had already been bombed out in Berlin several times. She managed to visit her mother and grandmother in their village at weekends even after it became a war-zone, because she got military permission. One weekend, the train tracks were bombed, and she was stranded in her village as the Russians advanced. She, her mother and her grandmother went to a cellar to seek shelter from shelling. They heard tanks rolling by and knew they were Russian. All three women were raped.

> And as we were then all hauled out of the cellar and as they stood there with their machine guns, my mother said, 'Well, now we'll probably be shot.' And I said, 'It's all the same to me.' It *really* was all the same to me. I mean, we had nothing more to lose... But then we weren't shot. A Russian officer came and thundered terribly to his guys. In Russian, I didn't understand, but one saw the results. They all left with very long faces and didn't bother themselves more with what they'd dished up. So anything additional was left undone. At least for this day. In the weeks to come, others arrived and then the *same thing* happened again. Do you think it happened just once? We always kept getting other troops.

She and her mother and grandmother were put to forced farm labour for the Russians in exchange for food. When the Kalmucks arrived, she told

Alison Owings, the Russian commander 'ordered the local populace to stay off the streets' because they had 'freedom to plunder'. She narrowly avoided another rape after being grabbed off the street by one of them. But she remembers acts of kindness from some Russian soldiers – 'Stalin pupils', who 'arrived in town and spoke some German and were nice to children and even slipped her some bread crusts so that she could give her rationed slices of bread to her mother and grand-mother': 'I mean, of course that happened but it doesn't annul the other,' she said.[9]

As the German armies had done before, the Russians plundered the occupied territory, removing food, livestock, machinery and people. Thousands of women were taken for forced labour for the Russian army. Irene Burchett was twelve when the German army defending their village vanished. The Russians took all their livestock and looted their possessions. She was forced to work as cook to the soldiers. Her father was saved from being shot because a White Russian testified he had helped him. Others in the district were shot, and Irene Burchett had to bury the dead. Several days after the invasion, the Russian soldiers roamed the village rounding up people. Irene and her sisters, cousin and father were among them. Two thousand prisoners, mostly women and girls, were sent to the East. At first they travelled on foot, and then in freight trains. Almost starved of food, many died on the way. Her father was taken away along the route, and she never saw him again. Their final destination was Chelyabinsk, a Soviet labour camp in Siberia.

Irene Burchert worked in a tile factory. They never had enough to eat but had just enough not to starve to death. Nevertheless, of the 2000 who had arrived with her, only 800 were alive at the end of the first year. Most died of disease. She had to bury the dead: 'Every night a wagon was driven by with bodies in it, naked. A little bit of straw over them. And my sister and some [other prisoners] went and dug a large, deep hole. The next day the corpses were in it with a little bit of straw over them. And we had to dig a new hole.'[10] She remained in the camp until her release in 1949.

Brutality

As the Russians advanced, the Nazis attempted to remove evidence of the genocide in the death-camps scattered through Eastern Europe. In Auschwitz, as at other camps, some of the crematoria had been blown up in autumn 1944. As the Russians advanced in January 1945, 65,000 prisoners remained in Auschwitz and over 700,000 prisoners, the majority Jews, were still incarcerated in camps.[11] A substantial number were women.

Nearly every concentration camp containing women had its small section of women camp guards – booted and uniformed – who added to the misery of prisoners' lives. Inmates testify to the brutality of these women. 'In my experience the matrons were cruel, more vicious than any SS man,' Susan Cernyak-Spatz recalled. 'These women who, as I later read, ranged from baronesses and countesses to prostitutes, were the most vicious. You rarely found SS men who played with their dogs in which the point was for the dog to get the prisoners' derrières, but the matrons did.'[12] Irma Griese, one of the few female guards at Auschwitz, engaged in sado-masochistic sexual practices with the prisoners. Hildegard Lächert, according to the testimony at her trial, assigned inmate Maria Kaufmann-Krasowski to wash floors and beat her mercilessly with a whip until she was 'only scraps of a human being' and then barked the order, 'Get this piece of filth out of here!' At Ravensbruck, largely a woman's camp, there were 2000 female assistants along with the SS guards. 'Only one NS sister treated me decently. And she was transferred for punishment,' Margarete Armbruster remembered.[13] Lotte Müller, a 'political' prisoner at Ravensbruck, told Alison Owings that all the female guards had a club or a riding whip for hitting people. One guard, a Frau Lehmann, was once 'in a towering rage and with an inhuman look on her face' was thrashing prisoners with a club, hitting out at everyone. Then she stopped and said, '"Ach, you all want to leave, don't you? I also have to give my child something to drink. It's time" ...She had to nurse her child. When she was gone I told the girls, "She must have sour milk in her breasts, this woman." That is a *woman*... Such a thing happened. They are *beasts*, is what they are. It's simply unbelievable that human beings can be that way.'[14]

The stark brutality of those women perpetrators who exercised a long-term reign of terror in the camps is barely understandable, even in the context of the general brutalization that Nazism tapped in the German population, particularly during the war. Like those soldiers for whom cold-blooded killing became a habit, and who justified their actions in the name of 'survival of their race' in the fight against the 'Jewish–Bolshevik conspiracy', they participated in the decay of morality that marked the entire system.

Not all women chose their part in the killing machine. By the latter stages of the war, women who were simply drafted to war work found themselves sucked into concentration camp duties. Anna Fest worked at a pharmaceutical factory which did research on typhus (later connected to the medical experiments in Buchenwald, though she did not know this). With the declaration of 'total war' in 1944, her factory was ordered to release a certain proportion of women for mobilization. She was reassigned to a job which, she was told, was to 'watch over foreign work forces', and was sent for two weeks' instruction to Ravensbruck concentration camp. During this time, she was inducted into the SS. One day she witnessed guards beating prisoners and was about to jump up in protest. A guard sitting next to her said, "'Obviously you are tired of living. Stay seated if you can and look away. You have no idea how many who have rebelled are already prisoners themselves." Of course, I didn't say another thing.' She was not assigned to Ravensbruck, but to a satellite work camp for Hungarian Jewish women who were making explosives. She escorted them daily to and from work and claims she tried to treat them with respect, though she witnessed other female guards treating prisoners roughly. No one at this camp died during their stay there, and she was exonerated after Allied investigation, having spent two years in prison after the war.[15]

Wives of SS officers were often stationed with their husbands at or near the camps. With some exceptions, such as Ilse Kochs, wife of the commandant of Buchenwald, they were not indicted for crimes after the war. Claudia Koonz suggests that these wives, like those of Nazi leaders, lived within their own domestic sphere, cut off from their husband's public role. She cites Albert Speer on the leaders' wives: 'In general the wives of the regime's bigwigs resisted the temptation of power far more than their husbands. They did not lose themselves in the latter's fantasy world. They looked on at the often grotesque antics of their husbands with inner reservations and were not caught up in the political whirlwind in which their men were carried steeply upward.'[16] Lower down the line, something similar applied. The perpetrators themselves separated their personal lives from their work. Home, wife and family were a haven. Rudolf Hoss, commandant of Auschwitz, lived with his wife and family in the grounds of the camp. 'When I saw my children happily playing or observed my wife's delight over our youngest, the thought would often come to me: how long will this last? My wife could never understand these gloomy moods of mine, and ascribed them to some annoyance connected with my work,' he wrote in his memoirs.[17] Koonz surmises, 'As the Nazi state destroyed morality in the public sphere, wives and relatives were supposed to guard an emotional "space" for the men who oversaw the killing operations. "Each partner performed the function prescribed for it by nature," as Hitler put it. These wives did not directly participate in evil, but, on the contrary, fulfilled "nature's role" by normalizing a masculine world gone amok.' They also 'gave the individual men who confronted daily murder a safe place where they could be respected for who they were, not what they did… The family continued to offer a haven from public horror for the men who arrested, deported, tortured and killed those they defined as enemies of the *Volk*.'[18] Nazi wives, in accord with the Nazi view of women, created 'a buffer zone for their husband's jobs'. Whether this also absolved them from seeing what went on, or making any moral judgement of their own, is another question.

When the Russians approached, the death marches began as the eastern concentration camps in their path were emptied. Hundreds too weak to move were shot. Long columns of prisoners, starving and frozen, often barefooted, were forced to walk hundreds of miles at gunpoint. Hundreds more were shot by guards on the way: 'It was as if they were shooting at stray dogs… They didn't care and shot in every direction and without any consideration. We saw the blood on the white snow and carried on walking.'[19] A low estimate of those who perished *en route* is quarter of a million, of whom half were Jews.[20] Those who survived were distributed to the death camps at Mauthausen,

Sachsenhausen, Buchenwald, Dachau and the grossly overcrowded Bergen-Belsen, where they were found by the advancing Allied troops in April 1945.

Defeat and Humiliation

By March 1945, few believed any longer in victory, and faith in Hitler had all but evaporated. At a remembrance ceremony for the dead of the war in Markt Schellenberg, close by the Berghof, on 11 March, 'when the leader of the Wehrmacht unit at the end of his speech for the remembrance called for a "Sieg Heil" for the Führer, it was returned neither by the Wehrmacht present, nor by the Volkssturm [Home Guard], nor by the spectators of the civilian population who turned up. This silence of the masses had a depressing effect, and probably reflects better than anything the attitudes of the population,' a police observer commented.

In a desperate attempt to get more troops, all available older men had been called up into the Volkssturm, though guns and uniforms were scarce, and boys from the Hitler Youth as young as eleven were drafted into active service, facing not only the aerial bombing but machine-guns, artillery fire and tanks. Food was scarce everywhere. Mathilde Wolff-Mönckeberg recalled how she and her husband picked out five small potatoes each per day, and bread was so scarce she couldn't provide a sandwich for her husband on his night duty.[21] Goebbels wrote in his diary for 1 March 1945: 'We shall very soon be forced to reduce by 35–50 per cent the ration of the most important items, fat and bread. As a result they will fall below the tolerable minimum subsistence level... To all of our people's miseries that of hunger will now be added.' Coal and electricity were also in short supply, so heating was minimal, and cooking difficult.

Hitler refused to believe all was lost. Bormann sent out endless exhortations on his instructions to continue the fight, threatening severe punishment to 'any scoundrel... who does not fight to the last breath', and, to the Party local leaders: 'The Führer expects that you will master every situation in your *Gaue* [districts], if necessary with lightning speed and extreme brutality.'[22] His wife Gerda, an optimist and fanatical Nazi to the end, had recently declared to him: 'Every single child must realize that the Jew is the Absolute Evil in this world, and that he must be fought by every means, wherever he appears.'[23] She was now sending him encouraging missives:

> One day, the Reich of our dreams will emerge... In some ways, you know, this reminds me of the 'Twilight of the Gods' in the Edda... The monsters are storming the bridge of the Gods... the citadel of the Gods crumbles, and all seems lost; and then suddenly a new citadel rises, more beautiful than ever before... We are not the first to engage in mortal combat with the powers of the underworld, and that we feel impelled, and are also able, to do so should give us a conviction of ultimate victory.[24]

Hitler remained optimistic, delivering a new slogan on 16 April: 'Berlin remains German. Vienna will again become German and Europe will never become Russian.'

Bombing raids intensified. In Berlin, women retreated to the cellars, only occasionally going above ground to fetch provisions. Lilli Gentzen, the butcher's daughter, remembers: 'When the war reached its close, we had been living in the cellars for at least two or three weeks. Sometimes we went into some ground-floor flats to cook some food, but overall we lived in the cellars. I was scared to death, because they said, when the Russians come they will kill us all. So I was petrified with fear.'

In April, with Russian troops encircling Berlin, few believed that anything other than defeat was in store for them. Nevertheless, the Battle for Berlin was hard-fought, with the Russians pounding the city and meeting strong resistance from the small number of German soldiers (45,000), the Volkssturm (40,000) and around 3000 boys from the Hitler Youth,[25] gathered up on Hitler's order to make a last stand, to retrieve a final victory. Hitler's last public appearance on 20 April, looking puffy, drawn and ill, with one hand behind his back shaking uncontrollably, was to congratulate a little gathering of troops, including a line of small boys in uniform, for their bravery in fighting off Russian tanks.

When the Russians came, Lilli Gentzen was in the cellar with a group of other women:

The first Russian came down into the cellar and he lifted his hand, and I thought, 'He is going to kill me.' But instead he gave me some chocolate. But then the others came, and they were far worse.

I was seventeen years old. I was in a small cellar, and a Russian soldier scared all the other people away. And he poured a glass, a pint full of vodka for me. Instinctively, I emptied the vodka on the ground when he wasn't looking, but he looked up and I pretended I'd drunk it. Then he pulled me on to one of the beds. In a corner was an elderly woman. I was clinging to the bed post, he had a gun at my head, and this woman said, 'Lilli, sacrifice yourself, sacrifice yourself.' And I said to the Russian, 'Shoot, shoot, why don't you shoot?' And then he dragged me on to one of the beds and tried to touch me. But suddenly he was ill, and he vomited all over me. I quickly squeezed out, past a huge Russian in the doorway, and found a bed where lots of women were huddling together. And I stayed there the whole night. And all through the night I could see his torch searching the cellar for me, calling 'Lilli, Lilli.' And I didn't really know what they wanted from the women.

She found out from the other women next day what it was the Russians really wanted.

Her mother managed to escape and reach their flat. While she was packing a pram for her two-year-old sister with things for their escape:

There was a knock at the door, another Russian, who this time wanted to rape my mother. My little brother stood next to her and my mother was full of courage and said to the Russian, 'Not now,' and made an appointment with him. She said, 'Come at such and such a time.' He said, 'Yes, yes,' and I was hiding in the larder listening to this conversation. She got rid of him and we left as quickly as we could... We crossed the courtyard, and ran along the street which was littered with dead horses and steel helmets and an inn was burning and some Russians approached us. My mother had put a headscarf round my head so they couldn't see my face. The Russians ordered us, 'Sweep the streets,' and I was too proud at first. But my mother yelled, 'Sweep, go on, sweep!' and we swept the streets and they left us in peace.

Over 100,000 women were raped in Berlin alone.

In Hitler's bunker, 50 feet underground, were his personal staff and secretaries, along with a fluctuating number of leaders and officials, On 20 April they had gathered for the gloomy occasion of Hitler's fifty-sixth birthday, and then gradually they dispersed, or made their escape. Attempts by several of his entourage to persuade Hitler to leave Berlin had failed. 'Only here can I attain a success, and even if it's only a moral one, it's at least the possibility of saving face and winning time,' he told Goebbels on 25 April. 'Only through a heroic attitude can we survive this hardest of times.'[26] With Russian troops advancing to the very heart of Berlin, and the noise of artillery fire audible day and night, the commander of the Battle for Berlin, General Weidling, found Hitler, face like a 'smiling mask', with both hands and one of his legs constantly trembling, unable to rise from his seat.[27] With each new missive, Hitler raged against betrayal and treachery – by the commanders, his armies and the German people. His personal secretary Traudl Junge remembers: 'In the last days he was like a dead man really. He was not a leader who took any decisions, or had any influence. He was very lethargic.'

The women on his staff, and Eva Braun, formed a small group of unwaveringly loyal supporters. Only with them would Hitler eat his meals. Traudl Junge, with Hitler's other secretaries, had been in the bunker for over ninety days. Eva Braun had flown from Munich in March or early April, and moved into the room next to his, determined to be with him at what she believed to be the end. 'She adapted herself entirely to life in the bunker. She was always neat, beautifully dressed, and invariably warm and helpful to everyone; she never wavered to the end,' Albert Speer told Gitta Sereny. 'I tried repeatedly to get her out of Berlin. I liked her so much; I wanted her to be safe.' On three different occasions, he offered her a seat in the ever rarer planes out of Berlin. 'She persistently refused and finally told me, with a big smile, to stop pestering her.'[28] After his birthday gathering, she took everyone up to Hitler's first-floor apartment for a small party, where they danced to the only gramophone record they could find: 'Red Roses Bring You Happiness'. 'We drank champagne and laughed loudly, but it was a very hollow kind of laughter,' Traudl Junge noted.[29]

On 22 April, Hitler for the first time conceded the war might be lost. News that the Russians had reached the city's inner defences provoked a torrent of rage, which subsided into despair. Hitler had already decided to take his own life. Suicide was the only honourable exit for him. 'It's all over, it's the end, There's no hope left,' he moaned to the women he had summoned – his secretaries, Gerda Christian and Traudl Junge, his female dietician, Constanze Manziarly, and Eva Braun. They were horrified at his admission of defeat. 'We had expected it,' Traudl Junge said, 'but now that it came, we were struck dumb.'

Hitler told them that they must leave. Traudl Junge describes the scene: 'The first to... break the silence was Eva Braun. Without faltering, she walked over to Hitler, took his hands in hers and smiled very sweetly. Gently, as if she were comforting a child, she said, "You know perfectly well that I'll never leave you. Why are you asking me to go?" Then the Führer did something that even his closest friends had never seen him do. Ignoring us completely, he kissed Eva on the lips.' All the others refused to leave. 'When we answered, "No!" he took our hands, pressed them tightly in gratitude and said, "If only our generals had been as brave as you."'[30]

Eva Braun had accepted her fate – to die with Hitler. That day (22 April), she wrote to her lifelong friend, Herta Schneider: 'These will be the last lines I write, and indeed, the last sign of life from me... We are fighting here to the last, but I fear the end is approaching threateningly closer and closer. Please leave the mountain. It is too dangerous a place for you to be when all this comes to an end. I cannot describe to you how sorry I feel for the Führer.' She sent her friend her jewellery with instructions about her will: 'I die as I have lived. It is not hard for me. You know that,' and ended with a PS: 'Perhaps everything will turn out *right* again, but *he* has lost faith and we, I fear, are hoping in vain.'[31] The next day, she wrote to her sister, bequeathing to her items of her jewellery.

When Albert Speer came to see her the following evening they shared a bottle of champagne and cakes and had a chat. Speer had already been told by Hitler that he did not want his body to be displayed as a trophy by the enemy and had ordered it to be burned. Eva Braun would die alongside him. Speer found her calm. They talked about people they knew, and places they'd been to. She was pleased Speer had come to be with Hitler. At one point, 'she put her hand on my arm just for a moment, and said she was really happy to be where she was and that she was not afraid. Oh, that girl...' Speer recalled. He described her as the only one to show dignity, even a kind of gay serenity. When she bade him goodbye, 'she wished me luck and sent greetings to my wife. It was extraordinary. Don't *you* think it was extraordinary?' he asked Gitta Sereny. 'On the face of it, a simple Munich girl, a nobody... and yet she was a most remarkable woman.'[32]

The faithful Goebbels had arranged for his entire family to move into the bunker to share Hitler's fate. His wife Magda arrived on the twenty-second with their six children. In this bizarre 'family' atmosphere, with children playing in the corridors outside, and the din of artillery and collapsing buildings just audible, Hitler and Eva Braun discussed, at lunch with the secretaries, the best way of committing suicide. Hitler thought 'the safest way is to put the barrel of the revolver in your mouth and pull the trigger. The skull is shattered in pieces and death is instantaneous.' Eva was horrified by this idea. 'I want to be a beautiful corpse,' she protested. 'I'm going to take poison.' Then she asked, 'But will it hurt? I'm terrified of a slow and painful death. I may have made up my mind to die courageously, but at least I want it to be painless.'[33] After this, Traudl Junge and Gerda Christian asked for, and were given, cyanide capsules in case of the worst.

Joseph and Magda Goebbels had already agreed to kill themselves, and their six children. 'We knew that their parents were going to kill them,' Traudl Junge said. 'Of course, *they* didn't know. One of them told an orderly who played with them that they were all going to have an injection so they wouldn't get sick. So you see, they had prepared them.'[34] Goebbels gave one explanation for his action in a personal testament on the thirtieth: he, with his family, could not leave Hitler alone in his hour of greatest need, with treachery everywhere: 'There have to be at least a few who will stay unconditionally loyal to him even unto death.' He had to end a life 'which for me personally has no further value if it cannot be used in the service of the Führer and by his side'.[35]

Magda Goebbels, held up among the leaders' wives as the icon of German motherhood, the Nazi ideal woman, had been tormented: 'If our state goes under then it is the end for us. My husband and I have come to terms with life. We have lived for a National Socialist Germany and we will die with it.' What she could not come to terms with, biographer Johannes Frank reported, was:

> ...the future of the children. Certainly, reason tells me that I must not leave them, unprotected, to a future in which they, as our children, will be the victims of Jewish revenge. But when I watch them playing around I cannot bear the thought of killing them. That must be the most difficult thing of all to ask of a mother. When Hilde said, 'Good night,' to me she put her arm round my neck and whispered in my ear, 'Is it so bad, Mutti, that you have to sigh so much?' Of course they don't know what the situation is. But they still sense it.

Goebbels had tried to console her by invoking Frederick the Great, who 'imagined himself on a distant star and from that point of view the events on our tiny planet, however incredibly important they may seem to us, appear very insignificant'. 'You are probably right,' his wife answered softly, 'but Frederick the Great had no children.'[36] By the time they reached the bunker, her doubts had been resolved. As a loyal Nazi wife, she must support her husband. Still trapped in the Nazi fantasy, she allowed fear of 'Jewish revenge', as she called it, to drown her maternal instincts in an act that was yet one more outrage to all natural and ethical order.

Hitler and Eva Braun were married in a brief ceremony after midnight on the morning of the twenty-ninth, witnessed by Bormann and Goebbels. It had been Eva Braun's wish for years, but Hitler, 'married to Germany', had refused, and kept her concealed from public view in the background of his life. Now, with her standing loyally by him at the end, and with nothing to lose for himself, Hitler had agreed. 'It is her wish to go to her death with me as my wife,' he explained, distancing himself from the decision. 'This will restore to us what my work in the service of my people had taken away from us both.' The small group gathered to celebrate with sandwiches and champagne. Traudl Junge was there for the celebration – secretive to the end, he hadn't told her beforehand of the ceremony: 'Nobody said anything. We couldn't very well toast their future.'[37] Hitler married Eva Braun, in her opinion, 'for the history books. He wanted to give a last satisfaction for her, after she had for years stood beside him with no meaningful place.' Hitler had dictated to her his final political and personal testaments. As she typed, she was shocked: 'Here we were, all of us doomed, I thought – the whole country doomed – and here, in what he was dictating to me there was not one word of compassion or regret, only awful, awful anger. I remember thinking, "My God, he hasn't learned anything. It's just the same."' Nicolaus von Below, Hitler's adjutant, who witnessed the testaments, 'found his self-deception really depressing and his repeated anti-Semitic invectives embarrassing'.[38]

On the afternoon of 30 April, after saying farewell to his 'inner circle', Hitler and Eva Braun retreated to his study. Ten minutes later, the others entered. The couple were both slumped on a couch. Shortly afterwards their bodies were carried up to the courtyard of the Reichschancellery and, following Hitler's instructions, doused with petrol and burned.

While the drama was being enacted, as the door closed behind Hitler and Eva Braun, Traudl Junge could stand it no longer, 'All I wanted to do was to get out; I felt I was suffocating... I wanted terribly not to be so frightened.' As she rushed away, she remembered the Goebbels children. She found them, looking lost and glum around the kitchen table, and gave them their lunch. 'And then, suddenly, there was the sound of a shot, and then dead silence. The children, startled, I think, were motionless for a second, and then Helmuth shouted gaily, "Bang on!" How right he was.'[39]

Just after 5.00pm the next day, Rochus Misch, a telephone operator, saw Magda Goebbels walk past, and disappear into an upstairs room with her six children aged from twelve to four, all wearing white nightgowns. Later she went up again with the doctor. Half an hour later she came back, crying. After each child had been given a shot of morphine, Dr Stumpfegger had crushed a phial of prussic acid into their mouths. Later that evening, Magda and Joseph Goebbels went up into the Chancellery garden and bit on the poison capsules. A shot was fired into each body.

The Soviet troops entered the Chancellery garden the next day.

With Hitler's death, the occupants of the bunker were free to make their escape. For Traudl Junge it was a release: 'We'd lived in the bunker in something like a state of trance. I realized that I didn't have any more emotions. I wasn't scared, there was no hope. I was just numb, functioning as if I was on automatic.' But Hitler's death brought an immediate change. For her, it was the discovery of her will to survive. She decided not to take the poisoned capsule: 'I didn't want to end in that mousetrap, or for my family to never hear anything more about me.' For everyone, Hitler's death left 'a vacuum in the bunker. The man who controlled the marionettes was dead, and suddenly everyone had to start to think for themselves again.' She joined the groups who tried to get out of the 'trap'. 'We had been locked up in the bunker, and had no contact with the outside world, for a relatively long time. And when we got out, I faced for the first time the stark reality of this incredible war. I saw complete destruction.'

For many, Hitler's death was a betrayal. At first he was reported to have fallen 'at the head of the heroic defenders of the Reich capital'. The communiqué to the troops in Berlin was blunt. It declared: '…the Führer took his own life and thereby abandoned those who had sworn him loyalty', and called on them to cease fighting.[40] For others it was a profound shock and a shattering of long-held beliefs. Committed Nazi Jutta Rüdiger heard the news when she was sitting by a lake in the mountains: 'I thought, how can it be that Hitler is dead? I couldn't imagine that the world could go on. But then I realized that after all, the world keeps turning, but just with a different set of rulers.'

Berlin was in ruins, with the remains of shattered buildings rising above the rubble for mile after mile. Ilse Schmidt remembers her return:

> I went to Wannsee and from there, you couldn't get any further, so I walked along the railway tracks. The destroyed Berlin I will

never forget. These skeletons of buildings. It was a feeling of utter annihilation. The war had destroyed the city. I was destroyed. The people were no longer there. All the people I loved were gone. And then I came home and knocked on our front door and my father opened the door, and said, 'Thank God you are back.' My father had no idea that I was still alive. It was Christmas, one day before Christmas, and as always there were red apples in the cupboards, polished red apples, and my sister and stepmother and father were the only people who were still left. And then I saw the empty chairs and that was horrible. None of them came back, my cousins, my uncles, my mother. It was a desolate feeling – all gone, all destroyed.

Homeless refugees, mainly women and children with their few remaining possessions, trudged wearily along the roads of Germany, not knowing where to go or where they would find shelter. Two-thirds of all homes in the country were destroyed. Cities lay in ruins. Everywhere there was hunger – and in many places, starvation. People begged or scratched a living where they could.

Hitler's legacy to the depleted German nation was that four million soldiers – sons, husbands, brothers, uncles – were dead. Hundreds of thousands more were marched off – cold, demoralized and starving – as prisoners. The majority never returned. Over a million women were widowed by the war, left to build what life and home they could for their children. Millions of children were orphaned.

Many young women who grew up under Nazism felt bitter and betrayed. Not just because so much was destroyed. Their youthful longing to believe in a higher ideal, to sacrifice themselves for the greater good, and to have pride in their nation, had been cruelly manipulated. They resented that Hitler had scarred their youth. Lilli Gentzen, seventeen at the war's end, says: 'They stole the best years, the most beautiful years, when you are young. That's why we were so desperate to enjoy ourselves afterwards. I wanted to dance. I finally wanted to get something out of life.'

For those who had quietly opposed Hitler, it was a new beginning. Socialist Elly Napp welcomed the defeat: 'I only had one feeling of incredible liberation because everything that had oppressed me before fell away. Once again, I could say who I was, where I came from, what I thought. I didn't have to be cautious whenever I opened my mouth any more.' Others were haunted all their lives by the horrific scenes they had witnessed, and by their powerlessness to do anything, even as the most basic tie between a mother and her children was being forcibly severed. Many kept silent. Others looked away as their nation descended into barbarism. Those who spoke up paid the price in prison, concentration camps, exile or death. Many more did not even see at the time the sheer injustice of what they were participating in, so imbued had these young women been by the siren voices of the times.

On the streets of Berlin and every other major city, the young joined the old in the shadow of twisted metal and skeletal buildings that had been homes. Dusty, undernourished and worn out, each became one link in the long chain of women who handed buckets one to another. It was the women who laboured to clear the rubble and rebuild from the ruins.

At the beginning of the Third Reich, women had welcomed Hitler's promise of glory as wives and mothers, who would bear the children to build the Thousand Year Reich. They had been seduced by the pledge of security in their homes, a safe haven for their companion husbands, in which their daughters would flourish, enriched by National Socialist values and their mission for the *Volk,* and their sons would achieve glory as warriors defending the homeland. If this meant sacrificing their lives, it was for the greater good of the 'national community'; women should not weep, but be proud that they and their sons had fulfilled their duty.

But Ilse Schmidt, who worked at the front lines, alongside nurses, for most of the war, reflects: 'How much disaster we brought on ourselves!' One episode stands out:

> We were in the Ukraine, standing beside a burnt-out tank, where there was the dead body of a Russian soldier. And the nurse whispered to me, 'That means another mother crying for her son.' And we saw a German plane shot down and we called, 'Get out of the plane.' And again this pilot died. And that was

another mother mourning her son. And it was not just the German mothers, it's the Russian mothers, and everyone who took part in that war. How much destruction was caused by the National Socialists!

NOTES

1 SD Report, Stuttgart, 8 August 1944; Noakes, *Nazism 1919–1945*, p. 578
2 Cited Kershaw, *Hitler: Nemesis*, p. 747
3 Burleigh, *The Third Reich*, p. 787
4 Kershaw, *Hitler: Nemesis*, p. 760
5 ibid., p. 762
6 Steinhoff, Pechel and Showalter, *Voices from the Third Reich*, p. 420
7 Owings, *Frauen*, p. 127
8 Cited Kershaw, *Hitler: Nemesis*, p. 763
9 Owings, *Frauen*, p. 406
10 ibid., p. 149
11 Kershaw, *Hitler: Nemesis*, p. 767
12 Cited Koonz, *Mothers in the Fatherland*, p. 404
13 Cited ibid., p. 404
14 Owings, *Frauen*, p. 164
15 ibid., p. 318-341
16 Cited Koonz, *Mothers in the Fatherland*, p. 415
17 Cited ibid., p. 416; Rudolf Hoss, *Commandant of Auschwitz: Autobiography of Rudolf Hoss,* Popular Library, New York, 1964 p. 34
18 ibid., pp. 418–19
19 Cited Kershaw, *Hitler: Nemesis*, p. 768
20 Burleigh, *The Third Reich*, p. 783
21 Beck, *Under the Bombs*, p. 185
22 Cited Kershaw, *Hitler: Nemesis*, pp. 790–1
23 Bormann, Martin, *The Bormann Letters: January 1943–April 1945*, Introduction by Hugh Trevor-Roper, Weidenfeld and Nicolson, London, 1954
24 ibid., pp. 177–8 (7 February 1945)
25 Burleigh and Wippermann, *The Racial State*, p. 791
26 Cited Kershaw, *Hitler: Nemesis*, p. 810
27 ibid., p. 1032 note
28 Sereny, *Albert Speer*, p. 505
29 Galante and Silianoff, *Last Witnesses in the Bunker*, p. 142
30 ibid., p. 3
31 Frank, *Eva Braun*, p. 286-287

32 Sereny, *Albert Speer*, p. 532
33 Galante and Silianoff, *Last Witnesses in the Bunker*, p. 5
34 Sereny, *Albert Speer*, p. 523
35 Goebbels, Joseph, *Tagebücher 1945. Die letzten Aufzeichnungen*, Hoffman and Camper, Hamburg, 1977, pp. 555–6
36 Frank, *Eva Braun*, p. 287
37 Sereny, *Albert Speer*, p. 537
38 ibid., p. 537
39 ibid., p. 539
40 Cited Kershaw, *Hitler: Nemesis*, p. 832

BIBLIOGRAPHY

Books:

Aly, Götz, *'Final Solution': Nazi Population Policy and the Murder of European Jews* (Arnold, London, 1999)

Barkai, Avraham, *From Boycott to Annihilation: The Economic Struggle of German Jews*, *1933–1943* (University Press of New England, Hanover N.H., 1989)

Beck, Earl R., *Under the Bombs: The German Home Front*, *1942–1945* (The University Press of Kentucky, Kentucky, 1986)

Beevor, Anthony, *Stalingrad* (Penguin, London, 1999)

Bessel, Richard, *Life in the Third Reich* (Oxford University Press, Oxford, 1987)

Blandford, Edmund, *Under Hitler's Banner* (Airlife Publishing, Shrewsbury, 1996)

Bleuel, Hans Peter, *Strength Through Joy: Sex and Society in Nazi Germany* (Secker & Warburg, London, 1973)

Bloch, Eduard, 'My Patient, Hitler', *Collier's* (15 March 1941)

Bock, Gisela, 'Racism and Sexism in Nazi Germany: Motherhood, Compulsory Sterilization, and the State', in Renate Bridenthal, Atina Grossmann and Marion Kaplan (ed.), *When Biology Became Destiny:*

Women in Weimar and Nazi Germany (Monthly Review Press, New York, 1984)

Bormann, Martin, *The Bormann Letters, January 1943– April 1945*, Introduction by Hugh Trevor-Roper (Weidenfeld and Nicolson, London, 1954)

Bridenthal, Renate, Atina Grossmann and Marion Kaplan (ed.), *When Biology Became Destiny: Women in Weimar and Nazi Germany* (Monthly Review Press, New York, 1984)

Bullock, Alan, *Hitler: A Study in Tyranny* (Odhams, Harmondsworth, 1964)

Bullock, Alan, *Hitler and Stalin*, *Parallel Lives* (Fontana, London, 1991)

Burleigh, Michael, 'Saving Money, Spending Lives: Psychiatry, Society and the "Euthanasia" Programme', in (ed.), *Confronting the Nazi Past: New Debates in German History* (Collins and Brown, London, 1996)

Burleigh, Michael (ed.), *Confronting the Nazi Past: New Debates in German History* (Collins and Brown, London, 1996)

Burleigh, Michael, *The Third Reich: A New History* (Macmillan, London, 2000)

Burleigh, Michael and Wolfgang Wippermann, *The Racial State: Germany 1933–1945* (Cambridge University Press, Cambridge, 1991)

Clay, Catrine and Michael Leapman, *Master Race: The Lebensborn Experiment in Nazi Germany* (Coronet Books, London, 1996)

Diehl, Guida, *Die Deutsche Frau und der Nationalsozialismus* (Eisenbach, 1933)

Domarus, Max, *Hitler. Reden und Proklamationen 1932–1945* (Süddeutscher Verlag, Munich, 1965)

NAZI WOMEN

Elling, Hannah, *Frauen im Deutschen Widerstand 1933–1945* (Röderberg, Frankfurt, 1981)

Fest, Joachim, *Hitler* (Penguin, London, 1977)

Fest, Joachim, *The Face of the Third Reich* (Penguin, London, 1972)

Frank, Johannes, *Eva Braun: Ein Ungewöhnliches Frauenschicksal in Geschichtlich Bewegter Zeit* (K. W. Schütz, Preussisch Oldendorf, 1988)

Fromm, Bella, *Blood and Banquets: A Berlin Social Diary* (Harper and Row, New York, 1942)

Galante, Pierre, and Eugene Silianoff, *Last Witnesses in the Bunker* (Sidgwick & Jackson, London, 1989)

Gellately, Robert, *The Gestapo and German Society: Enforcing Racial Policy 1933–1945* (Clarendon Press, Oxford, 1990)

Godl, Doris, 'Women's Contributions to the Political Policies of National Socialism', in *Feminist Issues* (1 January 1997)

Goebbels, Joseph, *Tagebücher 1945. Die letzten Aufzeichnungen* (Hoffman and Camper, Hamburg, 1977)

Goebbels, Joseph, *The Early Goebbels Diaries*, *1925–1926*, (ed.) Helmut Heiber (Weidenfeld and Nicolson, London, 1962)

Goebbels, Joseph, *The Goebbels Diaries*, *1939–1941*, (ed.) Fred Taylor (Hamish Hamilton, London, 1982)

Goebbels, Joseph, *The Goebbels Diaries*, *1942–1943*, (ed.) Louis Lochner (Greenwood Publishing Group, London, 1948)

Goebbels, Joseph, (ed.) Elke Fröhlich, *Die Tagebücher von Joseph Goebbels* (Saur Verlag, Munich, 1987)

Goldhagen, Daniel Jonah, *Hitler's Willing Executioners: Ordinary Germans and the Holocaust* (Little, Brown and Co, London, 1996)

Grunberger, Richard, *A Social History of the Third Reich* (Penguin, London, 1991)

Gun, Nerin E., *Eva Braun: Hitler's Mistress* (Leslie Frewin, London, 1969)

Hamann, Brigitte, *Hitler's Wien: Lehrjahre eines Diktators* (Piper, Munich, 1996)

Hammer, Joshua, 'Hitler's Children', in *Newsweek International* (20 March 2000)

Hanfstaengl, Ernst, *15 Jahre mit Hitler. Zwischen Wiessem und Braunem Haus* (Piper, Munich, 1980)

Hanfstaengl, Ernst, *Hitler: The Missing Years* (London, 1957)

Hanfstaengl, Ernst, 'I Was Hitler's Closest Friend', in *Cosmopolitan* (March 1943)

Hanisch, Reinhold, 'I Was Hitler's Buddy', in *New Republic* (5, 12 & 19 April 1939)

Hayman, Ronald, *Hitler & Geli* (Bloomsbury, London, 1997)

Heiden, Konrad, *Adolf Hitler* (Europa Verlag, Munich, 1936)

Heiden, Konrad, *Der Führer* (Gollancz, London, 1944)

Heineman, Elizabeth D., *What Difference Does a Husband Make? Women and Marital Status in Nazi and Post War Germany* (University of California Press, California, 1999)

Hitler, Adolf, *Mein Kampf* (Hutchinson, London, 1969)

NAZI WOMEN

Hoss, Rudolf, *Commandant of Auschwitz: Autobiography of Rudolf Hoss* (Popular Library, New York, 1964)

Hoffmann, Heinrich, *Hitler Was My Friend* (Burke, London, 1955)

Jetzinger, Franz, *Hitler's Youth* (Hutchinson, London, 1958)

Joachimstaler, Anton, *Korrektur einer Biographie: Adolf Hitler 1908–1920* (F.A. Herbig Verlag, Munich, 1989)

Johnson, Eric, *The Nazi Terror: Gestapo, Jews and Ordinary Germans* (John Murray, London, 1999)

Kaplan, Marion, *Between Dignity and Despair: Jewish Life in the Third Reich* (Oxford University Press, Oxford, 1998)

Kaplan, Marion, 'Keeping Calm and Weathering the Storm: Jewish Women's Responses to Daily Life in Nazi Germany, 1933–1939', in Dalia Ofer and Lenore J. Weitzman (ed.), *Women in the Holocaust* (Yale University Press, Connecticut, 1998)

Kershaw, Ian, *The Hitler Myth: Image and Reality in the Third Reich* (Oxford University Press, Oxford, 1987)

Kershaw, Ian, *Hitler: Hubris, 1889–1936* (Penguin, London, 1998)

Kershaw, Ian, *Hitler: Nemesis, 1936–1945* (Allen Lane, London, 2000)

Kersten, Felix, *The Kersten Memoir* (Hutchinson, London, 1956)

Kirkpatrick, Clifford, *Women in Nazi Germany* (Jarrolds, London, 1939)

Kitchen, Martin, *Nazi Germany at War* (Longman, London, 1995)

Klabunde, Anja, *Magda Goebbels, Annäherung an ein Leben* (C. Bertelsman, Munich, 1999)

Klee, Ernst, Willi Dressen and Volker Reiss, *Those Were the Days: The Holocaust through the Eyes of the Perpetrators and Bystanders* (Hamish Hamilton, London, 1991)

Klemperer, Viktor, *I Will Bear Witness: A Diary of the Nazi Years, 1933–1941* (Random House, New York, 1998)

Knopp, Guido, *Hitler. Eine Bilanz* (Siedler, Berlin, 1995)

Köhn, Ilse, *Mischling, Second Degree: My Childhood in Nazi Germany* (Greenwillow, New York, 1977)

Koonz, Claudia, *Mothers in the Fatherland: Women, the Family and Nazi Politics* (St Martin's Press, New York, 1987)

Kubizek, August, *Young Hitler: The Story of Our Friendship* (Tower, New York, 1954)

von Lang, Jochen, *Bormann: The Man Who Manipulated Hitler* (Weidenfeld and Nicolson, London, 1979)

Langer, Walter, *The Mind of Adolf Hitler: The Secret Wartime Report* (Putnams, New York, 1972)

Large, David Clay (ed.), *Contending with Hitler: Varieties of German Resistance in the Third Reich* (German Historical Institute and Cambridge University Press, Cambridge, 1991)

Lebor, Adam, and Roger Boyes, *Surviving Hitler: Choices, Corruption and Compromise in the Third Reich* (Simon & Schuster, London, 2000)

Lipstadt, Deborah E., *Beyond Belief: The American Press and the Coming of the Holocaust 1933–45* (Free Press, New York, 1986)

Lochner, Louis, *What About Germany?* (Dodd, Mead, New York, 1942)

NAZI WOMEN

Lukacs, John, *The Hitler of History* (Bradford Books, New York, 1997)

McFarland-Icke, Bronwyn Rebekah, *Nurses in Nazi Germany: Moral Choice in History* (Princeton University Press, New Jersey, 1999)

Manvell, Roger, and Heinrich Fraenkel, *Heinrich Himmler* (Heinemann, London, 1965)

Maschmann, Melita, *Account Rendered: A Dossier of My Former Self* (Abelard Schumann, London, 1965)

Maser, Werner, *Hitler: Legend, Myth and Reality* (Harper and Row, New York, 1973)

Meissner, Hans-Otto, *Magda Goebbels: The First Lady of the Third Reich* (The Dial Press, New York, 1980)

von Müller, Karl Alexander, *Im Wandel einer Welt: Erinnerungen 1919–1932* (Munich, 1966)

Noakes, Jeremy, *Nazism and High Society*, in Michael Burleigh (ed.), *Confronting the Nazi Past: New Debates in German History* (Collins and Brown, London, 1996)

Noakes, Jeremy, *Nazism 1919–1945*, vol 4, *The German Home Front in World War II: A Documentary Reader* (University of Exeter Press, Exeter, 1998)

NS Frauen Warte (1938–40)

Ofer, Dalia, and Lenore J. Weitzman (ed.), *Women in the Holocaust* (Yale University Press, Connecticut, 1998)

von Oven, Wilfried, *Mit Goebbels bis zum Ende* (Dürer-Verlag, Buenos Aires, 1949–50)

Overy, Richard, *The Penguin Historical Atlas of the Third Reich* (Penguin, London, 1996)

Owings, Alison, *Frauen: German Women Recall the Third Reich* (Penguin, London, 1995)

Peukert, Detlev, 'Youth in the Third Reich', in Richard Bessel (ed.), *Life in the Third Reich* (Oxford University Press, Oxford, 1987)

Picker, Henry, *Hitler's Table Talk* (Weidenfeld and Nicolson, London, 1953)

Pine, Lisa, *Nazi Family Policy 1933–1945* (Berg, Oxford, 1997)

Pine, Lisa, 'Hashud: An Experiment in Nazi "A-Social Policy"', in *History Today* (July 1995)

Pine, Lisa, 'Girls in Uniform', in *History Today* (March 1999)

Pine Lisa, 'Nazism in the Classroom', in *History Today* (April, 1997)

Pryce-Jones, David, *Unity Mitford: A Quest* (Weidenfeld and Nicolson, London, 1976)

Rauschning, Hermann, *Hitler Speaks* (Thornton Butterworth, London, 1939)

Rhodes, James R., *Chips: The Diaries of Sir Henry Channon* (Weidenfeld and Nicolson, London, 1967)

Richardz, Monika (ed.), *Jewish Life in Germany: Memoirs from Three Centuries* (Indiana University Press, Indianapolis, 1991)

Riefenstahl, Leni, *The Sieve of Time: The Memoirs of Leni Riefenstahl* (Quartet, London, 1992)

NAZI WOMEN

Rosenbaum, Ron, *Explaining Hitler: The Search for the Origins of His Evil* (Papermac, London, 1999)

von Schirach, Baldur, *Die Hitler-Jugend* (Berlin, 1934)

von Schirach, Baldur, *Ich Glaubte an Hitler* (Mosaik Verlag, Hamburg, 1967)

von Schirach, Henriette, *Frauen um Hitler: Nach Materialien von Henriette von Schirach* (F.A. Herbig Verlag, Munich, 1983)

Schoenbaum, David, *Hitler's Social Revolution: Class and Status in Nazi Germany 1933–1939* (W.W. Norton, New York, 1980)

Schroeder, Christa (ed.), *Er war mein Chef: Aus dem Nachlassder Sekretärin von Adolf Hitler* (Anton Joachimstaler, Munich, 1985)

Schwarz, Gudrun, *Eine Frau an seiner Seite: Ehefrauen in der SS-Sippengemeinschaft* (Hamburger Editions, Hamburg, 1997)

Das Schwarze Korps

Sereny, Gitta, *Albert Speer: His Battle with Truth* (Picador, London, 1996)

Shirer, William L., *Berlin Diary, 1934–1941* (Sphere Books, London, 1970)

Shirer, William L., *The Rise and Fall of the Third Reich* (Simon & Schuster Inc, London, 1959)

Siber, Paula, *Die Frauenfrage und ihre Lösung durch den Nationalsozialismus* (Georg Kallmeyer, Berlin, 1933)

Speer, Albert, *Inside the Third Reich* (Weidenfeld and Nicolson, London, 1970) von Stahlenberg, Elisabeth, *Nazi Lady: The Diaries of Elisabeth von Stahlenberg* (Blond and Briggs, London, 1976)

Steinhoff, Johannes, Peter Pechel and Dennis Showalter, *Voices from the Third Reich: An Oral History* (Da Capo Press, New York, 1994)

Stephenson, Jill, *Women in Nazi Society* (Croom Helm, London, 1975)

Stephenson, Jill, 'Women, Motherhood and the Family in the Third Reich', in Michael Burleigh (ed.), *Confronting the Nazi Past: New Debates in German History* (Collins and Brown, London, 1996)

Stibbe, Matthew, 'Women in the Nazi State', in *History Today* (November 1993)

Strasser, Otto, *Hitler and I* (Cape, London, 1940)

Thomas, Katharine, *Women in Nazi Germany* (Gollancz, London, 1943)

Thompson, Dorothy, *I Saw Hitler* (Farrar and Reinhart, New York, 1932)

Toland, John, *Adolf Hitler* (Doubleday, New York, 1976)

Trevor-Roper, Hugh, 'The Mind of Adolf Hitler', introduction to *Hitler's Table Talk, 1941–1944* (Weidenfeld and Nicolson, London, 1953)

Ulshöfer, Helmut (ed.), *Liebesbriefe an Adolf Hitler, Briefe an der Tod* (VAS, Frankfurt, 1994)

Unger, Michael, 'The Status and Plight of Women in the Lodz Ghetto', in Dalia Ofer and Lenore J. Weitzman (ed.), *Women in the Holocaust* (Yale University Press, Connecticut, 1998)

Wagener, Otto, *Hitler – Memoirs of a Confidant*, (ed.) Henry Ashby Turner (Yale University Press, Connecticut, 1985)

Waite, Robert G. L., *The Psychopathic God Adolf Hitler* (Da Capo Press, New York, 1977)

Website:

http://mars.wnec.edu/ffgrempel/curriculum/publications
– Gerhard Rempel, 'The Development of the Hitler Youth and the SS as Nazi Party Affiliates'

INDEX

abortion 89–90, 210
Appel, Marta 108
Armbruster, Margarete 224
Auschwitz 190, 191–2, 224, 226
Austrian invasion 149–50

Baarova, Lida 69–71, 125
Barkai, Avraham 107
BDM *see* League of German Girls
Bechstein, Helene 31–3
Behrens, Manja 121, 125
Below, Nicolaus von 234
Berlin 200, 228, 230–1, 235–6
Berner, Luise 103
Bierbaumer, Karl 103
bigamy 120–4, 210–11
birth rate 86–7, 89, 90–1, 124,
   209–10
Blersch, Dr Margret 112
Bleuel, Hans Peter 213–14
Bloch, Dr Eduard 13, 16
Bock, Gisela 90, 114–15
Boden, Margarete 125
Borch, Susanne von der 131–2, 135,
   152–4, 165, 166–7, 205
Bormann, Gerda 121–2, 227–8
Bormann, Martin 57, 121–3, 125,
   148, 186, 211, 227, 233–4
Borsig, Ernst von 31
Boyes, Roger 208
Brandmayer, Balthasar 24

Brandt, Anni 58
Braun, Eva 51–60, 96, 98, 124
   bunker 230–4
   marriage 233–4
   suicide 231, 232, 234
Bridal Schools 91–2
Brixius, Martha 107
Bruckmann, Elsa 31, 33, 66
Buck, Dorothea 113–14
Burchett, Irene 223
Burleigh, Michael 178

Cammens, Minna 81
Carnap, Helen von 34
Cernyak-Spatz, Susan 224
Channon, Sir Henry 'Chips' 142
Christian, Gerda 231, 232
concentration camps 81–2, 182,
   189–90, 223–7
corpse marriage 212
Czechoslovakian invasion 150–1,
   157
Czechs 184
Czellitzer, Margaret 155

Deutschkron, Inge 108, 188
Diehl, Guida 76, 79, 88
Dirksen, Victoria von 34–5, 66
divorce 115–16, 120
Döhring, Herbert 59
Dolfuss, Engelbert 168

Dortmund protest 203–4
Draber, Gertrud 91–2, 190
Dresden bombing 201–2
Drexler, Anton 27

Eckart, Dietrich 29
Ertl, Hedwig 95, 130–1, 134–5, 136
    Jews 102, 108–9
    letters to soldiers 187
    Poland 164–6

Fest, Anna 225
Fest, Joachim 21, 23, 32
Finckh, Renate 131, 134
food shortages 143, 163, 198, 199
Frankenfeld, Regina 222–3
Frank, Hans 39, 166
Frank, Johannes 233
French prisoners 177–8, 180–1,
    184
Frick, Wilhelm 114
Friedländer, Vera 193
Fromm, Bella 35

Galen, Bishop Clemens 112
Gang-Saalheimar, Lore 155–6
Gansser, Emil 31
Gentzen, Lilli 154, 188, 200,
    228–30, 236
Goebbels, Joseph 15, 62, 65–6,
    67–71, 74, 125, 130, 197, 219
    allied bombs 199
    BDM 137, 138
    beauty culture 98
    Berlin 230
    Jews 151, 152, 189–90
    and Leni Riefenstahl 64
    Olympic Games 141
    opulence 147–8
    partisans 173
    rations 227

Rosenstrasse protest 193
selective breeding 110
Slavs 158
Soviet invasion 172
Stalingrad 195
Star of David 188
suicide 232–3, 235
Goebbels, Magda 64, 65–71, 125,
    232–3, 234–5
Göring, Emmy 57–8, 86
Göring, Hermann 57–8, 86, 130,
    156
    jokes about 208
    opulence 147
    Russians 178
Griese, Irma 224
Groth, Verena 105
Grynszpan, Herschel 152
Gun, Nerin 53

Haferkamp, Wilhelmine 146, 179–80
Hamann, Brigitte 18, 22, 33, 60
Hamburg bombing 199, 201, 202
Hanfstaengl, Erna 30, 34
Hanfstaengl, Ernst 'Putzi' 29, 32, 34,
    42, 46, 76
Hanfstaengl, Helene 34
Hanisch, Reinhold 20–1, 23
Hanke, Karl 70
Heineman, Elizabeth 212
Hess, Rudolf 31, 47–8, 121
Hilgenfeldt, Erich 93
Himmler, Heinrich 35, 74, 130, 168,
    175
    abortions 90
    BDM 137
    contraception 89
    foreign workers 181
    Lebensborn homes 211
    marriage 125, 210
    motherhood 88, 116–19

Poland 164
polygamy 120–1, 123–4
race theory 103
youth gangs 214
Hitler, Adolf 71–9, 227–8
    allied bombs 199
    army service 24, 27
    Austrian invasion 149–50
    BDM 136–7
    beauty culture 98
    Berghof 32, 55–6, 59
    Berlin 228
    bigamy 123
    Brown House 31
    bunker 230–5
    childhood 14–18
    children 129
    conscription 161, 162, 177,
        184–5, 198
    corpse marriage 212
    Czechoslovakian invasion 150–1,
        157
    and Eva Braun 51–60, 96, 98,
        124, 230–3
    final speech 220–1
    food shortages 143
    and Geli Raubal 40–9
    Göring's wedding 86
    illegitimate children 210
    Jewish goods boycott 107
    Jewish Question 109
    jokes about 208
    and Leni Riefenstahl 63–5
    and Magda Goebbels 65, 66–71,
        125
    and Mimi Reiter 37–9
    mother's death 13
    Munich ladies 29–33
    Nero Decree 219
    Nuremberg Rally 95, 130, 137–8
    Opposition women 79–83

    oration 27–9
    peoples' doubts 197
    photographs 34
    Poland invasion 158
    polygamy 116
    prison 32, 34, 37
    and Renate Müller 61–2
    Russia 196
    sexual abstinence 20–3
    and Stefanie Jansten 17–18
    suicide 231, 232, 234, 235
    and Unity Mitford 62
    Versailles Treaty 141, 150, 151
    Vienna Academy 18–19
Hitler, Alois 13, 14–16
Hitler, Klara 13–14, 15–17, 18, 19
Hitler, Paula 13, 15
Hitler Youth 89, 129, 136, 138, 144,
    153–4, 157, 172, 199, 227, 228
Hoss, Rudolf 226
Hoffmann, Heinrich 34, 39, 42,
    43–4, 45, 46, 48, 51–2
Hoffmann, Henriette see Schirach,
    Henriette von

Jansten, Stefanie 17–18
Jetzinger, Franz 17
Jews 21, 23, 101–2, 151–2, 228
    BDM 135
    blood purity 104–9
    deportation 189–93
    exclusions 110, 115
    executions 168–73, 174
    Kristallnacht 152–5
    Olympics 142
    pauperization 166, 187–8
    Poland 164, 166
    Star of David 188
Johnson, Eric 104, 193, 207
Juchacz, Maria 81
Junge, Traudl 59, 75, 76–8, 96, 137

bunker 230, 231, 234, 235
cyanide 232
war 161
war declaration 158

Kahrau, Helga 119
Kahr, Brett 14, 16, 19, 40–1, 47
Kaiser, Hugo 96
Kaplan, Marion 109
Kardorff, Ursula von 200
Katscher, Liselotte 82–3, 112–13,
    158, 161, 205, 218, 221–2
Kaufmann-Krasowski, Maria 224
Kershaw, Ian 13, 22–3, 24, 47
    allied bombs 199
    Eva Braun 57
    Geli Raubal 40, 43, 44
    Klara Hitler 15–16
    Maria Reiter 39
    oration 27–8
Kersten, Felix 118–19
Kirchner, Johanna 81
Klemperer, Victor 105, 142, 191
Kochs, Ilse 225
Köhn, Ilse 106
Koonz, Claudia 193, 225, 226
Kretschmer, Karl 174–5
Kristallnacht 152–6
Kubizek, August 'Gustl' 17, 18, 19,
    20, 21, 22–3
Kuhn, Rita 106, 148–9, 155,
    191–2

Lächert, Hildegard 224
Landau, Edwin 108
Landau, Felix 168–70
Lapp, Hugo 173
Lasch, Lotte 80, 90
League of German Girls (BDM) 95,
    102, 129–39, 144–5, 147, 187
    allied bombs 199

Himmler 123–4
    marriage 211
    Poland 164–7
Lebensborn homes 117–19, 120,
    211
Lebor, Adam 208
Ley, Robert 93, 97
Liebenfels, Jörg Lanz van 21
Lingen, Maria von 154, 219–20
Lochner, Louis 76
Lohniger, Helga 82
Lueger, Karl 21
Lukacs, John 30, 47

Majlca, Julian 182
Manstein, Erich von 172–3
Manziarly, Constanze 231
marriage loans 84, 86, 103, 110,
    144
Maurice, Emil 41, 42, 44
Meissner, Hans-Otto 66, 70
mentally ill 111–14
Meyerowitz, Alfred 193
Meyer-Semlies, Ursula 146–7, 154–5
Misch, Rochus 234
Mitford, Unity 62
Mother Schools 94
Müller, Josef 208
Müller, Karl Alexander von 27
Müller, Lotte 224
Müller, Renate 61–2
Munich Agreement 150

Napp, Elly 79–80, 179, 201–3,
    204–5, 206, 236–7
Napp, Kurt 80, 202
Nauman, Josef 23
Neumann, Camilla 191

Olympic Games 141–2
Oven, Wilfried von 137